A MALE GUIDE

TO

WOMEN'S LIBERATION

Books by Gene Marine

AMERICA THE RAPED (1969)
THE BLACK PANTHERS (1969)
FOOD POLLUTION (with Judith Van Allen) (1972)
A MALE GUIDE TO WOMEN'S LIBERATION (1972)

Gene Marine

A MALE GUIDE
TO WOMEN'S
LIBERATION

HOLT, RINEHART and WINSTON
New York
Chicago
San Francisco

ACKNOWLEDGMENTS

Grateful acknowledgment is made to the following publishers and authors for permission to quote from the works listed below:

Myron Brenton, *The American Male*. New York: Coward-McCann, Inc. Copyright © 1966 by the author.

Simone de Beauvoir, *The Second Sex*. New York: Alfred A. Knopf, Inc. Copyright 1952 by the publisher.

Helen Dudar and others, "Women in Revolt," *Newsweek,* March 23, 1970. Copyright © 1970 by the publisher.

Eva Figes, *Patriarchal Attitudes*. New York: Stein and Day. Copyright © 1970 by the author.

Shulamith Firestone, *The Dialectic of Sex*. New York: William Morrow and Company. Copyright © 1970 by the author.

Betty Friedan, *The Feminine Mystique*. New York: W. W. Norton and Company. Copyright © 1963 by the author.

Lucy Komisar, *The New Feminism*. New York: Franklin Watts, Inc. Copyright © 1971 by the author.

Published simultaneously in Canada by Holt, Rinehart and Winston of Canada, Limited.

Library of Congress Catalog Card Number: 72–78118
ISBN: 0–03–001046–2
First Edition

Designer: Nancy Dale Muldoon
Printed in the United States of America

FOR

→

April, Craig, Sheila, and Kevin

This is one I'd really like you to read. And when you've read it, I'd like you to talk to each other about it—especially brother to sister and sister to brother. Ask the questions that are most difficult to ask. Say the things that are most difficult to say. Please.

PREFACE

Because my wife is an active feminist, some of her acquaintances may assume that she has more responsibility for any of the failings of this book than is actually the case. Of course, without her presence I would be far more retarded in my understanding than I am; she is responsible in that abstract sense if the book contains any successes. And she did take time out to look over the manuscript and point out several blatant masculinisms and not a few spots of bad writing. But otherwise it's all mine, a competent enough reporting job mixed with some grumpy opinion and, I hope, a little compassion. For the reader, too.

I suppose that whatever ability I may have to listen, to try to understand, starts way back there with my mother and my sister Dee and a little later with my sister Nil and my sister-in-law Dorothy. Since then a lot of women have helped me along a tortuous path, in large and small ways. Among many—some of whom I know only by their first names—who have provided personal insights over the past few years, I must risk offending some by mentioning only seven: Susanne Bodenheimer, Bea Cohen, Susan Griffin, Debra Long, Eve Merriam, Jessica Mitford and Hanna Pitkin.

Finally: No man can live to be forty-five, with any sort of social history, and then attempt to deal honestly with the ideas of women's liberation without suffering recurrent shocks. I have found my own history all too often in what follows, have recognized with despairing frequency my own actions, my own patterns. It would be grotesque to apologize to women for past oppressions of which I now find myself guilty. But I feel some need to say, in case any of them should happen to glance with understandable skepticism at what I have written here, that I really do wish I hadn't been quite such a son of a bitch.

GENE MARINE

BERKELEY
MARCH, 1972

PART ONE

Male Is Normal

1

U LTIMATELY, of course, we can learn only from them.

We cannot tell each other about sensations none of us has ever felt, frustrations none of us has ever known, the myriad daily differences to which none of us has ever given more than a passing thought. We cannot learn about blacks by reading books written by whites, beyond certain limits; we cannot learn, beyond certain limits, about life in the Trobriand Islands by reading Malinowski.

At the same time, if we are to rely on the written word for a beginning, it is difficult to begin learning from women. For one thing, their writing is mostly intended for other women—a fact that introduces subtleties with which most of us are not yet ready to cope. For another, their books and articles do not stress the same things, and in fact often seem to be in conflict with each other.

Sometimes the conflict is real. Shulamith Firestone's book, for example, is largely the detailed argument of a particular position within the women's movement.[1] * Sometimes it's simply that differ-

---

* Throughout the book, references are to the author's name only, except where it's necessary to distinguish among two or more works. That distinction is sometimes made in a chapter note. Where an author has written one book and some shorter pieces, reference is to the book unless otherwise stated. Complete citations are in the Bibliography.

ent authors are stressing different parts of the overall movement. But to somebody looking for a starting place, it's confusing.

There is a passion, an excitement, in the women's movement that men can feel and understand, but the more factual and rigorous, the better argued books miss that element—and it is crucial. You can get some idea of what I'm talking about by reading Helen Dudar's report in *Newsweek,* in which a "straight reporting" job turns out to be a very personal thing.

And finally, if we are just beginning to try to learn, we have no way to distinguish among the urbane but uncompromising work of Eva Figes, the sometimes important but ultimately unsatisfactory approach of Germaine Greer, and a great deal of useless nonsense, like Julie Ellis or the Hinckles. Nor do you have any way of knowing whether my opinions, as just expressed, are any good.

What puts us off even more, I think, is that women's liberationists write reasonably well about everything but men. Some of what they say just doesn't quite ring true; some seems to betray inexperience or unfortunate personal experience; some is simply nonsense.

Maybe it's necessary nonsense. Maybe women who feel that they are emerging from a state of oppression (we'll get to some words like "oppression" later) feel also a need to overstate their criticisms, in order to restore dignity. Maybe the more outrageous criticisms carry their own excitement; maybe they're needed to attract other women, as young blacks were attracted by the audacity of the first Black Panthers who dared to challenge the rule of white police in the ghetto. But it is nonsense all the same, and it keeps us from learning from those works which are not written for us anyway.

Still, we want to know. Clearly, Kate Millett, Betty Friedan, Eva Figes, Bella Abzug, Ti-Grace Atkinson are not stupid women, or insincere. Clearly they are not all compensating for being ugly or fat or pimpled, as one stereotype would have it—we have seen pictures of Atkinson and Millett and Firestone, Eve Merriam and Aileen Hernandez and Gloria Steinem, and that explanation won't hold up.

Since there is no formal organization called "women's liberation" to which women belong, and many women definitely in the movement belong to no organization at all, it is impossible to say how many women are women's liberationists. The National Organization of Women has over 15,000 members. A conservative guess would be that at least 100,000 women are directly and actively involved. But there is more to it than that.

4

Certainly most American women are not interested in the movement. Roper found about two years ago that 69% of American women don't think that women are "discriminated against and treated as second class citizens"; 83% don't think a "wife should be breadwinner if better wage earner than husband"; 76% don't think "men's clubs and lodges should be required to admit women," and 84% still think men ought to hold doors and give up seats for women.[2] About a year later Gallup said that 65% of all women think that American women get as good a break as men.[3]

The figures have changed since then; more women now feel or see discrimination and are willing to say so. But even those two-year-old figures indicate that there are sizable dissenting minorities. If they are not active—and obviously they aren't—they are there to be reached. And another of our problems as men, I think, is that we lack something that all of them have: a kind of instant access to the subject. On first encountering the movement, Steinem writes, women "share with each other the exhilaration of growth and self-discovery," after which a second enlightenment follows:

In the second stage, when we're exhausted from dredging up facts and arguments for the men whom we had previously thought advanced and intelligent, we make another simple discovery. Women understand. We may share experiences, make jokes, paint pictures, and describe humiliations that mean nothing to men, but *women understand*.

I have been present often enough while feminist women talked to other women who had no previous experience of the movement, and it's true. They do.

Although the result is sometimes astonishing to any male who happens to be on the scene, there's no reason for us to regard it as magic. It's true of us, isn't it? Leaving "humiliations" aside (most of us don't talk to each other freely about our humiliations), don't we constantly share experiences and make jokes that mean nothing to women—and don't men understand? The only thing that seems really to be different is that we grow up used to that understanding—and women do not.[4] They are discovering an enormous pleasure that is ours by birthright, and I don't blame them for feeling a little resentful about having been denied it all this time.

In any case, however, Steinem's delighted discovery that "women understand" is the flip side of the fact that men do not; and so we

5

will have to take other routes. Do not fear; it is not my intent to create male women's liberationists, for I am no such animal myself, and it is possible that the creature has yet to evolve. Nor can I provide the descriptions or make the arguments that a good female friend might provide and make—assuming that you were willing to "open up" enough, to give her enough time, and to keep coming back for more effort despite a number of inevitable emotional explosions on both sides.

No. I mean only to say that I think I have figured out this much about it, so far, "this much" being a little more than most American men have had a chance to deal with. Not many American men could take the time to fight their way through the Bibliography for this book, even if they were lucky enough, as I am, to know some very patient and some very remarkable women—in my case, one in particular.

If you want to make the try with me, you're going to have to wait for the good parts about sex objects and lesbianism and not wearing bras. They don't make sense without some kind of basis, which is why the press can make fun of them so easily. Even the relatively simple call for "equal pay for equal work" (we all agree with that one, right?) doesn't really make sense if all you've got going for you are statistics. They help in a courtroom, but not in understanding what's happening with women.

Besides, unless you start with a couple of ideas, you get lost just trying to find a place to start. The reality of the women's movement, like the reality of anything else worth knowing about, is structural: it's like one of those scaffoldings made out of pipe that you see on the outside of buildings that are being renovated. If you were going to describe that scaffolding, made out of interconnected and interdependent pieces of pipe, there's no one piece of pipe you can start with; you have to have the idea of it all fitting together before you can even start the description.

But while reality is structural, language is linear, and that's what we have to overcome. So we have to start in the dim recesses of ourselves. There are a great many reasons for this, of which the most pressing is perhaps that in this culture, women are pretty much whatever we say they are.

2
▼

THERE is a thing called an Embedded Figures Test, of which you have taken at least one version: See how many faces you can find in this picture of a forest, and send in your answer with two box tops and win (maybe) a magic decoder.

There is a thing called a Rod and Frame Test, in which it is your job to make a rod go straight up and down (or straight across), while the psychologist tilts a frame that's around the rod, to see whether you can be fooled into making the rod straight relative to *the frame,* instead of making it straight relative to *you.*[1]

There are tests involving series of numbers—you've taken those too, probably.[2] Like: Which number comes next in the series:

2, 4, 6, 8, 10 . . . ?

Got it? Try this one:

1, 3, 6, 10, 15, 21. . . .

A little harder, but you probably got it. Now that you have the idea, try one more:

14, 18, 23, 28, 34, 42, 50. . . .

No? Does it help if I tell you that the next three numbers are 59, 66 and 72?

It doesn't help, of course, if you've never been in New York City. But even if you have, I doubt whether you thought of the local stops on the IRT-Broadway-7th Avenue Subway.

Dirty trick, huh? There are, of course, a lot of jokes and riddles that work on the same principle. You get your mind "set" a certain way, and then you can't solve the problem unless you can "break the set" (*Q.*: If the removal of a growth in the abdomen is an appendectomy, and the removal of a growth in the throat is a tonsillectomy, what's the removal of a growth on the head? *A.*: A haircut). The Embedded Figures Test and the Rod and Frame Test are not exactly set-breaking problems, but they're related; they have to do with the ability to perceive something independently of its immediate context.

One psychologist, in an attempt to explain learning, used a very simple analogy involving building blocks.[3] You start piling up these "blocks" of knowledge when you're little. As you get older, you can then learn only things that will fit in place on top of the block structure you have already built. Really to learn something new—to break a set not in a riddle but in your perception of the world—is an extremely difficult process, because you have to tear down part of your block structure and rebuild it in such a way that it will accommodate your new block. Many people just can't do this, and it doesn't do any good to yell at them or to go over your impeccable logic again and again.

Everything about how we learn is still pretty tentative to psychologists, but if this analogy is right, it means that we need our block structures; they are our entire perception of the world, and if they are taken away, we are, in a sense, cast psychologically adrift. This seems to be the reason it is so difficult to shake long-standing prejudices of any kind. Beneath that dogged clinging to "wrong" block structures is fear, fear that there won't be anything adequately satisfying to replace it.[4]

Most of us keep getting the women's movement all wrong because it's like a block that won't sit on top of the blocks we already have in place. We have, in fact, a cultural block structure, made up of things we have all learned as "true," things we all know. We have to break that cultural set, to tear down a part of that structure at least tentatively, in order even to begin to follow the arguments of women's liberation.

8

Contrary to the myth that women's liberation is made up of man-haters, the women in the movement spend a disproportionate amount of time, on an individual basis, trying to explain the movement to men. Some of the funniest writing in women's liberation publications (and there is a lot of humor inside the movement [5]) has to do with women telling other women about their attempts to explain their position to men. For a male reader, of course, it's funny like Lenny Bruce was funny; you laugh, but you wince at the portrait of yourself at the same time.

But before you get to that point, you have to break the sets, and the difficulty of breaking them is what keeps women from being much more successful in their attempts to explain. In the course of trying, they've developed a few techniques that sometimes work—although if they don't work, they bring out all sorts of defensive and sometimes surprisingly angry reactions.

One is the simple technique of reversal, used in one widely reported case by women who leaned against buildings in the Wall Street area and whistled at men. A classic example (fellow reporters, *please* look this one up) is Dorothy Sayers' essay, "The Human-Not-Quite-Human," in *Unpopular Opinions*. It's a "news story" about a man, written as news stories are in fact written about women.

A second popular technique is the Black Analogy—pointing out to men that attitudes they wouldn't tolerate with regard to blacks are considered acceptable with regard to women. As we will see, there are dangers in that one (a lot of blacks don't like it). Still another technique is to attempt to push men into giving their reactions to being forced to do things (e.g., housework) that women are expected to do every day. The classic in this category is the essay by Pat Mainardi.

None of these techniques, however, is by any means an automatic set-breaker ("But, baby, it's not the same *thing*!"). Given the genuine difficulty we all have in breaking sets, we shouldn't be surprised that some women, after their tenth or fiftieth attempt to explain, become angry or strident or bitter.

Nor should we be confused, incidentally, by the fact that some women can't take a joke, aside from the fact that it's hard to regard your own put-down status as funny. The women's liberation movement, in all its many forms, is nonetheless a movement. And every movement—the radical Left, the radical Right, Moral Re-Arma-

9

ment, general semantics, natural foods, the Young Republicans or Weatherman—always includes a sizable number of solemn and dedicated followers who are very nearly faddists and who are inevitably totally without humor. If you happen to have run into one, don't judge women's liberation by her, any more than you would have your own deeply held beliefs judged by their least appealing adherents.

So, as they say in the counter-culture, you're going to have to struggle. Lift those blocks, break those sets, go away and get a little drunk and come back and try again. Happily, you don't have to break them all just yet; the best I can do here is give you a start on the first few blocks (one of *my* tricks is to keep jarring you a little by saying "her or his," where you're so used to seeing the masculine word alone that you don't notice it). On the other hand, the first block is the hardest—because if you can't move it, you can't understand any of the rest of it.

I am going to call it masculinism.

3 ⬇

THERE are no "male chauvinist pigs" in this book.

"Pig" is an unfortunate counter-culture term, which by now has become so widely applied to anything "Establishment" as to have lost its original meaning. It comes, for those who may not know, from the Black Panthers, who applied it to white policemen in an attempt to demonstrate to other ghetto residents that they had enough dignity to call "pigs" the same cops who called them "niggers." I would prefer to reserve its application to those policemen who earn it, of which there continue to be far too many.

I am also something of a language snob, and I cannot accept "male chauvinist," chauvinism being to me a word that means simply undue, blind patriotism. The fact that some dictionaries accept the wider use does not persuade me (there is a well-known dictionary that permits the use of "infer" to mean "imply," too).

I have trouble with "patriarchy," also, because I keep getting this picture of an old man with a white beard squatting in the middle of a village, or sitting on a porch surrounded by great-grandchildren. A somewhat better term that women in the movement use for the same thing is "sexism," described by Dudar as "the women's lib term for male supremacist and an offense to the language we will have to learn to live with" (as, she might have added, is "women's lib"). We probably will have to learn to live with it; but it's intended as an analogy to "racism," and to me it seems that "race" has a clear meaning, while "sex" carries all sorts of other overtones.

The point is that we do need a word that is analogous to "racism." Because what we are really troubled with in this country is white racism (analogously, "male sexism"), and because it is directly opposed to feminism, I've settled on "masculinism." But they all mean about the same thing, and it doesn't really matter that much.[1]

We are now back to set-breaking, and to one aspect (by no means one of the more controversial aspects) of the Black Analogy. The easiest way, for many men, to begin to break the masculinist set is to understand racism.

We don't, in our ordinary everyday speech, make a careful distinction between bigotry and racism. But we have to be able to follow it. It is relatively easy (the stress is on "relatively"; breaking any kind of set is never easy) for a white American not to be a racial bigot. It is much more difficult not to be a white racist, and that difficulty has to do directly with set-breaking.

A bigot is a person who believes certain (usually stereotyped) things about members of another race which are not true, and who acts on those erroneous beliefs. He (or she) "knows" these things— that Orientals are good at art, that black people have rhythm and/or smell bad, that Navajos are all alcoholics—and can sometimes cite particular experiences to "prove" it. Germaine Greer offers a splendid example of simple bigotry when she writes of "that most virile of creatures, the buck Negro."

Like all the rest of us who live according to existing block structures in our heads, a bigot will resist learning the truth about these matters, and usually cannot be argued out of them. But enough association with Orientals who can't draw a triangle or with blacks who can't find the beat in a Motown record and with whites who do not believe these things and do not act on them, will have its effect relatively quickly. The discovery that truth is not all threatening means that most of the block structure doesn't have to be disturbed after all.

A racist, on the other hand, is simply anyone who lives in a racist culture and does not recognize the manifestations of that culture's racism—and living in a racist culture means that the block levels go way down deep. You can have the best will in the world, and not believe a single stereotyped thing about blacks, and belong to the NAACP, and give money to the Black Panther Defense Fund, and still be a stone racist.

More likely, in this day and age, you'll be aware of a few of the culture's racist forms and oblivious to the rest. One of the problems when you really have to go deep to break a set is that you can understand the problem intellectually and still find yourself unwilling really to work at applying the understanding in your daily life. That is a little worse than not understanding it at all; you don't have innocence as a moral "out."

So what is this "racism"?

Racism is the assumption, built into the culture and drummed into our consciousnesses from the earliest moments of our lives, that *white* is *normal*.

I don't think that I have ever been really bigoted—for as long as I can remember, anyway, I seem to have been engaged in angry and futile arguments with bigots—but I was nearly forty before I think I truly recognized the difference between bigotry and racism and recognized myself as a racist, a characteristic I have been trying ever since to get rid of as far as I'm able. Some of the easier-to-understand examples of American white racism are disappearing, and younger white readers may not recall them, but there is always another and more current example.

During virtually my entire life, for example, I have walked down the streets of shopping districts and looked into windows at clothes on white mannequins. It never occurred to me that they were *white* mannequins. They didn't look to me like attempts to represent white people. They were simply attempts to represent people.

Nor were they put into the windows by people who decided not to use black mannequins. Nobody said, "Let's use white mannequins because most of our customers are white." Nobody ever thought about it. They simply used mannequins that looked like *people,* just as I saw mannequins that looked like people.

People were white. Black people were black. Different. Variations from the norm.[2]

But you can bet that black people saw *white* mannequins in those windows.

Take another example: Never until very recently did it occur to me that Santa Claus is white. A sizable proportion of American children are not white, but being a part of our culture celebrate, or at least live through, Christmas. The child who is not white sees that Santa Claus is white. To me, of course, as a child, he was never white. He just *was*.

So is God on the ceiling of Sistine Chapel (in Dino de Laurentiis' big movie, *The Bible,* Eve was a blonde, an extremely unlikely native of the Middle East). So, at least a few years ago, were all the people in all the illustrations in general-circulation magazines and all the people in advertisements printed or televised or even broadcast. And because in a racist culture *everybody* is white unless somebody says they aren't, then as far as most of us are concerned white was the color of Saint Augustine and Alexandre Dumas and Pio Pico, the last "Spanish" governor of California.[3]

Nor did it bother me a few years ago when Johnson and Johnson marketed a product called "flesh-colored Band-Aids." They *were* the color of flesh, just like crayons labeled "flesh" in the big 64-crayon box I had as a kid. Some people had different flesh—but I didn't even think about them as variations from the norm. I didn't think about them at all when I looked at the Band-Aids.

None of this ever met my consciousness until I began to understand that it is a cultural phenomenon, some of it deliberate, but most of it simply unconscious and based on an unconscious assumption, and that it is in fact destructive in its effect. Once I learned to recognize the phenomenon and call it by name—racism—the examples became overwhelming in their frequency; and after a time they began to force themselves on my consciousness.

As recently as 1971, a group of black artists protested *The Dick Cavett Show* on the ground that it paid insufficient attention to black culture and black art. The hapless Cavett, who seems to have understood the protest quite well, was required by his network to read a list of his past black guests—almost all of whom were entertainers who had made it in *white* culture. The idea of reading that list, as a defense against a charge of bigotry that had never been made, was itself, of course, pure racism.

If you can't see the difference, that makes you a racist, all right; but it does not make you *guilty* of racism—not as we usually use the word "guilty." All of us who are white Americans are conditioned into racism. We are guilty of it only when we make no at-

14

tempt to understand it or when we have a glimmer of understanding but don't do anything about it.

Most of us are still not aware that America is a culture of *structural* racism, which has to be overcome consciously and with effort.[4] When I was doing a story in Chicago a few years ago and a citizen told me that "the people of Chicago are not prejudiced against blacks," he was perfectly sincere. So was a friend, who does network television news, who told me once that "people are tired of hearing stories about blacks." Neither of them seemed to be aware, so pervasive are the effects of structural racism, that blacks *are* people— more than 30%, for instance, of "the people of Chicago."

So: Racism is the assumption, built into the culture and drummed into our consciousnesses from the earliest moments of our lives, that *white* is *normal*.

Masculinism is the assumption, built into the culture and drummed into our consciousnesses from the earliest moments of our lives, that *male* is normal.

If we were primarily concerned with racism rather than with masculinism, we would probably have to spend some time on the ways in which the two are more intimately connected. No bigot ever asked me, for instance, whether I would want my *brother* to marry one.

Some women will feel that I have not put my definition correctly. They see the unconscious assumption in the culture as being, not that "male is normal," but that "male is better." I think that this skips a stage in the process, at best.

That male is normal means that male activities are normal human activities—the ones that count, the ones that are meaningful; and if the normal activities are the male activities, then males are likely to be better at them. Beyond that, once the assumption is there, it is the males who will be trained for those "normal" activities, while women are for the most part trained for activities which can be performed perfectly well by the mentally retarded.

We don't have to worry, at this point, about how such theoretical distinctions are thrashed out. What is important is that there are cultural masculinist assumptions just as there are cultural racist assumptions, and that these extremely deep assumptions become so much a part of our learning processes that virtually all of us, female and male, are profoundly conditioned by them. They appear, to most of us, to be not only true but obvious.

It is because masculinism runs so deep in American culture—at least as deep as racism, possibly deeper because the conditioning starts much earlier (a black child knows she's female before she knows she's black)—that American feminists, even the mildest of them, find themselves required to use words that we find uncomfortable, like "revolution." Firestone, who is not one of the mildest of them, puts it this way (emphases hers):

> The reaction of the common man, woman and child—*"That?* Why, you can't change *that*! You must be out of your mind!"*—is the closest to the truth. We are talking about something every bit as deep as that. This gut reaction—the assumption that, even when they don't know it, feminists are talking about changing a fundamental biological condition—is an honest one. That so profound a change cannot be easily fit into traditional categories of thought, e.g., "political," is not because these categories do not apply but because they are not big enough: radical feminism bursts through them. If there were another word more all-embracing than *revolution* we would use it.

Firestone isn't saying, in this passage, that feminists *are* talking about changing a fundamental biological condition, which is by definition impossible.[5] If they actually were, we could justifiably treat them with lofty disregard. What she is saying is that the reaction is so profound that the rest of us treat feminist arguments as though they *were* attacks on fundamental biology.

The best single example I know of that shows how deep our masculine assumptions run in the culture is in a study, described by Chesler, conducted by Inge Broverman and some colleagues. The study involved a group of psychotherapists of various kinds—psychiatrists, psychologists and social workers. The Broverman investigators made up a list of 122 pairs of traits (like: "very subjective" *vs.* "very objective"), and took their list to the therapists.

The therapists were supposed to take each pair of opposed traits and break them down to a scale of seven (like: "extremely subjective, moderately subjective, slightly subjective, neutral, slightly objective," etc.). Having done that with all 122 pairs, they were then supposed to indicate, on each of the 122 scales, where they thought a mentally healthy adult would fall.

So far, so good. But the investigators then asked the panel of therapists to do it over again, indicating the characteristics of a healthy *male* and those of a healthy *female*.

Note that they were not being asked to describe men and women as they actually are, but as the experts thought they *ought to be* in order to be described as mentally healthy. The results (with no significant differences from male and female therapists) were quite simple. A healthy *adult* is a healthy *male*.

There is no ambiguity in this study. According to this group of psychological experts, a mentally healthy woman in this society is not an adult. This has to be nonsense; but it is nonsense according to which (for example) therapy is given to the overwhelming number of those American women who seek help for any self-perceived mental difficulties. Their "cure" is to be shaped into non-adults.[6]

You could make some sort of argument that a particular woman, if she wants to get along in a distorted culture and avoid frustration—if she wants to adjust to her condition rather than improve it—will be happier if she demonstrates what the therapists see as "female" characteristics. But then you will have to face the question whether a mentally healthy adult is one who accepts her or his society as she or he finds it, or whether a mentally healthy adult is one who tries to improve things. After all, men who try to change society get frustrated too.

Nonetheless, the Broverman result is clear. A healthy adult has "male" characteristics. In other words, male is normal.

And if male is normal, female is not.

The "supernormal" woman may appear to belie this. Adrienne Koch once quoted *The Radcliffe Report on Graduate Education for Women* regarding "the only woman member of a famous symphony orchestra," who "was engaged as a flutist because she far excelled the male applicants for the post. Her superiority demanded acceptance, and without question."

Koch commented: "I hereby propose that this solution be known in American history as the 'magic flute' position on female underprivilege." [7]

But the Magic Flautist (more language snobbery) is not really an exception. The women we know, who are not Madame Curie or Marian Anderson or Sirimavo Bandaranaike, are of course subnormal in our terms: our wives, our lovers, our girl friends, our sisters, the "girls" in the office, the waitresses at the lunch counter, the woman across the street. We don't honestly believe that they can do whatever we can do.

What now become interesting are the *ways* in which women are felt to be "subnormal." Broverman's was only one study. There are literally dozens of studies of how college students perceive women, how housewives perceive women, how various kinds of professors perceive women, how employers perceive women, how teachers perceive girls, how parents perceive female children—there is a study about everybody's perception except that of the household Siamese.

Not surprisingly, virtually all of them agree. Not only do they all assign to women characteristics that in men would be regarded as subnormal. Virtually all of them define women in terms of men to begin with. Women are *"less* aggressive," or *"more* intuitive," or *"not as good* at abstract reasoning." In some studies they have no characteristics of their own at all.

"We say that . . . women are home-loving, conservative, timid, devious," says one writer.[8] But "conservative" and "timid" are comparative terms. You cannot be timid unless there is a "standard person" in someone's head who, if not brave, is at least not timid. In our culture, that unmentioned, unseen, unnoticed standard person is male. Male is normal.

Chesler describes the Broverman study as finding women to be "submissive, emotional, easily influenced, sensitive to being hurt, excitable, conceited about their appearance, dependent, not very adventurous, less competitive, unaggressive [and] unobjective." Terman and Tyler, studying the studies on sex differences among children, found girls described as sensitive, responsive to the environment, ingratiating, likely to conform to social pressures, sympathetic, compassionate toward the underprivileged, anxious, without very high levels of aspiration, unstable, neurotic, submissive, timid, emotional, easily frightened, passive—and, in explicit comparison to boys, more nervous, lacking self-confidence, and possessed of low opinions of themselves and of females in general.

Remember that last trait, by the way, and remember that it is borne out by a number of studies. It becomes important a little later on.

Jo Freeman cites the Terman and Tyler study among many others in a thorough review of her own [9] and adds that in another study, women perceived their own sex as

uncertain, anxious, nervous, hasty, careless, fearful, dull, childish, help-less, sorry, timid, clumsy, stupid, silly and domestic. On the more positive side, women felt they were understanding, tender, sympathetic, pure, generous, affectionate, loving, moral, kind, grateful and patient.

Most studies don't give us such neat lists, but you get the same words over and over. Meredith Tax is among the writers who have noticed that these words don't only describe *women* as our culture perceives them. Put a handful of these words on a list, hand them to a psychiatrist of one or another kind without telling her (or him) where you got them, ask her (or him) what they describe, and the chances are that you'll be told that they're the characteristics of a schizophrenic.

Women are not only subnormal relative to men. In the terms usually applied to healthy American adults—gender unspecified—women are crazy.

Of course psychiatrists do not perceive all women as crazy. Those characteristics, in practice, mean "schizophrenia" only when they're present in men. In women they mean that the patient is cured!

But, you say—at least I assume you've said it by now—"I know a lot of women, and they *are* like that, whether they ought to be or not." Of course they are. They are conditioned in the same places and by the same people as you are. It is like Arlie Hochschild's story of the primitive society in which "the stories passed down through the generations portrayed the elders as wise, courageous and powerful, and then it was found that the elders were the story-tellers of the tribe." But it is much deeper than that, as Greer notes:

Because the difference is so wholeheartedly believed in, it is also experi-enced. As a conviction it becomes a motive for behavior and a continuing cause of the phenomenon itself.

In other words, given the structural masculinism of the society, you get an inevitable and quite vicious circle.

This conditioned set of assumptions about how women "naturally" are has been raised to an art form by the Freudians—an art form that would indeed be comic if so many people had not been tragically hurt by it. Marie Bonaparte, who follows Freud almost slavishly (the choice of words can be allowed to stand), writes of the extent to which female sexual enjoyment is "essentially" masochistic with such fervor and conviction that one almost wants to send Zorro around with his whip to keep her happy for a couple of weeks.

Helene Deutsch, often regarded as *the* Freudian authority on women, says that "intellectual" women are "masculinized"—they have let their "warm, intuitive knowledge" yield to "cold unproductive thinking." She was pretty intellectual herself, and possibly she thought of her own thinking as cold and unproductive—a train of thought whose logic will lead you to some odd conclusions about her writing her huge book in the first place. But I doubt whether most of us consider all of our masculine thinking to be cold and unproductive.

In fact, if you take away the adjectives, what she says is that the intellectual woman has allowed intuition to give way to thinking. We're left, in other words, with nothing but a dictionary definition of "intellectual"—an intellectual woman is one who acts intellectually— and a perfectly sane way of dealing with certain kinds of problems. Other problems are better dealt with, of course, by allowing thinking to give way to intuition, except that when *we* do that, we call it "having a hunch."

Male Freudians are pretty good too; Theodore Reik, for instance:

I have come across some women in analytic practice who lacked the faculty of being catty. They were either emotionally perverted, masochistic, homosexual, or neurotic.[10]

That about covers everybody. I wonder, by the way, whether Freudian Reik ever read Freudians Bonaparte and Deutsch, who insist that women are supposed to be masochistic.

Mary Ellmann notes that Bruno Bettelheim "characterizes the male mind as *expansive* and *exploratory* and the female mind as *interiorizing*." She can't help adding that "it is ludicrously clear that he envisages a mental copulation between the two." But the shrink who gets the gold-plated clock-bellied Venus lamp for giving himself away is Karl Abraham, whose 1920 essay on women won the admiration of Freud himself, and who in one sentence told us all we need to know about who he thought was important.

"Frigidity," Abraham wrote, "is a form of aggression against the man by disappointing him."

The only possible comment is another quotation, this time from Greer. "Freud is the father of psychoanalysis. It had no mother."

Women's liberationists don't like shrinks, generally speaking, for a simple and important reason. Psychiatrists, believing as they apparently do that certain differences between men and women come with the lease, naturally treat any woman with a problem as though the problem is somehow inside herself, in her inability to conform to the pre-existing Freudian definitions. If she doesn't think the role is right for her, it's "masculine protest." Thus Simone de Beauvoir's note that "when a little girl climbs trees it is, according to Adler, just to show her equality with boys; it does not occur to him that she likes to climb trees."

But the women's movement argues that more often than not, the trouble is not within the woman herself, but in the society. The trouble is there because of what the society is doing to her; and it is the society, not the woman, that must change if justice is to be done to each person as an individual. A society in which healthy adults are healthy males, and in which women to be "natural" must have the same characteristics as male schizophrenics, must have something wrong with *it*—and why should she pay fifty bucks an hour to a shrink who tells her that she's the one that has to change?

As I said before, reality is structural and language is linear. As a result we have wandered a little way from those lists of "male" and "female" characteristics, which most of us think of as natural differences. Look around us: Is it not *true* that women are, say, more passive? How do we know that it's not natural?

There are a lot of ways to tell. One is to go back, with a little care, to the Black Analogy. Another is to try to show that even *physiological* differences may not be *innate* or *necessary* differences, even when it seems "obvious" that they are. A third is to examine the conditioning process itself and to see just what has happened to you and me, and to the women we love, since the day we were born.

We shall take them in that order.

4
↓

ONCE, many years ago, I read a slim volume on logic, written for college freshmen (whom if I were a real feminist I should probably call "freshpeople"). It warned against certain faulty practices—common forms of argument that are in fact illogical and against which the reader should be on his guard. Most of us were of course delighted to learn all those new dishonest tricks for winning arguments, which I suppose was not the author's intention; but I recall particularly one that had to do with analogy. What it said about analogies was that it is illogical to argue with them.

If I compare a man who is repressing anger with a boiler that is being heated, and if I say that, like the boiler, my man is going to "blow up" when he reaches a certain pressure, you may disagree about the man. But it is silly to base your argument on the idea that boilers have other characteristics that I left out of the analogy. I didn't say that the man *is* a boiler. I said that he resembles a boiler *in certain respects,* and (by implication) *only* in those respects.

It's extremely common for the women's movement to draw analogies between the position of women in America and the position of blacks in America. Everyone who is concerned, on any sort of intellectual level, with racial differences has studied Gunnar Myrdal's classic *An American Dilemma*. Surprisingly few remember that there, in a long Appendix, is a careful delineation of parallels between the situation of women in America and that of blacks. Since then, a proliferation of studies, as well as a number of perceptive essays, have demonstrated that the analogies are not at all far-fetched.[1]

But they are analogies. They are not attempts to argue exact similarities.

The Hares quote two black women. One simply says, "The things white women are demanding liberation from are what we've never even experienced yet." True, certainly, in part; especially true if you're talking about a concern with middle-class "oppression" such as that described by Friedan. "The white Lib movement," says the other black woman, "is racist. They want to equate their oppression to that of black people. When has a white woman been lynched?"[2]

Linda J. M. La Rue makes the same point somewhat less bluntly:

> Let it be stated unequivocally that the American white woman has had a better opportunity to live a free and fulfilling life, both mentally and physically, than any other group in the United States, excluding her white husband. Thus, any attempt to analogize black oppression with the plight of the American white woman has all the validity of comparing the neck of a hanging man with the rope-burned hands of an amateur mountain climber. . . . What does the black woman on welfare who has difficulty feeding her children have in common with the discontent of the suburban mother who has the luxury to protest washing the dishes on which her family's full meal was consumed?

Of course. There are not a dozen women in the liberation movement who would disagree. Some might feel that *some* black men have it better than *some* white women, but that is not to argue with the generalization. Others may feel that, in an abstract sense, the oppression of women is more basic than even the oppression of blacks; but even they would certainly not argue that life in America is harder on women as a class than it is on blacks as a class. That would be silly.

But: If some aspects of the treatment of women can be more easily understood by looking at the ways in which it is similar to the treatment of blacks, and if those similarities do indeed seem to be valid as far as they go, then surely we must be free to use that method of looking at the problem. And surely, if we find that both groups are oppressed (regardless of degree or of differences in method), then what we want is for both groups, and any other oppressed groups, to be freed. No one wants women freed at the expense of blacks, or blacks at the expense of women.

Consider what most men traditionally say about women, and what most whites have traditionally said (before it became unfashionable) about blacks. They are in many ways like children. They are inferior in analytic intelligence. They are emotional. They have never produced an artistic or scientific genius. They are wonderful people in their places. The overwhelming majority are content to stay in their places. Most of them don't want what the liberationists say they want. Shirley Chisholm, who will probably not have been nominated for President by the time you read this, told a House subcommittee in 1970:

To keep them in their place, the same characteristics are imputed to women as to blacks—that they are more childish, emotional and irresponsible than men, that they are of lower intelligence than men, that they need protection, that they are happiest in routine, undemanding jobs, and that they lack ambition and executive ability.[3]

Jo Freeman [4] refers to Gordon Allport's "classic study on *The Nature of Prejudice*," noting that Allport devoted an entire chapter to "Traits Due to Victimization." He was writing primarily about Jews and blacks; Freeman notes that among those traits of the victimized he included

such personality characteristics as sensitivity, submission, fantasies of power, desire for protection, indirectness, ingratiation, petty revenge and sabotage, sympathy, extremes of both self and group hatred and self and group glorification, display of flashy status symbols, compassion for the underprivileged, identification with the dominant group's norms, and passivity.

You will have noticed that that fits very closely the list that Terman and Tyler came up with for girls in their study of the literature on sex difference. Freeman noticed it too. She also pointed out that there is a similarity in the way we regard work roles: The lower-ranked group—black or female—"is defined as not being able to do

24

certain types of prestigious work, but it is also considered a violation of propriety if they do." [5]

We really show our own lack of logic when we talk about the work women can do and the work they can't do. How many times have you heard it said—or said it yourself—with a quite serious and insistent vehemence: Women *can't* drive trucks, or work in warehouses, or be executives, or work on high-rise construction, or be competent doctors, or whatever. It's not prejudice; they just really and truly cannot do the job the way a man can. They're not built right. They're emotionally unsuitable. They just *can't*.

Think about it. If there is really some natural reason that women can't do it—then what are we yelling so loud for? If they can't, they won't. No prohibition, legal or unofficial, is necessary.

What we really mean, alas, is just what we (or our big brothers, or our fathers) meant when with equal sincerity we said the same thing about blacks. It isn't that they can't. It's that we don't want them to.

The effects of cultural oppression on blacks are also not all that different from the effects on women. Prior to the civil rights movement, the southern black, denied the opportunity of violence, had to get what he wanted by passivity, ingratiation, flattery, and—not too often and usually in subtle ways—through the partial withholding of what he had to offer to the white. Any married man will recognize the pattern immediately.

The black acts that way much less often now—and one result is that a lot of American whites have a reaction that can only be described as fear. The resurgent blacks scare the hell out of a lot of us whites. We don't regard them as grown-up children any more. And when we see women who do not act like the grown-up children they are supposed to be, I suggest that our reaction has more than a touch of fear in it.

Certainly an early reaction of almost every male is hostility—and if that does not apply to you, you're a rare exception. That hostility brings us back to Simone de Beauvoir, who found another similarity between the "black situation" and the "woman situation":

As a general rule, the superior caste is hostile to newcomers from the inferior caste: whites will not consult a Negro physician, nor males a woman doctor; but individuals of the inferior caste, imbued with a sense

25

of their specific inferiority and often full of resentment toward one of their kind who has risen above their usual lot, will also prefer to turn to the masters.

Knowles and Prewitt, describing institutionalized racism, point out that in a structurally racist society you don't have to make any individual choices to be a racist. The choices are already built in—you just go along, unthinking, with the "normal" way of behavior. Clearly this, too, applies to structural masculinism.

And it applies not only to men. Women, too, accept the norms of the society—and the vicious circle spins again, just as it did as long as blacks believed what the whites said about them. The pattern becomes: He (or she) can't have the job because he (or she) can't do it; and the evidence that he (or she) can't do it is that there aren't any of them in those jobs.

We whites, as individuals, often insist that we do not oppress blacks. We men, as individuals, are likely to insist that we do not oppress women. But we do—every time we let structural, institutionalized oppression go by without challenge. And the patterns of oppression, despite the obvious differences, are remarkably similar.

The word "oppressed," if you are not used to the rhetoric of the Left and of the women's movement, may bother you, since it carries in its everyday usage some suggestion of that conscious and deliberate persecution of which you probably don't feel guilty. Some writers think you are guilty; Atkinson argues that if women are oppressed, there is only one group left over to do the oppressing, and that's that.

The alternative—that because the oppressive practices are institutionalized, it is the institutions that do the oppressing—doesn't work too well either; that leaves nobody guilty, and is what some people on the Left would call (I think correctly) a liberal cop-out. The truth is no doubt somewhere in between: institutions continue to exist if, once we understand them, we allow them to continue to exist—and there's no point in arguing about whose fault it was yesterday.

Let us for the moment settle for this: If individuals within a group are unfree, kept down by something they cannot themselves fully control, kept thereby from becoming whatever they have the ca-

26

pacity to become, it seems fair to say that they are "oppressed," whether we are any more precise or not. Fanon in Algeria and Kurt Lewin in America, among many others, have pointed out that oppressed peoples share a number of characteristics, as we've already noted. One of those characteristics is that the oppressed people themselves see their differences as deficiencies.

When I spent a part of 1965 in a black community in Georgia, one of the most painful perceptions was the realization that black girls of twelve or thirteen or fourteen, whom *I* saw (in a purely old-fashioned masculinist way) as quite lovely, saw themselves as ugly. Surrounded since birth with only one ideal of female beauty—the white woman in the advertisements and in the movies and on the television—they struggled achingly to come as close to that model as they could and were twisted bitterly every day by the fact that they could never, ever, come close at all.

When one young woman of fourteen later came to New York to stay with us for a time, and in that far more advanced black culture picked up the new hair style then called an "Afro," she wore it home —only to be forced by the jeers of her black girl friends to abandon it after a few days for the hair-straightening operation that would bring her illusively nearer the white model.

It is, of course, precisely because this pattern was so widespread, because so many blacks were so deeply convinced that white standards were in fact normal standards, that some black activists began to insist on the concept that "black is beautiful." [6] And it did not only affect black women's view of their own appearances. It affected the perception by all blacks of their overall value relative to whites. It is only seven years since 1965, but it is already difficult in this day of black assertiveness to remember how thoroughly American blacks had interiorized the norms of white society.

And, just as blacks genuinely believed for so long in white norms (and as many still do), so do most women today genuinely believe in male norms. So much so that (with a sizable boost from the Freudians, to whom women are "incomplete men") they, too, see their differences not simply as differences—which bring their own different but equally valuable possibilities—but as deficiencies. And in both groups, even those who know they're doomed to failure go on desperately trying.

This means something that (although we asked you to remember it from the Terman and Tyler study on sex differences some pages back) most women will deny, and that you may at first want to deny too. In any case, if you ask the nearest woman, chances are that she'll tell you it's nonsense. But it's not.

Women hate what they are.

Understand me. Those black girls in Georgia might have said that they hated being black—or at the very least that they chafed under the frustrations of being black and longingly envied whites— but they would not have admitted that they hated being women or being, particularly, black women. They wouldn't have admitted it because they didn't really know it.

But it was true all the same, and their behavior made it quite clear. They were doing their best to turn themselves, not into whites, but into white women; not into women that free black men might have desired, but into women that white men might desire—and thus, into women that might be desired by black men who had also accepted white norms.[7]

Similarly with white women. If they liked what they are, they would insist on being what they are—and the bottom would drop out of the businesses that provide them with false eyelashes, depilatories, brassieres, eye shadow, hair coloring, nail polish, girdles, lipstick, eye liner, impossible shoes, fake moles, stuff for covering up real moles, mascara, foundation makeup, hair spray, perfume and that most absolutely ridiculous of all cosmetics, vaginal deodorants.

Outrage from some of you about here, I think. "What the hell is wrong with wanting to look nice? If those women's libbers want to be a bunch of bags, that's their business, but looking nice doesn't mean . . . "

Come on, buddy. You're supposed to be struggling. First of all, who says they look nice? You do. And because you do, they do. They want to look nice because we say that they should; and they want to do certain things which we all call "looking nice" because we, not they, decide that those are the things that "look nice."

Yes, I know. They don't do it for men. Oh, some do—the girls who work in the office while they look for a husband, and the secretaries who make it to the body-shop bars after work. But most ordinary women—people's wives, and the kids' mothers, and the people who go shopping—they look nice just because they think they should, and because it's right, and, of course, for each other. Don't they?

Do they? Really? In their heads, no doubt, but remember we're talking about a pattern that is built into the culture and conditioned into every one of our heads.

When that kid from Georgia went home from New York with an Afro, she didn't straighten her hair because the whites didn't like it. She straightened her hair because other black kids didn't like it. Each of those girls did not like what she was—a female with kinky hair—and what's more, they didn't like what other black girls really were—females with kinky hair.

Your "ordinary" woman does not like what she really is, and she does not like what *other* women really are. They don't think it's nice for a woman to go downtown without her makeup on. And where did they get the idea of what "looks nice"?

From a lot of places; mostly from their mothers, no doubt. But culturally, where are the ideals? In the magazines. On the television. In the movies. And who are the model women in the magazines, the television, the movies—the women who represent the cultural patterns to which "ordinary" people try to adapt? They are, in short, the women who get the men. Either they are women (in television ads, for instance) who have obviously achieved hard-working husbands, nice kids and pretty homes—and who keep them—or they are women who attract good-looking men. The fact that the standards persist for "looking nice" even when a particular woman is not man-getting or man-holding doesn't change the fact that that's the pattern that determines that standard.

It is a cliché that women do not, by and large, like each other; easy friendships like those among men are rare, though women who are thrown together (as in suburban tracts) may prefer each other to loneliness. It is not so obvious that they do not like themselves— that they do not like what they really are—and that they do not like other women especially when the other women are more nearly themselves.

If you are really willing to struggle with it a little, you will see it —and you will see, too, how much they deceive themselves, how much they twist their own perceptions, to fit the norm. Because without that fit, they would be more desperately alone than they think they can bear.

Jo Freeman again, from the same essay as before:

> This combination of group self-hate *and a distortion of perceptions* to justify that group self-hate is precisely typical of a minority group character structure. It has been noted time and time again. . . . These traits, as well as the others typical of the "feminine" stereotype, have been found in the Indians under British rule, in the Algerians under the French and in black Americans [emphasis added].

If blacks, though, had this distorted perception, this self-hate, and if the whole black movement from Martin Luther King through Malcolm and Eldridge to today has changed that (at least for some blacks, especially younger ones), is there a similar experience for women who break the patterns of *their* conditioning? There sure is.

Writing about the black experience, Kirsten Amundsen notes that despite some assessments that it didn't achieve anything, "the civil rights movement *did* achieve a degree of success. What is important in our consideration here is that it succeeded in changing the consciousness of large numbers of black people in this country."

It is not an accident that many people in the women's liberation movement came out of the civil rights movement, and it is probably not an accident that Amundsen used the phrase "changing the consciousness." The women's movement calls one of its central processes "consciousness-raising"—we're going to talk about it in detail somewhat later on—and its principal function is to bring about deliberately what the civil rights movement began doing for blacks more or less accidentally.

Without going into detail here, the consciousness-raising process in women's liberation has several purposes. Among them, the process is designed to show women that (1) they *are* oppressed, (2) it is not their fault, (3) it is most often society, not the individual woman, that must be changed if the woman's condition is to change, (4) they ought to be proud of what they really are and (5) they ought to like and feel solidarity for what their sisters really are.

Female, in other words, is beautiful. Again drawing on the analogy, Anita Lynn Micossi, who did a study of women "converted" to liberation, puts it precisely:

30

This increase in esteem for members of one's own sex is a measure of the increase in self-esteem (again, similar to the black experience) and demonstrates how relations with the world reflect one's relations to and image of self.

The black man or woman hears "black is beautiful" and says, "If black is beautiful, then by God *I* am all right, I am *not* really inferior or ugly or whatever, my culture and its standards are just as good as theirs, and my sisters and brothers are all right too. If black is beautiful, then *they* have been jiving me all these years." [8] And this is exactly what happens to women in the liberation movement.

We honestly believed, we whites, that a lot of those black characteristics were "natural." If a black kid in the South acted "deferential, devious, unassertive, and coy," [9] we honestly thought that it was because that's how black kids are. Well, we know better now, don't we? The question is whether we can learn from the analogy.

We use the same words for women and for oppressed minorities. We endow them (often falsely) with the same characteristics. We apply much the same treatment in some ways. In response, they develop much the same techniques of behavior. They themselves internalize our perceptions and values and make them theirs. Out of those perceptions and values they generate much the same feelings, including some degree of self-dislike.

Both patterns are structured into the society, similarly so, and even the fact that the methods of control are different does not destroy the fact that "control" exists. And finally, they have even developed, to some extent, the same techniques for liberation.

The analogies hold, at a surprising number of points; and the differences that we can all see don't invalidate the similarities. Nor, in ending the subject, should we let ourselves pretend that they are two entirely unrelated problems, even though black men, particularly, won't like the idea.

For just as the kids in Georgia got their models of American female attractiveness from the white culture, their ancestors for centuries got their models of male-female relationships from that same white culture. Blacks are as hung up in masculinism as whites are, and for the same reasons; they live with the same institutions.

We opened the chapter with a quotation from La Rue, making clear the differences between white women's and black women's problems. Perhaps we can permit her also the last word, for the moment anyhow, on the Black Analogy and the black experience:

Many suspect that Women's Liberation will enhance the distrust and dissension existing between black men and black women. I maintain that the true liberation of black people depends on their rejection of the inferiority of women, the rejection of competition as the only viable relationship between men, and their reaffirmation of respect for man's general human potential in whatever form—man, child or woman—it is conceived. If both men and women are liberated, then competition between the sexes no longer exists, and sexual exploitation becomes a remnant of social immaturity.

5

I WAS taking a break anyway, and I looked at the television, and there was Dr. Marcus Welby, telling a distraught husband soothingly that "women see these things with their own peculiar logic," while the husband nodded wisely.

It is bad enough to try to fight everything you were ever conditioned into at home or in school. Now I have to fight Dr. Welby, too. And while I've been trying to be nice about it, I know that ultimately I have to face some hostility from you. I may as well start now, with a sentence that—especially when it's true—is almost guaranteed to bring a hostile reaction from anyone, female or male.

You don't know what you think you know.

What I mean by that is that some of the things of which you are *absolutely certain* are untrue. The human psyche is not well adapted to having its certainties taken away, which is where the hostility comes from. If one set of certainties becomes untenable, we want another set right now.

How about this one: Men are bigger. You know that. Hell, you can see it.

But let's take a look at it anyway. To start with, as any cop will tell you who has ever tried to interview a group of "eyewitnesses," people see what they think is going to be there. And structural, institutional factors in the culture have a lot to do with what they think they're going to see, or what they think they've seen.

I know a good example that deals with racism; it sticks in my mind

33

from something I read ten or twelve years ago about perception psychology. A bunch of college students were told that they would be shown a picture for a while, and then asked questions about it—no tricks, just straight, "What did you see?" The picture was a street scene, in which a white man was wielding a knife against a black man. The questions were things like, "Was the white man wearing a tie?" And, of course, each student was asked for a general description of the scene.

More than half the students put the knife into the hand of the black man. And if by any chance that's what you thought I said the first time and had to go back to check—welcome to the club.

Believe it or not, we see men as bigger than they are, and we see women as smaller. Let me use myself in another example. I come from a large and close family, in which a lot of branches maintain some kind of contact; at a family gathering it's not unusual for me to see one of my sister-in-law's sister's kids. When I think of "women in the family," I think of perhaps twenty separate adults.

Now, aside from a few remarks on the sparsity of growth on the front half of my head, I've never heard anyone kid me about how I look. I look ordinary. Nobody has ever called me "shorty" or "skinny" or anything denoting unusual smallness in any dimension. But of the twenty or so "women in my family," all but two or three outweigh me.

Yet the members of the family will be genuinely surprised to read that, because they literally see me as bigger and see the women as smaller. So don't be too sure what you see.

Now we fall back a step. Never mind what I can see. Aren't there facts we can refer to—insurance company records, census figures, something like that? Isn't it objectively true that men are bigger?

No. It's statistically true that men are bigger, and that's an objective fact. No doubt, if I haven't aroused your hostility by talking about women's liberation, I can arouse it by talking about statistics, but that's how it goes.[1] Because one of our problems is our tendency to confuse a statistical statement with an absolute statement.

Charts are easy, though. Let's take all the men in America, from the biggest to the smallest, and all the women in America, from the biggest to the smallest, and see how the size distribution looks. You can use height or bulk or anything you want; it doesn't matter. It comes out something like this:

34

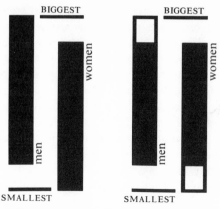

That's not to scale or anything, but it goes about like that. So we look at it and we say, "Men are bigger than women," and what we mean is, "The biggest men are bigger than the biggest women, and the smallest women are smaller than the smallest men."

Now that is obviously a statement of an entirely different kind. Elephants are bigger than Thomson's gazelles, but men are not bigger than women. Which leads you to shrug and say, "Okay, okay, that's what I meant, of course."

Ah, but: When somebody makes an absolute statement in a place where a statistical statement belongs, it often leads to trouble. It leads to trouble because people draw inferences from the (incorrect) absolute statement that wouldn't make sense if they were drawn from the (correct) statistical statement. Suppose, for instance, that we dramatize the existence of the biggest men and the smallest women by redrawing our simple chart to look like this:

As I said, it's not to scale, but there is one thing about it that's accurate. The common black section in the middle—the overlap section—is, in real life as in the drawing, *bigger than the two white sections put together*. In other words, there are more American adults within the overlap area than there are in the two biggest-men and smallest-women areas put together—by far.

We do not often say, in this culture, that there are some jobs that only women can do because of their small size. If we did, it might make sense to find some of the healthiest women in that white section of the chart and make them our astronauts. We do often say, however, that there are jobs that only men can do because men are bigger (or stronger, or both—a "strength" chart would look about the same).

And that, friends, is where we have drawn an inference from an absolute statement, which is incorrect, while an inference drawn from the correct information would not support the conclusion. In other words, it isn't so.

If it is a job that can only be done by a man who is bigger than any woman, then it makes sense. There are very few such jobs, of course, but it would certainly be difficult to find a woman big enough to be a defensive tackle for the Minnesota Vikings. The point is that this is not because "men are bigger." It is because the job calls for one of the biggest *humans* there is, and the biggest humans happen to be men in almost every case. The point is also that well over 90% of American men are not big enough to play defensive tackle for the Minnesota Vikings either.

There are women who can drive a semi with a set of doubles or a 35-foot van behind it (there are all kinds of women bus drivers), there are female longshoremen ("longshorewomen"?), and there are female lumberjacks. If you want to say of some kind of work, "A lot of women can't do that because they're too small," okay—but don't use that as a reason for barring all women, because it doesn't make sense. In fact, why not say, "A lot of *people* can't do that because they're too small?"

The idea of, say, a female cop walking a beat or a female fireman ("firewoman"?) climbing a ladder, axe in hand, still bothers a lot of us, of course.[2] That's partly because we're conditioned into this protective, no-honey-let-me-do-that role, and partly just because it's unfamiliar. So if we make it familiar, it won't bother us any more.

36

Like women typists. When typewriters first came out, the work was restricted to men because women were too frail to stand the strain of pounding those keys all day.

There's one more thing about men being "bigger" that we ought to keep in mind. "We do not know," says de Beauvoir, "whether woman's musculature or her respiratory apparatus, under conditions different from those of today, were not as well developed as in man." This has to do not with how individual female children are conditioned and trained, so that they grow up in a certain way, but more with how males and females have evolved over a long period of time because of the roles into which they fell during those thousands of years before we arrived at "civilization."

There is a lot of discussion in some segments of the women's movement about how it was back there in the caves (was human society originally matriarchal? and things like that). I don't really care how it was back there in the caves. That's not where we are. The point is that some differences, which may actually exist, may exist as adaptations to conditions that are no longer with us, so that there is no longer any reason to regard them as necessary.

Think about that. An *innate* difference may not be a *necessary* difference. That's another confusion we often run into when we talk about women.

Before we go back to the particular things we think that we know, we ought to take a look at this whole business about what's "natural" anyway. Certainly one of our objections to women's liberation has been that some of those nutty females want to defy their natural roles. What is this "natural" we keep talking about?

The level-headed Figes deals with this question somewhat dryly and, I think, rather neatly:

> What is a "natural" man or woman? One is forced to answer that there is no such thing, unless one concludes that, since man is a social animal, his "natural" condition is to *be* artificially conditioned, with variations in time and place [her emphasis].

We talk about "natural food," but we don't mean going out and picking for our dinner whatever grows wild in a wilderness zone. All agriculture is artificial. We walk around *au naturel* in houses kept artificially, through an extremely complex process, at 72 degrees. We use expressions like "artificial rubber" or "artificial cloth" as though what we usually call rubber or cloth were "natural" substances any caveman (or cavewoman) might have found lying around.

Except for childbearing and what precedes it, it is semantically silly to talk about what is "natural" to women. Even if it weren't, what are we worried about, we men? If something about women really is natural, then by the very definition of the word it is not going to change—no matter what the women's liberationists do.

Is there nothing else "natural," nothing but vagina and womb? Yes, of course; some things. Some aspects of body structure that go along with the childbearing capacity. Cells—X and Y chromosomes and all that.[3] And there's the Barr Body.

The Associated Press advised me from Miami during 1971 that the International Olympic Committee, faced with the problem of being certain that female athletes are not male ringers, solved it by taking a wooden spatula, scraping cells from the gums of females, and putting them under a 1200-power microscope. If between twenty and sixty per cent of the cells have a "distinctive extra dot, called a Barr Body," the athlete is female.[4] Of course there is, as a doctor noted at the time, an easier way, without even a microscope.

It is necessary, however, to ask another question. I apologize for all these questions, but they are a necessary consequence of a genuine attempt to investigate a subject; if you don't ask them they have a nasty way of coming back and tripping you up later. The question: Is even a *physiological* difference "natural"?

Our text for this point comes from Kate Millett:

> We are hardly in a position to assess the existing differentiations, since distinctions which we know to be culturally induced at present so outweigh them. Whatever the "real" differences between the sexes may be, we are not likely to know them until the sexes are treated differently, that is, alike.

Sickle-cell anemia, a disease primarily of blacks in America, does not really result from a "natural," physiologically based difference between blacks and whites. It results from the cultural difference between living where there's malaria and not living there, and then from being descended from imported slaves and not being descended from slaves. Because it took place over a great period of

38

time, it would take similar centuries for it to disappear naturally—a process I hope we are too humane to await—but it would disappear.

So we ask now: What may have happened to the physiology of women in the same amount of time, not because they have always had those differences, but because of their having been treated differently somewhere, somehow? Are some of those *physiological* differences also *cultural* in origin?

And we answer: We can't tell. Which is what Millett said. We will have to treat everybody alike for a while in order to find out what the differences really are; and only then can we begin to find out where those differences came from.

How about hormones? You have heard about hormones; without hormones we wouldn't have birth control pills, or at least not the ones we (they) have. Women have different hormones, or anyway hormones in different proportions. They lead to what the doctors and psychologists call "secondary sex differences." You have to shave, but she doesn't, and she doesn't (usually) get hair on her chest either—although she does get something there that you don't (usually) get, complete with plumbing that exists in you only rudimentarily.[5]

Some of those hormones go with the simple vagina-and-womb difference, because their job is directly related to reproduction; those are the ones affected by the pills. But we look closer, and we see that what we call "sex hormones" also go to the brain. Aha! Different chemicals go to the brain; *ergo,* the brain is different. And that's not cultural, that comes with the original difference, right?

Well—let's say, right, *but.* Sex hormones do go to the brain, and they're not the same in you as in her. But again, we don't know just what that means in real life. This time the text is from the psychologist, Weisstein:

The . . . theory argues that since females and males differ in their sex hormones, and since sex hormones enter the brain, there must be innate differences in *psychological nature.* But this argument tells us only that there are differences in *physiological state* [emphasis in the original].[6]

What does that mean? Happily, she gives us an illustration about physiological states. Freshmen (freshperson?) psychology courses familiarize thousands of people with what is often called the fight-flight reaction—a physiological state. Confronted with a threat, you (and I, and she) come up with a little internal shot of adrenalin, and that induces some other changes; you know the feeling, that sort of racing-blood readiness if, for instance, an argument turns serious and a little ugly.

Looked at physiologically, that burst of adrenalin gets the body ready. It gets the body ready, in a number of ways, for a fight. It also gets the body ready, in a number of ways, to run like hell if that seems like a better idea—hence the "fight-flight" phrase. Some of them are the same ways—it increases the quickly available energy, for one. And under slightly different circumstances, the same shot of adrenalin just makes you feel good; you get a shot like that when somebody calls you on the phone and tells you that you've won the Irish Sweepstakes.

Same physiological state. But your *psychological* feeling may be entirely different. You may be eager for a fight, or you may be frantically searching for the nearest faraway place. In a danger situation, whether you fight or flee does not depend on the adrenalin shot; it depends on a lot of things, including what your old daddy told you was the right thing to do in a spot like this. You might be about my size and the same age; I might run; you might fight. Nothing to do with the physiology.

It's not only what your old daddy told you, either. There is also, and perhaps most important, the question: Who's watching? If the rest of the gang is watching, will I do what I would do if everyone were a stranger? Probably not. If (being hung up in cultural roles like most other people) I'm trying to impress a female with my manhood, will I do what I would do if I were alone? Probably not. You recognize those differences, don't you?

But let Weisstein tell you about an experiment:

Stanley Schachter and J. E. Singer gave a group injections of adrenalin, which produces a state of physiological arousal. . . . When they were in a room with a stooge who acted euphoric, they become euphoric; when they were placed in a room with a stooge who acted angry, they became extremely angry.

Very natural, that adrenalin. Not at all "natural," our behavior. So we can't go with the hormones and the brain—not quite. It depends too much on what is expected of us; and that, of course, is cultural.

Which leaves us with the difference—the set of differences—that we are absolutely certain of. And this time, we are certain, or there is no point in talking about people called "women" or "men" at all. It is simply this: We are "designed" differently, so that we fit together physically, in a way that has become through the processes of evolution and culture a pleasurable act for a lot of us. And, through that act, a child can be conceived, and a woman is so "designed" that the child can partially develop within her before it has to make it on its own out there in the open air.[7]

Again, an *innate* difference may not be a *necessary* difference. There are sperm banks.[8] There are test-tube babies, otherwise known as extrauterine pregnancies. There are even a few discoveries about those eggs females carry around—discoveries not at all good for the male ego—suggesting that we may not be even routinely necessary to the whole process of reproduction. "Parthenogenesis" is the word for that.

There are a few women in the liberation movement who seem to argue that parthenogenesis and extrauterine pregnancy are both absolutely necessary to women's liberation—that without them, liberation can never be "real." I oversimplify, of course, but if I read them correctly, Firestone and Atkinson both seem to make this argument. It is a theoretical argument at the moment and beyond our scope, but I can say that if one of them is the first women's liberationist you happen to run into in your studies, you can get a very distorted idea of the movement. Most women, whether they agree with that approach or not, aren't primarily concerned about it right now; there are other things up front.

So let's just assume that most of us, regardless of our gender or of how feminist we are, will reproduce conventionally, if at all. It is reproduction we're talking about—not just sex—because we are talking about natural differences, and those differences are geared toward reproduction, whatever other use we may make of them in the meantime.

At this point we have to understand a distinction—simple in theory, but demanding of almost all of us males that we really make an effort to break the sets in our heads. We have to get this one straight. I was made to understand it by Anne Koedt, who has

41

one of the sharpest minds in the movement, and I have borrowed her terms, although of course she isn't responsible for how I use them (or mess them up).[9]

There alongside you in bed is this body, different from yours, right? And the big difference is that if things happen in a particular way while you're both there, you can walk away from it and she can't. Her body has to carry (literally) the consequences. She *can* have a baby, in the physical sense of that phrase. You can't.

That does not mean that she *must* have a baby—either this time or at any other time. It only means that she can.

To say that she can have a baby is to describe a physical *capacity*. To say that she must have babies is to describe a *function*: That's what she's for. To say that she is "naturally" a mother because she's a woman is to describe a *role*: That's what she ought to do with her life.

What we do, we men, and we do it a lot, is to mix up the capacity with the function. Because women *can* have babies, we look at their bodies and say that that's what women are *for,* that's their function in the world. And some of us, anyway, get very uptight about any woman who steps out of the wife-and-mother picture; because we don't only expect her to perform what we see as her *function,* but we want her to play what we see as her *role*.

The idea that it's her *function* turns a capacity into a necessity. The idea that it's her *role* turns the supposed function into an institution.

Assuming that you're not too young or too old, and that you're not Jake Barnes or anything like that, you have the *capacity* to be the father of a child. You may not want to be. You may want desperately not to be. You can be a Trappist monk, but you have the capacity.

So I come along, and I say to you: You are built to father children. Therefore, it is your destiny, it is your natural function, to father children. It is *unnatural* for you to try to get out of it or to think that it should be only a relatively small part of a life much of which is devoted to something else.

If you decide that you want to have a good job before you get married—a job you intend to keep even after getting married and becoming a father—then you are denying your natural function. If you decide that you would rather be a bachelor, you are either sick or queer. If you say that you don't mind fathering a child or two, but you really regard your "real" work in life as more important, you are downright weird. If anything else in your life is not put well behind your principal function—which is fathering children—then there is something wrong with you; you are an unnatural man.

I say that to you, and what do you say to me? You say to me that I am out of my gourd.

And so you should, for you are quite right. I have noted your *capacity,* and proceeded to get all mixed up and think that your capacity is your *function.* Which, as you have quickly noted, is nonsense.

The usual male reply at this point is something about the man's duty to work in order to support the family. But that's cheating. We're talking about what is a natural difference between men and women, and about how, in discussing that subject, we often confuse capacity with function. Who brings home the bacon is obviously cultural, not natural; it's all the way over into "role." It may affect what we (or they) *decide* to do, but it doesn't affect what is *natural* to do.

Another technique for understanding is the absurd analogy. The trouble with the absurd analogy is that people always say, "But it's not the same thing." It is the same thing, though, except that the ridiculousness of the logic becomes obvious.

Put your arm straight down at your side. Now, keeping it straight, extend it in front of you, then over your head, then bring it down backward to your side again. Now extend it sideways across your body. Now over your head, then out to your side, then down again.

You have just demonstrated that you have the capacity for swinging through trees.

So is that your function? Do you argue that people who don't devote their lives to swinging through trees—at least as their first and most important duty, the thing they are obviously destined for—are somehow unnatural?

"But"—with a stubborn, dogged shake of the head—"it's not the same thing." Look: A little light is not going to go on over your head, and you're not suddenly going to say, "Gloryosky, Sandy, I never thought of that!" and change your life. Take the word of a reasonably bright brother who has lived for some time in close proximity to a pretty tough feminist and spent most of that time resisting. Every little crack in that wall of blocks we've built up comes after weeks, sometimes months, of resistance, hostility, and determined insistence that "it's not the same thing."

Logically, it is the same thing. A woman has a capacity for childbearing just as we all have a capacity for swinging through trees. A woman has a capacity for childbearing just as you have a capacity for child-fathering. No more, no less. Your anatomy is one thing and your destiny is something else again, no matter what your sex.[10]

But it takes somewhere from two minutes upward to father a child, and it takes nine months to bear one. That, too, is a difference.

It is not a difference, however, that automatically disqualifies a woman from doing anything else during her pregnancy. Late in the game, it would make some kinds of jobs a little clumsy—an eight-months-pregnant truck driver might have something of a bad time— but not most jobs.[11] We have cultural hangups in some places about things like pregnant schoolteachers (or cocktail waitresses), but the objections are not physical or natural. They can be changed if we want badly enough to overcome our cultural conditioning, and if for other reasons it seems worth it.[12]

The next step in the usual male argument reaches for half-understood biology. It is natural, the argument goes, for women to want to devote themselves to bearing children because that is how the survival of the species is guaranteed.

It would help considerably if we would stop getting our biology from the pop mishmashes of the Lionel Tigers and the Robert Ardreys (I would make the superb essay by Judith Shapiro required reading), but let us leave that aside for the moment and take a look at the logic. It might make some of the most masculinist among us wince a little if we examine what we're really saying.

The argument would allow men to roam the entire range of human culture—being the job-holders, the technicians, the artists, the scientists, the movers, the doers—while restricting women primarily to a function derived from their capacity. What that means is that the guy making the argument sees the human race as divided into two groups: men, and a different animal that exists only to breed more men. And, of course, to breed more breeders as well.

Most of us either do not really believe that women exist only to enable men to go on existing—or we don't know that that is what

44

we really believe. To say that they are also there in order to make us comfortable is merely to compound the arrogance.

Certainly, looking at things from a biological and evolutionary standpoint (perhaps a redundancy), there is a "drive" to perpetuate the species. But not, any more, an uncontrollable and absolutely predetermined drive. We still have to eat, but few of us any longer hunt or gather to obtain food. Similarly, through the use of our intelligence (which is also and equally a product of evolution), we consciously change the conditions of our reproduction.

As a matter of fact, although since the romantic age in Western civilization (a small part of the human race, remember) some writers have come up with an awful lot of mystic nonsense about reproduction and the perpetuation of the race, the biological probability is that we don't, as individuals, have a drive to reproduce at all. What we have, just like your neighborhood unfixed tomcat, is a drive to fuck. He doesn't go around looking for a heated female in order to perpetuate his species; it just happens that what he wants to do is also how the species gets perpetuated. With him—*and* with his mate—as with us, the fun comes at the start.

Of course, a lot of men and women in a lot of cultures, our own included, want children. Some of them want children enough so that they may think of it as a "natural" feeling. But there are also a lot of men and women in a lot of cultures, our own included, who do not want children. If it were a natural biological drive, there couldn't be so many people without it.

Finally, one of the obvious differences between being human and being, say, a garden snail is precisely our ability to overcome, or anyway to redirect or channel or sublimate, our natural drives for the good of the society in which we live. If the unbridled pursuit of a natural drive comes at the expense of the well-being of other people, we don't do it (or if we try, the other people stop us).

What is natural, of course, is the maternal instinct—isn't it?

Sorry, but no. We have talked about capacity and function, but we haven't talked much about role, because I'm saving it for later. The motherhood bit, however, is a cultural role; and just so you'll know what you're in for, here's the bare and for the moment unsupported fact: There is no such thing as a maternal instinct in humans. Very likely, there is no such thing as *any* kind of instinct in humans. If that makes you recoil a little, hold your indignation for a few pages.

So does that leave any natural differences at all? One—or, if you like, one set. It leaves us with the fact that men and women are biologically different in a way that makes it possible—not necessary, but possible—for them to have sex together and to conceive children together, and makes it possible—not necessary, but possible—for women to bear them.

And it leaves us with the fact that if there are any other absolutely inherent biological differences, there's no way to find them under the present layer of cultural conditioning.

And that's all.

There is no other difference between men and women about which we can say that we know it's a natural difference, free of cultural impact. A change in the present male-female divisions in our culture may do all kinds of things, over a few years, for what seem to be "natural" differences between men and women.

But if that takes care of what is "natural," it doesn't completely dispose of the fact that you don't know what you think you know. Regardless of natural *vs.* cultural, there are a lot of things we think we know about our culture, which on examination also turn out to be wrong, or at least misstated. Most of them belong in other sections, but we ought to look at how we "know" some of them—especially those that involve the statistical facts we were talking about earlier.

Or, to put it more interestingly, I would like to introduce you to what I call Jo Freeman's Rule.

When people in our culture do tests on men and women or on boys and girls, differences often show up. They are almost certainly culturally caused, but that's beside the point right now; the point right now is that they're there. Boys, for instance, tend to do better on mathematical or analytic tests; girls on verbal tests. Boys are better at picking out the number of faces hidden in the drawing of a bunch of trees—things like that. Tests that involve finishing a story about yourself, in which the first sentence is given, show that women usually tell low-achievement stories, while men usually tell high-achievement stories.

At least that's the way the tests are usually reported, and that's the way most of us read about them. But there is a curious thing about tests like that. In her essay, "Growing Up Girlish," Freeman found dozens of examples of this peculiarity, which is why I think of it as Jo Freeman's Rule. It's amazing how often it proves out:

The generalizations about women that result from comparative tests usually apply to only about two-thirds of the women tested.

Let's say that you've got a test designed to find out from a roomful of children how many of them have strong, aggressive career drives. If your sample is good, you are likely to wind up with results showing that about two-thirds of the boys have such drives, and only about one-third of the girls. You are very likely to slip into reporting that "boys are more achievement-oriented than girls"—the same kind of statement as "men are bigger than women." And you have just dropped one-third of the females.[13]

Now, one-third is one hell of a large minority. If we take a result that in fact applies to only two-thirds of the women, and then apply that result as though it were a valid statement about women *in general,* we are going to do one hell of an injustice to one out of every three women in the country, right?

Majority figures are conclusive in elections—and just about only in elections. Even there, smart politicians, if they want to get reelected and if the result was any closer than a landslide, pay almost as much attention to the minority who didn't vote for them as they do to the majority who did. We could with profit take the same attitude toward a lot of test results.

Jo Freeman's Rule doesn't apply to simple polls—pollsters might ask anything—but we can look at some polls in the same way, with some startling results. Mr. Gallup and his cohorts are very, very careful, when they distribute their results to newspapers, to provide all the proper statistical data and the right figures all along the line. But most newspapers don't have anybody on their staffs who would know a random sample from an obsolete Japanese battleship, and some newspapers are not above jazzing up Mr. Gallup's rather dry copy by putting a little juice into the lead. Add in the fact that most of us readers aren't sophisticated in the use of statistics either, and you can get a pretty misleading result.

Early in the book I referred to two polls, one by Gallup and one by Roper (remember that current figures are different and show more discontented women than these old figures did). The Gallup copy specifically said: "Two-thirds of American women, mothers included, believe they get as good a break in the world today as men do." The paper I took it from headlined the story:

MORE WOMEN THINK THEIR LIFE EASIER

That's not a very unfair headline—the story says "as easy," not "easier," but let that go. Nevertheless, the headline and the copy do tend to take your mind off the fact that one out of three women do not think they "get as good a break." And that's a *lot*.

The Roper poll story is even more interesting. The copy said that "three in four women reject the [women's] movement's claim that women are discriminated against." The figure in fact was 69% —much closer to two in three than it is to three in four. That may not bother you, but in the United States the difference right there is about 6,300,000 women, who just got erased from the face of the earth in a hasty lead.

On top of that, however, the headline on the story read:

Women Don't Feel Discriminated Against

How many people (female or male) do you think analyzed the figures? How many do you think read only the lead that said "three in four"? And how many do you think simply read the headline, saw that it was over a poll story full of impressive-looking figures, assumed that the headline was accurate—and now *know* that women don't feel discriminated against?

In fact, the story shows that 31% of American women either *do* feel discriminated against or say they "don't know," which at least means that they aren't ready to say they're *not*. That just happens to be *thirty-two and a half million women*.

Remember, these polls (if they're well done—and Gallup's and Roper's are well done) represent all women: your wife or girl friend, your mother, your Aunt Minnie, the black woman on welfare, the nice lady across the street, the machinist's wife in Dayton, Ohio (supposedly the "typical American"), the small-town Appalachian mother, that drum majorette with the impossible early-sixties bouffant hairdo you saw on that televised football game from Texas, and both Patricia Nixons—as well as the comparatively few young, middle-class students and "counter-culture" types.

48

Still think they're all "a few malcontents who want to be men," or "a handful of radicals who need a good session in the sack"?

I have only talked, in this chapter, about how we can be wrong about the things we are pretty sure we "know." I have not talked about one of the most common of psychological processes, the way in which we often distort incoming facts in order to make them fit comfortably on top of the blocks we already have in our heads. Sometimes we can look straight at a story in the newspaper and remember it differently ten minutes later—because to get it right would force us to an uncomfortable change.

But I think you know about that—and if you're being honest, you'll be making some sort of effort to apply that knowledge in the future when you read about women. So—having treated the Black Analogy and the fact that "obvious" differences are not so obvious— let's tackle the toughest one of all.

Let's look at how we got this way in the first place.

PART TWO

Congratulations!
It's a Girl!

6
↓

THE first time I told Judith that, snob that I am, I didn't like either the word "sexism" or the phrase "male chauvinism," she proposed that I come up with a substitute. The first one I came up with was not "masculinism" but "genderism." She didn't like it. Whenever I tried it on a woman in the movement, in fact, the response was a snicker, a pitying look or a derisive snort.

My chance to get back at them all came when I encountered Stoller, who knows the difference between gender and sex. Sex is biological; but:

> *Gender* is a term that has psychological or cultural rather than biological connotations. If the proper terms for sex are "male" and "female," the corresponding terms for gender are "masculine" and "feminine"; these latter may be quite independent of . . . sex.[1]

You *are* your sex. You *learn* your gender. You know, in fact, that you can rear a (genetic) boy to be more girl than boy, and vice versa. In extreme cases.

Why not, then, face the fact that in ordinary cases we also rear biological boys to be cultural men, and biological girls to be cultural women? And, if we do face it, why not examine the process to see whether it might in fact do some damage—to all of us?

For clearly a biological male is a biological male in Indiana or

53

Iran, Kurdestan or Keokuk, Dayton or Dar es Salaam. But a cultural man is something entirely different in one land than in another, as to some extent we will see. And while our culture may be better than some other cultures in some ways, it is by no means (as you will admit) the best existing culture in every existing way—and it is by no means beyond the need for improvement even in its own terms.

So we can admit, without feeling too threatened, that de Beauvoir is right when she says that "one is not born, but one becomes, a woman." Good or bad, how does it happen, and why do we care?

Second question first. We care because we rear children—or if we, as individuals, do not, our generation does. Some of you have done it already for better or for worse. Some of you are doing it now. Some of you will do it in the future. But it is important to all of you.

There is one thing that almost every one of us does when he comes across the phrase, "women's liberation." Almost every one of us thinks of it in terms of his own sexual relationships. A few of us may occasionally think of women who work in the same field as ours, but by and large we tend to think immediately of our "girl friends," or of the girl friends we will have in the future, or of the women with whom we live or will someday live. We think, in other words, of the women among whom we must move as *sexual* beings.

This should tell us a lot about ourselves (and our own hangups), but it is almost equally interesting to reflect that when we hear about "women's liberation" we do *not*, usually, think of our mothers, or of our sisters, or—most important of all—of our daughters.

I have two daughters, and I find, as I dig into this subject, that I think more and more about them and less and less about the women on my own generational level.[2] One such woman, Kirsten Amundsen, has probably spotted the reason for this:

A concerned father is particularly vulnerable, if it can be demonstrated, *as it can be,* that his daughter's chance for a more fulfilling and secure life is significantly reduced by the perpetuation of sexist practices [her emphases].

As it can be. Can it? I think so, but you will have to judge, and the time for that judgment comes considerably later in the book. At any rate, let's try to think less about the women we know—except as they may serve as examples of how the process has worked in

54

their cases—and more about the women our daughters, present and future, might become. Because that depends on what we do to them —and, of course, on what we do to our sons as well. Stendhal said this:

Pedants have for two thousand years reiterated the notion that women have a more lively spirit, men more solidity; that women have more delicacy in their ideas and men greater power of attention. A Paris idler who once took a walk in the Versailles Gardens concluded that, judging from all he saw, the trees grow ready trimmed.

Just as you, today, look at the women around you and say unthinkingly that that is how women "are." And just as a later generation of men will look at your daughter and say the same thing. But you trim that tree—and you trim it, not to her design, but to your own.

No, no, you say: My wife and I do it *together*. Yes. But who trimmed her?

Or, less flippantly: What I have been trying to get at is that women are conditioned into norms that are essentially male. I intend to go at some length into that conditioning process. And your wife, unless she is so unusual that you have little to gain from reading such a book as this in the first place, is a product of that conditioning just as you are. The difference is that you are male, and thus conditioned into norms that are tailored to your continuing supremacy.

So we are talking about a process in which—to use an example out of old China—women with bound feet share quite sincerely and honestly in teaching their daughters to bind their feet. But it was males, ultimately, who liked women with bound feet. It is really not quite fair to say that you and your wife, together, teach your daughter to bind her feet.

You would think that we could start with the birth of a baby. But if it only went that deep, if it began only with birth, it would be a lot easier to break. There are a few other things that come first— preconditions, you might say, into which that girl-child is born. One that ought to be obvious, but apparently isn't, is that we are talking about a particular culture.

There is no name for this culture, except to call it "ours." Our literary, musical and general artistic culture is, for example, what we usually call "Western." Few of us, even in this day of black studies, know of even the existence of the African empires of Songhay or Ghana or Mali, with their high cultures and universities. Few except literary intellectuals have ever heard of the *Tale of Genji,* though we have all heard of Turgenev or Dante or Cervantes. Oriental music sounds weird. Arabic music sounds monotonous until we find out what the beat is and try to count it, and then it's bewildering. And so on.

Our historical culture is very much English-speaking. We learn a little of the history of England, either in school or in the movies or in literature, but very little of the history of Europe (and virtually none of the history of Europe east of the Danube). We get those parts of Spanish or Portuguese history that have to do with the discovery of America, and that's about it.[3] It would be hard to imagine even PBS offering us a six-part dramatic series on a queen of Spain.

Other parts of our culture are strictly American (football, jazz), and some are regional or subcultural. But in any case "our" culture is vastly different from that of the Middle East, or that of Peruvian Indians, or that of the Nyakyusa of Malawi. All of which seems obvious until we start talking about sex roles.

As the previous chapter suggests, it seems almost unnatural to us that women should not be emotional, and sensitive, and intuitive. We cannot imagine living as Iranians—in a society which is extremely male-dominated, but in which everyone is equally convinced that men are "naturally" emotional, sensitive and intuitive.[4] We cannot imagine living in a culture in which descent and inheritance are through the wife, not the husband, or in which the location of the woman determines where the family will live; but both are traditionally true of the Hopi.[5]

Margaret Mead, of course, is famous for paying particular attention to this point. She has supported with overwhelming detail, in a number of studies, the point that what we call "feminine attributes" are masculine attributes in some other cultures, and in still other cultures are attributes which *nobody* is supposed to have. She concludes:

Many, if not all, of the personality traits which we have called masculine or feminine are as lightly linked to sex as are the clothing, the manners, and the form of head-dress that a society at a given period assigns to either sex.[6]

Which brings up another point about culture—obvious but often overlooked. You might argue, with reason, that we cannot after all

56

escape our culture. We cannot decide to be Hopi or Arapesh or Nyakyusa while we live in the middle of San Francisco or Abilene or Tallahassee. Even those younger Americans who are trying, in cities and in rural surroundings, to evolve new (for them) ways of living together or of rearing children are under no illusions that they can escape overriding facts like zoning, or school attendance laws, or even the behavioral norms of the "straight" world that necessarily surrounds them. Polynesian women may go around bare-breasted in *National Geographic,* you might remind me, but even if I told my daughter that it's okay, she'd still get busted.

Well, yes. She'd get busted today. Maybe not ten years from now. Or maybe ten years from now she'd get busted for wearing a mini-skirt (or a button that makes fun of the Vice-President). Other, less superficial changes take longer, but the point is the same: Cultures don't only exist in places; they exist also in times. And they change with times as they do with places—which every parent ought to remember, for we tend to rear our children to live twenty years behind the times, instead of in the world in which they actually find themselves.

But our conditioning teaches us to regard our culture as fixed. That fact, itself, is one of the preconditions into which that girl-child is born. Oh, we know that styles change, and there are inflations and depressions, and all that. But we assume that there are some basic things which, if they are not "natural" (and we do tend to act as though they were), are at least fixed within our culture. Our concept of the family is one of them. Here is Firestone:

> The nature of the family unit is such that it penetrates the individual more deeply than any other social organization we have: the family shapes his psyche to its structure—until ultimately, he imagines it absolute, talk of anything else striking him as perverted . . . most alternatives suggest a loss of even the little emotional warmth provided by the family, throwing him into a panic.

Possibly I got a little more emotional warmth out of my family than Firestone did out of hers, but that's aside. What is the point here? Does women's liberation want to abolish the family?

I won't say "no," because that would be misleading; but I certainly won't say "yes." Women's liberationists differ in their attitudes toward the family and their prescriptions about it, though they do agree that it is somehow basic. I promise more on this later.

At the moment, though, forget about abolishing the family. All that we want to note here is that the idea of the family, as somehow a basic unit, is very, very deep in our heads; if it's not the first of those building blocks, it's certainly in the first layer.

Possibly because it's so deep, you can get a pretty hot argument going in a roomful of anthropologists or ethnologists about whether the family is, in fact, "natural"—or at least, about whether it's universally present in human societies. What is not natural, though, or universally present, is the family *as we know it*. There are families and families. There are all kinds of living patterns involving people related by blood and/or marriage, and all kinds of provisions for the rearing of children. Mom and Dad and the kids in one unit is definitely a *cultural* form.

And that is what most of us mean when we use the word "family," or at least that's the basic unit to which most of us refer. Of course I still refer to my brothers and sisters and my parents as my family (in fact, as I said before, the word has a slightly wider meaning in my particular case and in the cases of a lot of people who retain some Old Country "extended family" concepts). But for most of us in America, the basis for that usage is that we all used to live in the same house together, in a mom-and-dad-and-the-kids form or in one of its accepted variations (which we sometimes call, interestingly enough, "broken homes" [7]).

This is, in our culture, the standard family, the one that exists in children's books, the one we grow up learning whether we actually grow up in one or not (stock character in sentimental drama: the kid who lives in an orphanage but dreams of being in a real family). That concept is there, in our culture, when your girl-child is born— and it immediately acts as a determinant in how you regard her. Every excited father makes plans for his kids; but I don't have to be explicit about how the plans you make for boys differ from those you make for girls. Just think about it for a minute.

Sociologists refer to this parents-and-kids-in-one-unit as the "isolated nuclear family." That's to distinguish it from the "extended family" of not too long ago, when grandparents lived in the same house, children grew up and got married and the sons brought their wives to live in the same house, and a pattern of mutual care and mutual involvement was accepted (usually, of course, with the women responsible for the "care").

The extended family has survived longer among poorer people, for reasons I trust are obvious, but it is just as obviously disappearing; among other influences, the continuing trend toward moving to cities has something to do with it. A lot of people think that the isolation of the nuclear family—isolation in the simple sense of living in a separate dwelling unit—has cost us a lot of things that we should be sorry to see go. It surely seems to have one effect that is directly relevant to what is going to happen to your girl-child. It leads away from cooperation and toward competition, as a value, as a way of life.

It is probably true that while we may teach our kids to cooperate with each other, we also teach them, in effect, that they're going to have to learn to compete with the kids next door. And of course we teach this particularly to our sons—which in turn has its effect on our daughters. They can see (at a remarkably early age) that they are treated differently—that those aspirations are not to be their aspirations—and they must learn soon that while those values dominate their world, they are shut off from pursuing them.

When everybody from grandma on down to the newest great-grandchild lived more or less together in a farm complex or in a small town, a lot of this emphasis on aggressiveness and competition was countered by the necessity for cooperation and, less tangibly, by a feeling of being less alone in the world. Existence was not so "obviously" root-hog-or-die. Life was not the nuclear-family pattern of the few of us *in here* and all of them *out there*.

Although I have several friends who live in communes, I have no desire to do so myself. I am forty-five, and set in my ways, and not certain that I am flexible enough to make the personal adjustments that would be required, or that I would be able to do the other things that I want to do. But if I had younger children and they lived with me—especially daughters—I think I might give it a try for their sakes.

For one thing, female children would have more than one model. In a nuclear family, if it's affluent enough, there may be a full-time governess or housekeeper or something to serve as an alternate model; but who wants his little girl to grow up to be a governess or housekeeper? And no matter what Mom's own accomplishments, even if she is a professional in some field of high attainment, the principal model she presents at home is still that of mother-in-the-single-dwelling-unit.

In a commune there are at least several women, all different, to serve as models; and as of today, if they're living in communes at all, they are probably women who have some other interests outside the home, which might make them more stimulating as models, giving the growing girl-child some idea that there might be some fate other than the cookbook and the vacuum cleaner—or, just as important, the isolation in the single home.

Models are important in a different way to girls (compared with boys), because there is another precondition into which your girl-child is going to be born: It is a world in which, except for a few teachers, female models outside the home hardly exist.

A boy-child does not see the world with our perspective, of course; but he does see it. There is television. There are, unfortunately, comic books. There are newspapers as soon as he can read at all. There are magazines and (one hopes) books. There is conversation around him. And in all of those perceptions of the outside world, that begin long before school, there are *men*—doing everything, running everything, active in everything: Richard Nixon, George McGovern, George Wallace, Willie McCovey and Brooks Robinson, Rock Hudson and Robert Young, Neil Armstrong, Norman Mailer, Hugh Hefner, the mayor and the chief of police and Steve Roper and Walter Cronkite and the president of General Motors and Chou En-lai and Ralph Nader and the reporters and the columnists and the radio and television announcers themselves and—well, go look at the front page of today's paper.

If there are women on that front page, or in the news, or on the tube, they are there because of what they *are,* not what they *do.* Aside from the obviously very rare presence of an Angela Davis or a Golda Meir, the woman on the front page is there because she shot her husband, or won a beauty contest, or was raped, or went on a trip with Clifford Irving.

So your girl-child will be born into a world in which there is indeed a Margaret Chase Smith—the "woman senator," notable primarily because she *is* the exception, the Magic Flautist. The nearest to athletic fame is Peggy Fleming or Billie Jean King, the nearest to journalistic renown is perhaps Barbara Walters.[8] In San Francisco, a McCovey home run is an eight-column headline on the sports page, and if it's a crucial game he makes the front page itself. When that happens to Billie Jean King, somebody call me.

When a woman does make the news, she cannot be a model simply by being there; she is invariably talked about as an exception (and often in unflattering terms). Dita Beard, the lobbyist who came to prominence in March, 1972, in the furor about ITT and Richard Kleindienst, was promptly described as "tough—hard-drinking, hard-talking and hard-working," "salty," "hard as nails"; and a congressman was quoted as saying, "Talking to Mrs. Beard is like talking to a man." [9]

Never mind the patent masculinism of the whole thing—including the statement by the congressman, a gratuitous insult, when you think about it, to any intelligent woman. Just look at what happens to a highly successful woman—probably another Magic Flautist— when she gains enough prominence to appear in the male world of models for children: she is described, actually, as not a woman at all, but a man who happens to be female. Or, to put it differently, she is described entirely in male terms—which in effect makes her, from the girl-child's point of view, not a model at all.

There are female models in popular entertainment—singers and actresses (and a few comediennes). Maybe that's why so many girls used to dream of getting into the movies, while relatively few boys ever thought about it, much less made it the stuff of their fantasies. Even in entertainment, though, the female talk-show hosts are all limited to "women's programs" (Dinah Shore cooks, Virginia Graham does *Girl Talk*), and the number of women musicians you could hide comfortably behind a Fender bass. [10]

There are women writers, but unless you are somehow connected with the business yourself I'll bet you can't name ten living female writers in English whose work is taken seriously in literary circles (mystery writers don't count). Even if you are, I'll bet you have to scratch for a few minutes. And if you're holding them up to your daughter as models, you're probably going to have to tell her what happened to Virginia Woolf.

Another difference: Your girl-child isn't going to be born, either, into a world in which there are models for her in the history books. Not that they have not existed, but their contributions, by and large, have been ignored and bypassed or even, perhaps, undiscovered. Queens won't serve; your daughter can't grow up to be Henry VIII's daughter. And past discriminations had their effects; Catherine Green was so affected that she was afraid to attempt to patent an invention in her own name, and with his cooperation chose instead to patent her cotton gin in the name of Eli Whitney.

Finally (leaving your wife out of it for the moment, because it's the state of *your* head that I'm concerned with), there are the pre-existing facts of what you want for children, especially what you want for your daughter. De Beauvoir says this of the girl-child in general:

> If she were encouraged in it, she could display the same lively exuberance, the same curiosity, the same initiative, the same hardihood, as a boy. This does happen occasionally, when the girl is given a boyish bringing up; in this case she is spared many problems. It is noteworthy that this is the kind of education a father prefers to give his daughter; and women brought up under male guidance very largely escape the defects of femininity.

Whether that is, in fact, the kind of upbringing that a father prefers to give his daughter is arguable (so is the bit about being "spared many problems," but that comes later). Maybe that was true in France in 1949. Some people think that here it's just the opposite—that it's the father who insists on his daughters' learning and playing the traditional feminine roles. But in any case, what *you* already want, consciously or unconsciously, is an existing precondition into which the girl-child is born.

We do know that the role of the father, the father's attitude, seems to make more difference than the attitude of the mother, even though studies, like those assembled and cited by Maccoby, are not at all clear about how that difference works. Possibly it varies with the education of the father and/or the affluence of the family unit.

Certainly those women who have attained prominence in some area outside the traditional female roles, and who have talked or written about their own lives, are nearly unanimous in discussing their fathers' interest in them *as people,* and in describing the ways in which their fathers were different from other fathers in their circles. And vastly different circles they were, from Jane Addams' father teaching her to memorize one life story at a time out of Plutarch to Bernadette Devlin's father sometimes doing the housework and the cooking in a poverty-ridden Catholic slum in north Tyrone.

And so into all these preconditions, your child (yours and your wife's) comes to be born, a girl baby in almost certainly a nuclear family, unable certainly to escape her culture and yours, but with a thousand options before her nevertheless. Different from a boy baby in no way of which we can be certain except for a physical difference that marks a capacity only, she (and you) will face outside pressures of fantastic enormity, pressures almost overwhelming. How can a single family overcome the myriad messages of the school, the people next door, the television, the billboards, the entire universe of print, the child's entire world?

Yet we know this one thing: *You, your* role, *your* concepts, *your* beliefs, are crucial.

7

"HERE'S your little girl," the nurse says to your wife, and hands her the baby. There is at least a pretty good chance that both the nurse and your wife hold the baby differently because they know it's a girl, and it's started already.[1]

I don't know how important that is. It isn't all women, and apparently they don't do it all the time; it's just a tendency. In any case, nobody knows whether that tendency, taken by itself, would do anything to the child's head later in life (there are all sorts of guesses about how treatment of tiny infants affects later behavior, but not a lot of knowledge).[2]

I mentioned it, though, because it does provide an indication that our beginning to treat boys and girls differently begins very early, and it is more or less unconscious. Men tend to be relatively undemonstrative about newborn babies in this culture (that's *our* conditioning), but before your wife brings the baby home, watch and listen to the women visitors when they see the child.

Although there is no way in the world to tell a male from a female baby with a diaper on, the words people, usually women, will use about the baby will differ once they know its sex. You'll almost never hear, "Isn't *he* a *pretty* baby?" Regardless of the baby's weight, the observer is likely to make some reference to a boy's apparent strength or sturdiness. If it's a girl, the remarks are much more likely

64

to be about appearance: hair color, complexion or some such attribute. And you'll see, too, that it's more than words; you can detect a whole difference in manner.

It's a fair bet, by the way, that your manner will be different when you tell the other guys at work about the new baby. Not any less proud—don't get me wrong—but *different*. You feel different about having a daughter instead of a son.

I can understand it, if your first child is a daughter, if you feel somewhere just a little (possibly guilty) twinge of disappointment. Most of us to some extent identify with our children, and it's obviously easier to identify with a child who is what we were. Those gags about buying baseball gloves or chemistry sets for newborn sons are based on something very real, even if it's only the desire to buy for ourselves, symbolically, the things we didn't have as kids.

It occurs to very few of us that there is really no reason why we shouldn't treat girls in exactly the same way. To us, daughters are simply not sons, and it just doesn't mean the same thing to us. Given that your wife also somehow sees a girl-child in not quite the same way she would see a boy, you just *know* that those attitudes are going to communicate themselves to the child very, very quickly—certainly before the baby can talk. And, in another way, so are the pink booties and the croonings of Aunt Minnie.

Certainly one of the things that communicates itself very quickly to a female child—although of course she is in no way conscious of it and is probably unable even to come up with the concept—is the absence of an attitude or a treatment that we almost automatically direct toward boys. From the time of birth, Sandra and Daryl Bem point out, we are almost certain to look at, and to think of, our children differently depending on their sex:

When a boy is born, it is difficult to predict what he will be doing twenty-five years later. We cannot say whether he will be an artist or a doctor or a college professor because he will be permitted to develop and fulfill his own identity. But if the newborn child is a girl, we can predict with almost complete certainty how she will be spending her time twenty-five years later. Her individuality does not have to be considered; it is irrelevant.

That may be overstated as far as your household is concerned;

65

but it is true for most households, and I'm sure you can see how close it comes to the truth in yours. Another investigation, by Aberle and Naegele, approached the same distinction from another direction. They studied a group of middle-class fathers—in the professions, in business, on managerial levels, etc.—with a view to finding out what those fathers wanted for their children. What is interesting to us is not what they wanted for daughters, but what they wanted for sons.

They wanted, of course (why "of course"?), responsibility, initiative, stability, and what Brenton calls "the guts to stand up for themselves." Admirable enough; we might want those traits for all our children. But they also wanted athletic ability. Exactly one parent in the entire sample did not list athletic ability as one of his goals for his sons; all the others had their hearts set on it.

I can recognize the feeling, too, from the pride I take in any sign of athletic ability in my sons, although it doesn't happen inside me in the same way with regard to my daughters. According to Aberle and Naegele, the fathers didn't want their sons to be athletes, necessarily; they wanted them to have athletic ability because if they didn't do well at athletics, they might become men who are insufficiently competitive or aggressive.

I think some of the men were giving the interviewers conventionalized answers; there is, I suspect, a certain element of the vicarious in the fathers' attitudes that they either didn't recognize or didn't want to admit. When my kid hits a baseball farther than I could ever hit one, there is a piece of me out there swinging.[3] But my motivation isn't important. What is important is that there is something that a startling number of fathers want for their sons—and that every daughter in the family grows up without the same kinds of encouragement for her efforts, athletic or otherwise.

Rear your daughter, *not* primarily to look nice and to know how to cook and to do well in school for its own sake rather than for any possible vocational use, but primarily with a view toward independence, responsibility, initiative, stability, and the guts to stand up for herself—and you may find yourself with a raging feminist in the house, but you will probably not wind up with a child who demonstrated all kinds of potential at twelve and finished at twenty-two with an existence no different from that of a million other girls buried entirely in their private lives.

In fact, you might consider that phrase—"finished at twenty-two" —and see how well it does indeed apply to the personality growth of a great many women. Then think about how negatively it would affect you if your son simply moved into a niche at twenty-two and stayed there for the rest of his life without becoming, or struggling to become, anything more.

At any rate, the difference in early treatment, the difference in attitude at the very beginning, is there. If you do have kids in real life, you know how quickly they can pick up the most subtle vibes from the adults around them, and how early in their lives this ability begins to show. You know how surprisingly early they will begin to act differently toward one parent—and how the nature of that difference is likely not to be the same in a girl as in a boy.

This is obviously not because they "know" that there are masculine and feminine roles. It comes long before. It's just that each child, female or male, learns quickly what will work with you, and it happens to be true that what will work with you is different if the child is female than if it is male.

So your own masculinism—I trust it's obvious by now that that is what it is, since it is clearly based on cultural expectations—has begun to have its effect on the kid even before she can talk. You don't play in the same way—men tend to toss male babies around, to play rough with them, in of course a gentle way, more than they do with girl babies. And the daughter, then, doesn't know that what she does in response is feminine; she only knows that it works with you, and every favorable response from you reinforces her acting in a certain way. So there is her mother, saying knowingly to a visitor, "She sure knows how to wrap her daddy around her little finger."

There may or may not be any real significance in the way people hold tiny infants, but you know intuitively, if you do have kids, that the difference in treatment starts very early, and that the difference in reaction on the kid's part starts just about as soon as the kid can react at all. If it doesn't seem to be true at first reading, think back. You can remember a very early time when it was obviously true, but you can't pinpoint a time at which it started. If you think about that experience for a minute, you can see that if there was a "start," it came very, very early.

I am not going to waste your time with "penis envy," which I think has been thoroughly enough discredited by now. Let's just say that it's a culturally based theory proposing the existence of a characteristic that a number of empirical studies have completely failed to locate.[4] But it's interesting to note that even the Freudians who accept this theory recognize that it is the preexistent attitudes of parents that make the theory seem at times to work. Writes de Beauvoir:

> Adler has insisted precisely on the fact that it is the valuation established by the parents and associates that lends to the boy the prestige of which the penis becomes the explanation and symbol in the eyes of the little girl.

In other words, she doesn't envy the *penis,* she envies the "valuation established by the parents and associates." She envies the boy —and who can blame her? The idea that this makes her somehow "sick" or "incomplete," instead of making her simply an accurate observer of the world she lives in, is a gratuitous male insult.

Before we let your hypothetical newborn daughter get too much older, there is one more point that is a little difficult to deal with. It's difficult to deal with because the people involved so often insist with such vehemence that it isn't true. It has to do with the fact that your daughter's mother (who in the nuclear family is more likely to stay home and to be both model and day-by-day influence) is a woman.

The trouble for men with reading the works of "liberated" women who talk about this is that they seem to us to overstate the frustrations of, say, our wives. There are a number of reasons for this; de Beauvoir, for example, may have been describing accurately the attitudes of French women twenty-five years ago in ways that are not really appropriate to American women now. She also tends to make what may be an unconscious feeling sound as though it is conscious. Take for example this passage:

> The great danger which threatens the infant in our cultures lies in the fact that the mother to whom it is confided in all its helplessness is almost always a discontented woman: sexually she is frigid or unsatisfied; socially she feels inferior to men; she has no independent grasp on the world or on the future. She will seek to compensate for all these frustrations through

her child. When it is realized how difficult woman's present situation makes her full self-realization, how many desires, rebellious feelings, just claims she nurses in secret, one is frightened at the thought that defenseless infants are abandoned to her care.

Well, now, surely it's not as bad as all that. We can scarcely credit, with reference to our wives and the women with whom we share parenthood, that they are in our culture "almost always" sexually unsatisfied, inferior-feeling, psychologically dependent, and nursing secret desires, rebellious feelings and just but unrecognized claims. What is wanted here is a little perspective—especially since our own wives tell us (don't they?) that they don't feel that way at all. And some of them obviously believe what they say.

So take it from the top. Are the women who are mothers in our culture sexually "frigid or unsatisfied"?

Well, we have Kinsey, and we have Masters and Johnson, and we have a few other interview collections of various kinds. True, the two big studies dealt mainly with white middle-class women; but white middle-class patterns tend to set our cultural norms, and to some extent are imitated "downward."

These studies tell us that "almost always" may be an exaggeration, but there *are* a hell of a lot of white middle-class women in America, including mothers, who are sexually unsatisfied. Being otherwise reasonably sane, a lot of them have learned to adjust to it and get along as best they can; and a lot of them like what they *do* get, even if it isn't what they *could* get. It's not even uncommon for women to come to believe in their own faked orgasms.

So there may be some frustration there, although it may very well be unconscious and even vigorously denied by a lot of women. And if the class bias really does bother you, the book by Rainwater *et al.* and Komarovsky's *Blue-Collar Marriage* make it quite clear that women a little further down the economic ladder lead, by and large, pretty lousy sex lives, being in many cases not so much partners as targets.[5]

Do women feel socially inferior to men? Surely we need no study for that. We have all lived long enough to be familiar with the wife who in social situations defers to her husband on all subjects that have to do with the world outside the home. We have all been at social gatherings at which the sexes (or, more accurately if technically, the genders) segregate themselves, and at which the men may talk about electoral politics or baseball or personnel problems down at the office or China or Africa or the relative merits of automobiles, but the women talk about housekeeping, cooking or children.

There are of course shy men, men who lack personal self-confidence, and there are women of great poise; but as a general statement (probably not even limited by Jo Freeman's Rule), a man, finding himself in a room full of strangers discussing anything out in the world, will get along—as you know if you have ever decided to wander alone into a strange bar. Put a woman in the same room (not necessarily a bar) and she is as likely as not to feel hopelessly lost, if not terrified.

And surely it is true that women have, as a class, "no independent grasp on the world or on the future"—especially women who fit the culture's "standard" role for the mother whose husband works while she stays home and takes care of the kids and the house. She is economically dependent. She rarely follows the political or social issues of the day beyond the superficial recitals of the evening news on television, if indeed she watches that. There is nothing that she *does,* outside her family role, in the sense that her husband *does* his outside work.

Finally, does she in fact nurse in secret all these "desires, rebellious feelings and just claims"? De Beauvoir's picture of the housewife-mother who is nothing but a seething mass of bitter frustrations hardly fits our knowledge of the women in our lives; and we do know at least a few of them well enough to know that. But is there *something* there?

Friedan, who based much of her famous book on an extensive series of interviews with middle-class women, certainly thought so; she called it "the problem with no name," and insisted that most such women recognized it—the problem being that so many of them thought it was unique to them. And there are a few cultural clichés, too, to which we might pay some attention.

There is the woman in the hospital to bear her second or third baby, who jokes half-seriously that it is worth the labor to get the rest in the hospital and to have someone else wait on *her* for a change. There is the wife who suddenly complains that she wants to go out somewhere, anywhere. There is a woman somewhere at whom all those ads for Compoz are aimed. There is the mother who plops into

70

a chair in her neighbor's suburban kitchen in September and says fervently, "Thank *God* they're back in school!" There is the airline advertising campaign for family fares that concentrates on the image of the dowdy wife in old robe and curlers, suddenly transformed by the idea of taking a business trip with her husband.

Clichés, it is well to remember in matters dealing with women, do not come from nowhere.

So it is possible that the overstated quotation from de Beauvoir, which we males are likely to read for the first time with impatient disbelief, is not all that far from true after all. In a given case—your wife, perhaps—we might be wiser to say at least that some of it may be true to some extent. That does not, of course, make her a monster to whom the care of an infant should never be given, lest all her children (and yours) become warped and misshapen mental gargoyles in their turn. Most kids do, after all, turn out rather better than we, their parents, secretly think we have any right to expect. But it does at least raise a question about your newborn daughter.

For just as, no matter how hard we try (and most of us of course don't try at all), we tend to identify much more strongly with sons than with daughters, so it would seem likely that mothers do the opposite. We see, more or less unconsciously, that our son's life opens out before him; in our imaginations at least, the vista is virtually unlimited. The possibilities exist in real life. A mother knows, however —whether she thinks about it consciously or not—that her daughter's life is almost automatically limited by the very fact of femaleness.

If the mother's sex life *is* unsatisfactory, she is likely to think (and as we've seen, not without some reason) that that's how it is for women. If she *does* feel socially inferior to men, she is likely to think that women probably feel, or even are, socially inferior to men. And so on down the catalogue of conditions and feelings we've just been talking about. Add in the fact that if she does have intimate conversations with other women (which is rarer than you think), they are more likely to confirm these ideas than to contradict them.

The limitations that we feel in our lives we put down to external forces. We think of what we could have been if we had gotten the breaks, if there had been enough money for a different education, if we had studied harder, or made a different decision about a job, or resisted pressure from our families, or learned public speaking. Those limitations, we promise ourselves, will not be there for our sons, insofar as it's within our power to remove them. That assessment of ourselves, that hope for our sons, conveys itself to them, repeatedly and unmistakably, during all the time they are growing up in our presence.

A woman, however, is almost certain to be aware that any limitations she feels in her life come at least in part from the simple fact of womanhood. And that assessment of herself, that knowledge about almost any woman, conveys itself just as often and just as unmistakably to her daughters.

Sometimes, we can see, this awareness takes a reverse twist; possibly to avoid being conscious of her life as limited, a woman sees its limitations as positive, as in some sense a "fulfillment" (confusing capacity with function again), and attempts to convey that to a female child. But the effect on the kid is limiting all the same. In Bengal, where as poverty has risen begging has become an acceptable and honored profession, some parents deliberately deform their children in order to give them a better start in life.

We don't have to believe in all or even most of the arguments of any school of women's liberationists in order to see that there is clearly injustice here. There is injustice not because we are pigs, determined to keep women in some second-class status; but there is injustice because it is an institutionalized pattern, structured into the way things *are,* and because we have not understood it, we have resisted understanding it for our own psychological reasons, and consequently we have not tried to do anything to change it.

It is a lot to overcome, for each of us, and our own apathy and self-justifications, and the apathy and self-justifications of other men, are by no means the smallest obstacles. School. The people next door. Television. The World Out There. Political scientists who interview a thousand *men* and then publish results about the behavior of *voters.*[6] The female translator of de Beauvoir into English, who cannot keep from adding a footnote saying that the wearing of pants by college women is unladylike.

But the girl-children are our daughters. As the present system is set up, like it or not, we are responsible for them and for what they become. There are something like 28 million children in elementary school, full time, right now. A couple of hundred thousand, at the absolute outside, are the subjects of any kind of effort to break the cultural stereotypes related to their "gender roles."

What's happening to the rest of them? What are they becoming?

72

8

THERE is one thing, so far unmentioned, that no woman can do, something that a man *can* do. Like the childbearing capacity, it comes with the lease.

No woman can remember having been a boy.

There is certainly plenty that is different about being a girl, and there is certainly a lot about it that we can know only by inference, or intellectually. On the other hand, while almost every one of the important books on the women's movement by women deals with childhood conditioning—the subject is hardly avoidable—they share one characteristic. They talk in detail about the conditioning of the girls (with which, of course, the authors are familiar), but discuss the conditioning of boys, usually, in only the most general terms. "More is demanded of boys because they are seen as superior." That kind of thing.

Not unimportant. But I wonder whether, since we have been boys, it might not be a little easier for us to understand that much of *their* conditioning comes about not because they are girls but because they are not boys. Or, to put it differently: Isn't it true that some of our concepts about rearing *children* are applied in practice only to *sons,* or at least applied more vigorously and carefully to sons? If that's so, then a lot of the conditioning of girls must result simply from the fact that they do not receive what the boys receive. What we received.

One thing that makes this idea interesting to me is that it covers the case of the family in which the only child is a girl, or in which the only children are girls. If the ideas in the parents' heads are still ideas which are unconsciously directed toward the rearing of boys, then one of two things will happen. The daughter or daughters will be treated, in a sort of compensation, partly as though they were boys (a pattern that tends to lead to more independent women), or the parents will hold back on some of those ideas, as if waiting for a boy to come along, and the girl will be conditioned not by observing a contrast but by feeling the result of a contrast that is never explicit.

It is a commonplace among psychologists that, among breast-feeders at least and possibly among bottle babies as well, weaning is a time of difficulty and perhaps of trauma. It is not quite such a commonplace that there is, in effect, a "second weaning" through which we must all go, one which probably hits boys in this culture harder than it hits girls. It has to do (since we are conditioned away from displaying the physical love that we ought to show) with the mother's whole body being withdrawn from physical contact with the child, and particularly the male child. Discussing this "second weaning," de Beauvoir writes:

The boys especially are little by little denied the kisses and caresses they have been used to. . . . The little boy . . . is told that "a man doesn't ask to be kissed. . . . A man doesn't look at himself in mirrors. . . . A man doesn't cry." He is urged to be "a little man"; he will obtain adult approval by becoming independent of adults. He will please them by not appearing to seek to please them.

Which of us does not even yet feel a twinge of the resentment, the frustration, that went with that treatment? Which of us—for all that we may have "had it better," for all that our lives may have opened out before us with infinite possibilities, for all that we may have been regarded as the superior gender—did not feel at some early point that girls had a measure of parental love that we did not have? Which of us, however we may have deferred with mixed pride and fear to our fathers' insistence on our masculinity, has not at some point been convinced that mothers loved girls better?

We got over it, of course, and quickly enough (insofar as we ever get over anything). But for a time it was there. Girls could be called

74

by masculinized names—Bobbie, Jackie, Sandy—but woe to the boy whose name sounded at all feminine. Girls could wear boys' clothing, for a while anyway, but not the opposite. Girls could for a while play cowboys and Indians, but we would at best get a weird parental look if we were caught playing house. In fact, girls could play with all the toys in the neighborhood, but if we had wanted to spend any portion of our time playing with dolls we would have been rushed in either to the family version of the woodshed or to the nearest shrink.[1]

That last has had an odd effect on some of us. As adults we have abandoned to women the simple joy of holding and cuddling a baby for the sake of the sheer love we feel—or even for the sensual pleasure to ourselves. Many of us are uneasy even at the idea of holding and stroking a purring cat, or of rubbing a piece of velvet over our faces. And thus as fathers we pass on to our children the unfortunate and crippling idea that "men don't do that," that providing physical love and nurture to a baby is somehow a pleasure reserved to women (whence it's a short step to the idea that it's "natural").

As children ourselves, some of us may have felt some resentment, too, at our parents' attitudes toward our minds. Not every male kid is inherently fascinated with the practice of swinging a tapered stick at a hard sphere, or with using an inflated bladder of some shape or other in a complicated, if pointless, series of physical maneuvers. But a lot of parents expect him to be, especially if he shows an "unhealthy" tendency to read or to listen to music too much. Before long, the kid himself is worrying about what he is—as Komisar notes:

> The boy who is fascinated by such prohibited interests begins to feel that there is something not quite right with him. Even his parents often push him to go out and play baseball or exercise with weights, and if they live in a private home they may install a basketball hoop over the garage.

How many of those ubiquitous basketball hoops are there because the son for whom they're intended wanted them there—and how many because the old man thought there ought to be one? It's a fine image, and an important question. And surely this, and not some "innate" tendency, is a part of why we have a cultural picture of women as being the ones who are interested in art or music, extending to the stereotype of Maggie dragging Jiggs to the opera or the one that has a bunch of overstuffed middle-aged women gathering in a hall to listen to a dry recital by a desiccated poet.

There is also, as Figes notes, the fact that there is no money in those fields anyway, and men must be breadwinners first of all.

Few boys are naturally ambitious, but the necessity of earning a living is drummed into them at an early age. Most parents also go on to point out that a specialized education makes it easier to earn a comfortable living, and that the pleasures of art and music, for instance, have to be balanced with the greater remuneration likely from the study of engineering. This, together with the law of supply and demand, ensures that we have enough engineers and that only the very gifted or very determined stick to music or fine art. The fact that we have almost no women engineers and very few women lawyers or physicists results from the notion that, since her real career is going to be marriage, a woman might as well study the things she really enjoys, like the arts.

Do you begin to get a funny feeling here? Does it begin to feel as though, despite the feminist sources, this all has to do with how little *boys* are to some extent twisted away from their natural tendencies in order to fit masculinist roles? Is it possible that some of you even feel a return of a few buried resentments about what you didn't get to do —or even about what you don't get to do right now?

I'll tell you a story. There was a guy in Florida in 1971 who had an insurance job. Good at it, too. But inside of him, buried there apparently by precisely the sort of pressure Komisar and Figes are talking about, there was a guitar player. He told his wife about it. She told him to forget it and keep bringing home that insurance company money. Still, it got to be too much for him. One day he up and quit his job and went to work in a night club playing the guitar.

In the middle of his gig his wife walked in with the family lady-from-Bristol and plugged him dead on the stage.[2]

Conditioning runs deep.

But we're supposed to be talking about *women's* liberation. It just seemed to be time to suggest that it doesn't all happen to them—that, if women *are* oppressed, they are oppressed not only by their (preconditioned) parents but by their simultaneously conditioned brothers. We are victimized too. It is, I suppose, some sort of paradox that we are victimized into the role of oppressor; but there it is. And by the time we're grown up it is difficult to do anything about it, so thoroughly are we convinced that that's the way it ought to be—no matter how much, sometimes, in secret, known only to ourselves, it hurts.

76

Enough, however, of feeling sorry for the oppressed rich while the poor go on starving. The real point of the difference in conditioning that oppresses females is in Figes' phrase, " . . . since her real career is going to be marriage . . . "

Ask an adolescent boy what he wants to be or do when he grows up. The answer might be anything. Ask a girl. I'll give you 8 to 5 that she says something about getting married.

Nothing wrong with getting married. Oh, I know there are new mores coming into play and all that, but they only change the definition, not the fact, of marriage. So some people don't bother with a ceremony any more, and they regard the union as temporary. The ceremony doesn't make the marriage, the life-pattern does; and the divorce rates make it clear that the more formal union isn't really regarded as permanent all that often either.

Nothing wrong with getting married, except . . . Can you imagine, at eight or twelve or sixteen, defining your future life in terms of someone else, possibly someone yet unmet? Can you imagine defining it in terms of whether you would be married or not?

Probably most of us figured we would be sooner or later. There is at least one recent study of college men showing that while a lot of them are attracted by the idea of spending a single life, most nonetheless believe that they will be married before they're thirty.[3] But never, never would it have occurred to any of us to mention that fact —our vision of our probable future marriage—in connection with a question about what we wanted to do or to be (maybe if someone had asked us what we wanted to *have,* we might have mentioned a wife along with a car, a house, a TV set and other objects).

So the girls and young women, too, are probably being accurate enough in predicting marriage for themselves. But they say that that is what they're going to *be.* Even those who intend to pursue some sort of career, to do something with their lives outside a kitchen or a nursery, are likely to put their marriages-to-come into their answers: "I want to be a nurse and be married and have two children." No male would ever answer that way.

De Beauvoir has a poignant phrase about it. The boy, she says, confronts "a future in which the unexpected awaits him." The girl, on the other hand, will become first wife, then mother, then grandmother, caring for her children just as she was cared for. "She is twelve years old," de Beauvoir writes sadly, "and already her story is written in the heavens."

77

And nothing more is demanded of her. She is not even encouraged, in most cases, to study, say, music or art; she is allowed to because it won't hurt what she's really going to do. Even among that small minority who are encouraged to expand their mental horizons a little further, the parents usually don't feel anything like the same disappointment if she doesn't do well as that they would feel if she were a boy.

So we are trained, however consciously or unconsciously, as the doers, the achievers, the free humans. Be a man, my son. Hit the bully back. Learn to throw a curve.[4] Get good grades so you can get into college so you can get good grades so you can get a good job so you can support a wife and kids so you can tell your sons to get good grades so they can get into college . . .

But of course, you know the pattern, don't you? In the stereotyped versions, it's Hit the Bully Back. In the more refined middle- and upper-class versions, it may be a little (just a little) less physical, but it's the same thing. Win the debate. Get the cup for the mantelpiece. It's not manly to cry—unless you're a college quarterback (a grown man of twenty-two) and come in second or third for the Heisman Trophy.[5]

And they are trained, our sisters—often literally our sisters, flesh of the same flesh, bone of the same bone, genes of the same parents, dwellers in the same rooms—to serve *us,* almost entirely by performing duties which they have learned thoroughly by the age of twelve.

That's what most girls in our culture are primarily trained for, aimed at, shaped to fit; and by the time they're old enough to answer with any perception a question about what they want to "be," they not only know it but they're molded into it. You, of course, want the best for your little girl, nothing but the best; it may just be possible, though, without your noticing it, that your wife is a little more cynical. She may, that is, see the female world a little more clearly than you do, as we suggested earlier.

And quite sincerely, such a mother (again in de Beauvoir's words) "will as a rule think that it is wiser to make a 'true woman' of her, since society will more readily accept her if this is done." Whether this is mother's motivation, or whether mother herself is simply a finished and polished and smooth-edged product of her own conditioning, the same thing happens.

The little girl—your daughter, perhaps—is discouraged from

78

playing with boys, encouraged to spend her time with other girls. At a considerably earlier age than that at which something similar happens to boys, she is encouraged or at least allowed to be in the presence of older women, themselves firmly fixed in the feminine role. The toys and even the books chosen for her (whether the choice is deliberate in the case of the books is arguable, but it's obvious about the toys) involve her quickly in that role.

She may in some households "share the chores" with her brother —but she's still likely to be tied directly to Mom, the model. Girls do the dishes, boys take out the garbage. On the farm or in the city, the kids' work reinforces, it doesn't break, the gender-role pattern. He's putting in time until he goes off on his own; she's learning her turf.[6]

Women tell her the things she "ought to know" about men (many of them mythical, but most of us don't even get that). She learns not only to cook and to sew and to run a vacuum cleaner but that she should "look nice." Much more than is the case with boys, she is dressed in clothes that demand care while worn, and thus, by implication, she is barred from certain kinds of physical play. Her hair is fussed over. She is repeatedly warned about how to stand, to walk, to sit.

Of course she is rarely told, explicitly, "If you stand or sit that way, you will not bring as high a price in the slave market of marriage." She is rarely told even, "If you stand or sit that way, men will not like you." She is told only, "If you stand or sit that way, it does not look nice," or at most, "it does not look feminine" or "ladylike." But obviously: Why else look "feminine" or "ladylike"? She is being trained to be an *object*. Like the little statue on the piano. Like the painting (or the poster) on the wall. Like the prize miniature Schnauzer in the dog show.

No, really. It *is* true, isn't it, when you look at it? We were told to "stand up straight," sure, for reasons of posture, related to health— and possibly, underneath somewhere in the murky recesses of the mind, for reasons vaguely related to an image of virility, who knows? But did your father ever tell you how to *walk,* how to *sit,* how to place your arms while standing still in a room?

With, of course, one exception. You would get told damned quick if you were doing something that looked *feminine.*

In the ninth grade I admired a male teacher, and it happened that he had a habit, when exasperated, of closing his eyes for a minute and then opening them with a different expression in them. I have a tendency, which has never quite gone away, unconsciously to mimic some habits of people I admire or am constantly around, and I picked up that one; but the teacher was twice the size I am now. Also, he was light of hair and skin.

Since I'm relatively small and dark, and have fairly long eyelashes as well, the same mannerism apparently struck people, when I did it, as effeminate. From adult male relatives and from male friends my own age I soon began to hear angry demands (they were always angry and they were always demands, which must mean something in itself) that I quit "batting my eyelashes." So we do get *some* training.[7]

But it is training in what not to do. It is designed not to fit us to an image but to keep us from breaking one that already exists. There's a big, and I trust obvious, difference. Girls have to be taught to fit their roles. We learn ours as normal, and need only to be cautioned not to deviate.

To put it on a somewhat higher level, girls are taught, so much more than boys are that it is really an entirely different process, to repress their natural movements, their natural reactions, in the interest of being ladylike or feminine or nice or whatever word mother (and sometimes father) happens to use. They are not really taught to walk with books on their heads, but they are taught the same things in subtler ways. After a certain time in her life, she can't play violently any more. She certainly can't fight.

"But *we* don't do that. *We* don't *believe* in repression."

You let her develop just as you would a boy, do you? You give her exactly the same encouragement, no matter what she wants to do? When she decides to take auto shop instead of cooking (or typing) in high school, and they give her a bad time, you go down there and fight for her, do you? [8]

Well, you don't, of course, but let's pretend you do. You tell her, "Go ahead, honey (do you call your son "honey"?), *be* a doctor or a physicist or a telephone lineman if that's what you want—we're for you all the way." Now what are the odds that you don't also tell her, "Just be sure that you don't lose your femininity"?

Okay, we'll stop pretending. Maybe, if I am a lot more successful at what I'm trying to do here than I'm likely to be, some of you will try in the future, but we both know that that's not how it is now. As of now, your son is reared to be as free as you can make him, and your daughter is reared to be a miniature Schnauzer.

But something more than a miniature Schnauzer trained to win the blue ribbon in the marriage dog show. For that she learns—is quite deliberately taught—how to stand, sit, walk, dress, apply makeup, talk quietly, behave responsibly, and under no circumstances to go to high school without a bra on. But she also learns that the ultimate purpose of all this is that her capacity is in "fact" a function: She will be a wife, and then she will be a mother. She must "run a household" —an operation which may take a lot of work, but which takes about as much intelligence as is demonstrated by a two-year-old "running" a toy automobile around the floor—and she must be The Mother of His Children.[9]

She is, in fact, so well trained for this role that there are still thousands, perhaps hundreds of thousands, of us who think that she does it by instinct. From the time that she is able to perceive anything at all about the world around her, the little girl can see quite plainly that mothers—females—take care of children. From that moment on, her mother and father, and the whole world around her, confirm that impression. She knows, as soon as she knows anything, that that is how it is, that that is what she is destined for. That is the first and in most cases the only model she has.

It is in her school books. It is on the tube. It is in the funnies. That is what women *do*; that is their vocation. And at home, she is given dolls before she can lift them, her helpful and intelligent and perhaps even educated mother cheerfully shows her how the diapers are changed and how the dolls are dressed—and probably along the way chats merrily about the other aspects of taking care of a real baby. When she arrives at child-bearing age and seems to know what to do, we call it "maternal instinct."

But your daughter is not a mother hyena or a salmon who will someday swim upstream. An instinct is a pattern which exists in the brain at birth; it is there *genetically*. It may not come into play until a later stage in life, but it is always and inevitably there, and if an animal of a species which has a particular instinct does not display it, it is because of brain damage or some other physical disorder.

Humans do not have instincts. None whatever. Or, at the very least, none has ever been observed to exist to date. We use the word by a wildly erroneous analogy with the behavior of some other animals; we've been making a lot of those analogies in popular books lately. But the development of the human brain along unique evolutionary lines has replaced instincts with other behavioral forms. There is no such thing as a maternal instinct, or any other instinct, in human beings.[10]

I know that *you* believe me, but when you tell your friends that, they are likely to argue. The trick is to argue back that if there is a human instinct, then *every* human—in this case, it would be every human female—must have it. It is quite clear that that is not the case with the so-called maternal instinct, and that the exceptions are too numerous to be attributed to physiological damage.

Yet the young mother is likely to feel as though there is such an instinct. She may say that on giving birth to a baby she feels "complete," or "fulfilled."

Obviously I don't know what she really feels. Equally obviously, she cannot really tell me. From my own knowledge I can make a pretty good guess that one of the things she feels is an enormous surge of both physical and mental relief that must in many cases be strong enough to be euphoric. But I am not cynical enough to assume that she thinks she feels complete just because she feels immensely relieved.

I *do* know this. Unless she has been so uniquely reared as to be virtually a freak, she has been told since she knew the difference between male and female that she *would* feel "complete" and "fulfilled" right now. She has been told, not only by her mother and her aunts and all the other adult women in the world (a few crazy feminists aside), but implicitly at least by the men too, and by the magazines and the newspapers and the radio and the television and the popular songs and the movies and her teachers and the school books and doctors and clergymen and almost literally everybody and everything else.

Tell somebody that you are going to burn him on the buttock, and then hold a piece of ice against him, and he will yell from the heat. At the very least it may be possible that the "fulfilled" feeling of childbirth—which, not incidentally, a lot of women say that they don't feel at all—is simply the heat of a piece of ice. That and our amazing determination as humans firmly and insistently to believe what we want to believe, however alien to fact, when the need is deep enough within us.

All her life, practically since she was a toddler, she has been told directly and indirectly that this is what she is *for*. All her life she has been told that this is what is expected of her. All her life she has been told that only this moment will bring the complete approval of the rest of mankind. Is it any wonder that she feels "complete"? She has finally done what has been expected of her ever since she can remember.

This is *not* to say that having babies is *bad*. Nor is it to say that it is, or ought to be, a bland and neutral experience, like eating a tuna sandwich on white bread. When (in our family system) both parents want a child, its birth can be a deeply satisfying, even thrilling, occasion—and in fact there is nothing but cultural or economic fear to keep a woman from feeling that deep satisfaction even if she is not in a formal family and has no desire ever to see the biological father again.

It is deeply satisfying, too, simply to hold a baby. A special satisfaction if it is one's own baby may be cultural, but *someone* provides *some* nurture to babies—not just food and care, but holding and love and warmth—in every culture, and there is even evidence that without it a baby cannot develop normally. Because we men deny ourselves, to a great extent, that nurtural role (it is a masculine role in some cultures), a woman in our culture is likely to feel that that is her role by nature.

It is our loss, and her gain. But it is not a built-in biological fact. Women are uniquely equipped to give the baby *milk,* but they have no natural monopoly on love or nurture. Obviously what happens here is that a common but very deep human satisfaction has been culturally transmuted into part of a role, and renamed "fulfillment."

We said earlier that fathers, whether they want to or not, are likely to identify with their sons. We can remember, certainly, that we identified with our fathers. "Following in father's footsteps" is another of those noticeable clichés.

We wanted (and were taught to want) to be strong like Daddy, big like Daddy; we wanted to smell like Daddy's tobacco, or his tweed suit. We wanted to be old enough to drink coffee or booze like Daddy, and more subtly, we wanted to be free like Daddy, to be on our own in the world like Daddy.

Girls, you will note, cannot want to be free or on their own in the world like Mommy. If there is a Daddy around, then Mommy is clearly *not* free or on her own in the world. No identification there.

But for us, there is another cultural cliché with a lot of meaning that comes into play right here—you've seen it in the movies, even if your own family was far too civilized for it ever to come up in fact. We wanted to be big like Daddy, and we wanted to be free like Daddy—and we wanted to beat Daddy up.

The plot of *Taras Bulba,* such as it was, turned a corner when Tony Curtis threw Yul Brynner into the river, although they of course did it playfully. You are now a Man, My Son. Those of us who don't throw our fathers into rivers, or (after respectfully taking several blows without response) come out on top in a fist fight à la Montgomery Clift and John Wayne, tend to have a few problems about whether or not we *are* men, since the culture provides us with no real rituals for that determination. Confirmations or Bar Mitzvahs don't really work that way any more. Take a look at the next Marine Corps recruiting poster you pass and you'll see how they try to play on this fact.

What has that to do with the girls? Simple. It is clear to every kid in the family, female or male, that the old man has the power. The daughter may identify with the mother, probably does, but that doesn't mean that she sees Mom in the same way we see Dad.

Dad has the power, and in his power we see our future power, the double image of the exhilarating future of freedom and the fearsome need to toss him into the river. Mom is loving, and kind, and nourishing, and easy to con—but she is nothing to be afraid of, and she is not really of consequence to our tomorrows. We will bring her trinkets on Mother's Day, and of course we love her; but she has really nothing to do with our becoming men or with our vision of ourselves as men.

To the girl, Mom is herself tomorrow, she is the identity-figure that Dad is to us. But to the girl as to us, the old man has the power. The difference is that we sense, we know, that somewhere in our future is a rebellion, a rivalry, a necessary overcoming. The girl knows, just as certainly, that no such rebellion, rivalry, overcoming is even possible for her. She is not *the same.* And so she can only admire the power, perhaps be awed by it, probably be inordinately grateful for any notice it gives her.[11]

The Freudian theory here, by the way, is that our rivalry with Dad has to do with Mom, and unconsciously has to do with Mom in the sack. I think that except for those of us who blindly accept whatever intellectual fashion is around, we know that that's nonsense. We feel the rivalry long before we know there's any such thing as Mom and Dad doing something in the sack. It's more like a case of a theorist taking a fact that is obviously already there and twisting it to fit the theory. Not on purpose, of course, but doing it just the same.

The girl is deprived (*not* by her sex, which would fit the Freudian theory, but by her *gender*) of all the influences from the outer world, including *Taras Bulba* and *Red River* and other good or bad movies, but including also the finest of literature and drama, that give her the direction of her future freedom. She is reduced to admiration devoid of potency. And while we try, more or less successfully, to become Men, what she becomes is simultaneously a twelve-year-old copy of Mom, and "Daddy's little girl."

Which of course Daddy likes, and therefore reinforces. So, for that matter, does Uncle Gene, or any other male figure the girl-child may admire.

What we are going to be at that stage, we boys, is somewhere outside, somewhere shrouded in the exciting pastel clouds of the future. We do not even know what the words mean that describe some of the possibilities before us: physicist, electrician, computer technician, longshoreman, personnel manager, Doctor of Philosophy. We can think only of the simple things we see: policeman, fireman, astronaut, cowboy, doctor, teacher.

For the old man does *something*, but whatever it is, it is something he does somewhere else. Even if he is (say) a policeman, he tells us that it is not like the policeman on television or in the school books. He doesn't tell us what it is like, because he can't even if he would. By the time we are old enough to perceive these things, he has been separated by years of learning, of training, from his childhood.

Ah, but the girl in the house. She is *never* separated from her childhood.

She is going to become, in effect, her mother; and her mother is right there for her to see. She can see everything her mother does, there is no mystery there, and in fact she is serving her apprenticeship at her trade simply by growing up with her mother in the same house, or flat, or apartment, or whatever. It is not even important that what her mother does is probably far easier for a child to learn than whatever her father does. The important thing is that the woman she's going to be is there already at ten years old, while the man we're going to become is still a mysterious figure, actually still beyond our ability to understand.

"It is sometimes held," says de Beauvoir, "that she is more precocious than the boy. In truth, if she is nearer to the adult stage it is because this stage in most women remains traditionally more or less infantile." Not a criticism of women, much less an insult (and not of course a reference to physical development); more like an accurate description rendered in genuine sorrow.

Judith Wells has written, drawing on her own experiences and self-analysis, a moving description of how a woman remains "Daddy's little girl" well into adulthood. It translates itself, simply enough, into an irrational but deeply felt need for the approval of a male—especially the approval of whatever male happens to be most important at the time. It is true, Wells notes, even when her work is intellectual and the male in question has no qualifications for evaluating it except his maleness.

In fact, this pattern runs so deep that most women, even those who are highly conscious of the role of conditioning, are unable to distinguish between the times when they are genuinely and maturely seeking the opinion of an authority in their field who happens to be male and the times when they are seeking the approval of an authority *because* he is male. It is intelligent to do one; it is yielding to your "role" to do the other. No wonder that women in the movement are often confused.

Of course most women aren't in the movement, and as a result they don't have problems like that. A great many of them don't even know that they spend a large part of their lives hunting around for one or another kind of male approval, and that they go on, in effect, being Daddy's little girl until the effect borders on the grotesque.

Those who do learn to spot the conditioning game, to understand what has been done with them, tend, as we've noted, to react with anger, or with bitterness. Those who go on to wry humor are fewer, and if you're trying to get through the writing on the subject, they're extremely welcome. A lot of women, for instance, have written about the influence of toys on the conditioning of male and female children in our culture. Karen Kearns, however, has a genuine eye for the absurd.

In one section of her article she describes wanting a chemistry set for two years, dropping hints all over the place to no avail, and finally "learning" that girls are no good at science anyhow. So she asked instead for a Harriet Hubbard Make-Up Doll.

Of course I got it, and lavished love and lipstick on that doll with all my childish energy. To this day I don't know what makes litmus paper turn colors, but I can apply eyeliner with the best of them.

Another section describes a day in F. A. O. Schwarz in New York City (which she describes unfairly as "the rich kids' store"; many of the items are really well within the reach of the upper middle class). There are costumes—Superman, Batman and NASA Flight Commander for boys, Dutch girls, Fair Princesses and ballerinas for girls.

The salesgirl told me, "The girls show no preference for roles—they or their mothers just pick the prettiest." I saw one mother drag her four-year-old daughter away from the Batman outfit and the groovy monster masks and say, "I think this ballerina outfit would be best, Clare."

Before you leave that quotation, think about showing no preference for roles but picking "the prettiest." You might even think about whether Batman costumes are or aren't "pretty."

Not that some people don't take the toy question seriously. The National Organization of Women in New York City has a group working on that—and a *New York Times* story represents them as saying that the toy industry, by confining boys to mechanical or gymnastic products and girls to dolls and homemaking equipment, is imposing predetermined roles on kids, and thereby lousing up the kids' personal development.[12]

Well, obviously they're imposing roles. We can't argue with that—and I don't think we can say that it's trivial. Look at it like this:

We all care about education, and about what our kids are taught. If what they're taught somehow cons them, somehow forces them into channels of thought or channels of behavior whether they like it or not, then we as parents resent that. At least we resent it if we know about it.

Once we see that this is what happens with gender roles, just as it is what happens if the teacher doesn't tell the truth about history, or if the school forces kids of a certain race into a certain kind of training, we ought, it seems, to resent that, too.

"Toys," says Kathleen Grady, quoted in the *Times* story, "imply roles. Why should children have to make decisions about roles at such a young age? Is everyone going to be able to be a mommy or a daddy in 20 years? It may not be ecologically feasible. Children should be flexible and try all sorts of things." [13]

The *Times* story tells us a lot. The president of F. A. O. Schwarz, Ernest Thauer, said that he took his three-year-old grandson into the store and told him to pick out a toy. It didn't faze Thauer in the least when the kid picked out a tea set. Instead, he put on the *Times* reporter a little with a straight-faced answer: "No, I'm not worried that he'll become a waiter."

Grady did say that the biggest resistance to "integrating" toy use came from the parents of sons when dolls were mentioned. "That really hangs them up. They're worried about homosexuality, about their sons being called sissies."

That one really grabs you too, doesn't it? And we can remember, can't we, how that pressure worked when *we* were kids. If there is a greater and more sustained pressure on male children, I can't imagine what it would be. And if you don't still feel it, then in this culture you're a strange male, and a highly enviable one.

Possibly the most indicative quotation in the story, however, came from an unnamed "spokesman" (that's newspaper for "public relations man," usually) for Fisher-Price Toys, Inc. It seems that F-P used to make a doll house, but they decided to break down the gender roles—and, I presume, double the market. They called it a "play family house" instead, and tried it out under the new name in a test nursery school.

The boys would pretend to be the father coming home from work; they would slam the door and demand dinner. The girls would just push the furniture around.

Tell the truth: Doesn't it chill you just a little?

I don't mind being flippant, because that's how I talk to other men; we all have our own games, we all play our roles in the best way we've worked out. But something serious is going on here. That's a *nursery school* that guy is describing. Kids too young for kindergarten—and if his description doesn't convince you of the destructive way in which we condition roles into our kids, then it's hard to see what will.

Seriously, can we give them no more sensitivity than that? No more intelligence than that? No more freedom than that? Do we have to build cultural cages around our kids, trap them in roles they didn't invent, roles for which they have no inherent need—just because we were trapped in them?

Well, we *do* every time we don't notice something—a sentence in the kid's English book, a commercial on television, any of the myriad daily impacts that reinforce those roles—and thus let our kid, female or male, absorb that impact without any comment or influence from us to counteract it. As I said before: There is so much to overcome.

And if you do overcome it, what are you doing? You're teaching your kid—female or male—to go out into her or his kindergarten or first grade or junior high school world with ideas that are sharply at variance with those of almost all the other kids. You're subjecting your kid, in other words, to the worst kind of pressure a kid can feel, the same kind that that girl in Georgia got when her hairdo was a year ahead of the times: the ridicule of the conformist majority.

And more. For she or he is also very likely to get it from the teacher, and from the principal, and from the parents of the other kids when she or he goes to visit, and possibly from your adult relatives and friends as well. It happens to any kid who behaves in any way that's different.

So what am I trying to do—get you to rear a neurotic kid?

Well, I'll tell you. You're already rearing a neurotic kid. The only question is the shape of the neurosis. The only hope is to give the kid, female or male, as much strength as you can to deal with it as the years go by.

Bring them up "straight," like we were brought up. What do you get? A society full of males almost all of whom have hangups about homosexuality or masculinity or both. A society of females so insecure because of that Daddy's-little-girl, male-approval horror that a previously nonexistent product like "feminine hygiene spray" can become a big seller overnight, dealing with a "problem" that nobody knew she had five years ago.

Do you really think that women who can all that quickly be stampeded into worrying about how they smell between the legs don't have "neuroses"? Do you really think that we, with our John Wayne hero-image that makes it sissy to be able to communicate our feelings, or even to admit that we have them, can be said not to be neurotic? Call it something else if you want to avoid the technical term —"fucked up" will do nicely—but whatever you call it, just about all of us are it.

Better, I suggest, a kid whose "neurosis" consists of being a little *saner* than most people. I don't say that that makes for an easy life; anybody different gets pushed around a lot, and a difference in the direction of sanity doesn't lead to an exception. Either Virginia Woolf or Lenny Bruce will serve nicely as an example that sanity does *not* lead to an easy life. But who has an easy life, and what makes that a desirable goal for our kids anyway?

There's evidence, by the way, for what I say about neuroses. We say, for instance, "He's all boy." What does it mean? It means, suggests Amundsen, that "he is aggressive, gets into trouble, or dirties himself." "He's all boy" does not *ever* mean that "he is showing tenderness, emotion, or affection." So we call him "normal." But here is Phyllis Chesler:

When little boys are referred to child-guidance clinics, it is for aggressive, destructive, antisocial and competitive behavior. Little girls come in for such problems as excessive fears and worry, shyness, lack of self-confidence, feelings of inferiority and so on.

To oversimplify, but only a little: If the conditioning "takes" to just a certain extent, he's "all boy." If it takes just a little too well, it's off to the shrink. My memory of the freshman-psychology definition of "neurosis" is precisely that the word describes a problem you have which, if it gets a little worse, sends you off to the shrink. And the pattern described by Chesler for little girls is fairly obviously the same thing. The "feminine role" is to be timid, submissive and inferior; condition them just a shade too much and it's clinic time.

Then there is Susan Gray, who studied middle-class kids in the fourth, fifth and sixth grades, and found a neat correlation. She picked out the boys who scored highest in "sex-appropriate behavior"—the ones who fit best the "masculine role" we seem to want for all of them. All boy, every one of Gray's subjects. She found that these were precisely the same male students who scored "highest" in showing inner anxieties. This is similar to the findings of Ruth Hartley in her psychological studies of eight- to eleven-year-old boys, most of whom she says were

in virtual panic at being caught doing anything traditionally defined as feminine, and in hostility toward anything even hinting at "femininity," including females themselves.[14]

Explain to me why we don't keep from producing these same anxieties in rearing our own children? Why do we keep pushing the boy to be a Man? And why don't we see that by pushing our sons that way, we are inevitably doing something—innocently enough, perhaps, but doing it anyway—to our daughters?

It's a normal part of growing up, you say. He *has* to learn it in order to be an adult (meaning, don't you, in order to be a man?). But who says he does? And who says it's normal? You say, the other guys (the other children or the other adults later—same thing) will think he's a sissy, or worse, they'll think he's queer. But who says they will? Isn't that your fear coming out? In fact, haven't you known some genuinely *gentle* men, whom in fact you have admired a little, whose sexual proclivities never occurred to you?

Your son may get a bad time from the superjocks among his peers. He may even have to deal with a conflict between what you say is good and what a neurotic society says is good. But he will be a lot better off than if he were feeling—as most boys do—a conflict between what we are repressing in him and the silly role into which we are forcing him.

Urie Bronfenbrenner, a leading authority on this whole subject, has a somewhat different way of distinguishing between how we rear boys and how we rear girls:

The differential treatment of the two sexes reflects in part a difference in goals. With sons, socialization seems to focus primarily on directing and constraining the boys' impact on the environment. With daughters, the aim is rather to protect the girl from the impact of environment. The boy is being prepared to mold his world, the girl to be molded by it.

You can't get much plainer than that. "Socialization," of course, is only another word for "conditioning."[15] Bronfenbrenner goes on to note that this is where *you* come into it, for "in fact, it is the father who is especially likely to treat children of the two sexes differently," and as far as girls are concerned, "the presence of strong paternal . . . power is particularly debilitating. In short, boys thrive in a patriarchal context, girls in a matriarchal one."

That last may be, I suspect, a little misleading. I don't take it to mean that the presence of strong paternal *influence* is necessarily debilitating. In fact, much of the material collected by Maccoby, as I mentioned earlier, suggests the opposite. Rather, I take it to mean that the exercise of paternal *power*—you, the old man, throwing your weight around and being the big deal—is debilitating.

I mentioned a study of eight- to eleven-year-old boys by Hartley. One of its principal purposes was to find out what *boys* think boys *are,* what boys themselves think that boys *do.* Another was to find out what the same boys think that *girls* are and do.

The startling part of the finding is that boys, at that age, are already quite convinced that what they are describing is fact, somehow built into the world. They don't use the phrase or the concept, but clearly they are already convinced that the differences they describe are "natural." Since no one ever contradicts them, of course they grow into adults with the same convictions.

Girls, the boys said, have to keep clean and must not play as hard. They can't go as far from home. They are afraid to go anywhere "dangerous" (rooftops and vacant lots are given as examples). They cry a lot when they're either hurt or scared. They play with dolls and like babies. They talk about clothes a lot. And they have to learn cooking, sewing and how to take care of children, but it's not very important for them to learn spelling and arithmetic.

Boys, the boys said, have to know all the things that girls don't know, like how to climb. What's more, boys

have to be able to fight in case a bully comes along; they have to be athletic; they have to be able to run fast; they must be able to play rough games; they need to know how to play many games—curb-ball, baseball, basketball, football; they need to be smart; they need to be able to take care of themselves.

Nor is that all:

92

They should have more ability than girls; they need to know how to stay out of trouble [!]; they need to know arithmetic and spelling more than girls do.

Since these are the general images that boys carry, I wonder first —being male—about the effect of all this on the boy who *can't* run fast, who is chosen last if he's chosen at all when the sides are picked for football games, who loses when the bully comes along. I don't mean the boy who (perhaps thanks to wise parents) has broken these images. I mean the boy who has *not,* but who can't live up to them either. Most of us, maybe?

But beyond that: You will have noticed the masculinist emphasis on athletics that came up earlier in the Aberle-Naegele study of middle-class fathers. You will have noticed, too, the obvious fact that boys see males as aggressive, competitive, curious and venturesome while girls are timid, tied to the home, uncompetitive and can't climb. Did you notice, though, that a part of the boys' vision of girls is already focused on the girls' future as wives and mothers—but no part of the boys' vision of boys is focused on *their* futures as husbands or fathers?

The first suggestion that leaps to mind is that that is the model they see at home—Daddy goes out and does something else, Mommy simply stays home and *is*. But it's deeper than that. A change in the home pattern isn't enough to crack the cultural stereotype. In another study,[16] Hartley queried 157 children, both of whose parents worked.

Our subjects clearly tell us that the basic homemaking duties are still the woman's; the money-getting role is still primarily the man's. Whenever women are perceived to have assumed the work-role, they are generally perceived to do so as "helping" persons within the family group. . . . Similarly, fathers occupied with domestic activities are seen as "helping" the mother in her myriad home-centered responsiblities, not supplanting her.

Or even sharing with her, as Densmore and Mainardi and others have noted. Always "helping." And when you do the dishes, isn't that how you think of it?

No one, of course, tells kids about Jo Freeman's Rule, either. Indeed, we do not school them in the perception of statistical facts at all. To them—as to most of us, alas—boys are *this,* girls are *that.* And it becomes, by a quite logical process, a self-fulfilling prophecy.

One difference which we see, though most of us are not familiar enough with the terminology to know just what we're seeing, is that, in psychological terms, boys are analytical, while girls are contextual.[17]

This means simply that boys are better able to break sets than girls.[18] I have heard Alan Watts say that the analytic intelligence is like a spotlight, aimed and direct, while the contextual intelligence is like a floodlight, diffused and illuminating (in a sense) the entire context rather than the single fact. After reviewing a lot of studies, Maccoby puts it this way—in what is, by the way, one of the most widely quoted passages in women's liberationist literature:

> I suggest that girls on the average develop a somewhat different way of handling information—that their thinking is less analytic, more global, and more perseverative—and that this kind of thinking may serve them very well for many kinds of functioning but that it is not the kind of thinking most conducive to high-level intellectual productivity, especially in science.

Before you look too smug, Maccoby's very next words (which oddly enough are not nearly so widely quoted) are to the effect that to phrase it in this way overstates the difference—that in fact many women think analytically and many men think "globally," or contextually. In fact, many of the studies to which she specifically refers do indeed seem to follow Jo Freeman's Rule fairly closely; their findings about "girls" refer to only about two-thirds of the girls, and their findings about "boys" to only about two-thirds of the boys.

But our concern is not only with what some girls *are,* but with how they get that way. "Global" or "contextual" thinking is sometimes referred to as "verbal," because people who fit that thinking pattern tend to do better on verbal tests, while "analytic" thinkers do better on spatial or mathematical tests. Freeman went back through some of the tests that Maccoby cited and sums them up this way:

> D. M. Levy has observed that "overprotected" boys tend to develop intellectually like girls. Bing found that those girls who were good at spatial tasks were those whose mothers left them alone to solve the problems by themselves while the mothers of verbally inclined daughters in-

sisted on helping them. H. A. Witkin similarly found that mothers of analytic children [not "boys" or "girls" this time, notice] had encouraged their initiative while mothers of nonanalytic children had encouraged dependence and discouraged self-assertion.[19]

The kid who is more or less left alone, whether female or male—the kid in whom independence and self-reliance are encouraged—is more likely to turn out "analytic." Boys are, in fact, much more often left alone and encouraged to be independent and self-reliant (and as we have noted, we teach them to see themselves that way). There is undoubtedly some degree of oversimplification in putting it quite that flatly, but surely the pattern is clear. We manufacture the differences that we later discover.

One kid asks for and gets an explanation of a phenomenon in the outer world. The other kid, left to herself or himself, has to find out, has to explore—and is less likely to accept the superficial appearance. Jo Freeman quotes one unnamed psychologist as saying that "the independent child is likely to be more active, not only psychologically but physically, and the physically active child will naturally have more kinesthetic experience with spatial relationships in his environment."

Or hers.

Levy's book is called *Maternal Overprotection,* but certainly it must be obvious by now that in male terms, all girls are "overprotected." That is, we treat them in a way that we would consider overprotective if they were boys. Assuming that you don't really want to retard your daughter—and that is the right word, if what you're doing is limiting the possibilities for her development—it seems that one of the things you have to learn to do is to "underprotect" her a little more.

Because the answer, certainly, is not to protect boys more. Aside from whatever other effects that might have, you would wind up retarding the boys too. In the book she edited, Maccoby noted that "for *both* sexes there is a tendency for the more passive dependent children to perform poorly on a *variety* of intellectual tasks, and for independent children to excel [my italics]." And in "Woman's Intellect," she quoted another psychologist who was asked how an intellectually active woman develops: "The simplest way to put it is that she must be a tomboy at some point in her childhood." [20]

95

You are needed less than you think, Dad, and so is Mom. A lot of love, sure, but only the most rudimentary guidance and control. When you get to Firestone, you will be fascinated by her account of the Dauphin, born in 1601, a boy of only average intelligence, but one whose upbringing was by luck completely recorded.

He played the violin at seventeen months. Nobody pushed him; but nobody told him to leave the delicate thing alone because he was too young, and someone was around to answer his questions. He played, at the same age, a game called mall, which involved using a mallet to knock a wooden ball through a hanging ring.[21] He played tennis. He played strategy games. He talked at sixteen months, learned to read at three years and to write at four.[22] At four and five years old, he played adult card games and practiced at archery, and at six he played chess.[23]

"At all times," Firestone concludes, "just as soon as he was able to walk, he mixed as an equal with adults in all their activities . . . professionally [*sic*; I assume he didn't get paid] dancing, acting, and taking part in all their amusements."

He also played with dolls. Which didn't seem to give him any great traumatic hangups when he became Louis XIII, although he did exile his mother for five years (she came back, bringing Richelieu). Anyway he married Anne of Austria and helped to produce a son to succeed himself.

So maybe you don't have quite the resources of the court of Henry of Navarre. But that's arguing with the analogy again; you get the point. Obviously there are limitations to the possible development of any child. But within the limits we can't do anything about, we can—while we wage our own fights to make the world a little better—provide our kids with as much freedom, as much independence, as we can manage, give them love but otherwise leave them alone as much as we safely can, and provide all the stimuli we can think of.

We don't want a population of analytic thinkers. Intellectuals who write on this subject sometimes bias their writing in that direction. Women, especially—seeking the information that will help them to achieve their own liberation—are likely to be (at this point) themselves analytic thinkers, analytically aware of the obstacles to women's development, and aware mostly of those that were in *their* way.

We want a world in which those who are best at analytic thinking do it in freedom and without discrimination; in which those who are

96

best at the verbal and contextual (the artists and poets belong there, after all) can do the same; and in which parents can be proud not because their daughters are "Daddy's little girl" and their sons are "all boy," but because their children are free to become whatever they have the capacity to become.

If the rest of the world will let them.

9

$\blacktriangledown$

M OST of us do not look at children's books. We may come into contact with them; we may even read them to our children, if we
have children of appropriate age; but we do not see what is in them.
If we did, we'd have a hard time saying that certain roles are "natural"
to the sexes; the conditioning is so blatant that it does the feminists'
arguing for them.[1]

I'm talking about today's children's books—both the ones they use
in school and the ones you yourself go out and buy in a bookstore.
Some of the subtler forms of conditioning, of course, go back as far
in the culture as does masculinism itself—and even then, it is a rare
person among us who notes the depth of the conditioning patterns.

In adult literature, George Eliot (and after her, Virginia Woolf)
noted the recurrent pattern in which the blonde and passive heroine
wins out over the independent, bold brunette.[2] Walter Houghton
pointed out that the Victorian wife-mother was supposed to be
"pure" and decidedly not sexy and was often pictured in white; the
mistress (embodying evil) was sexy, dark and wore lush colors. It's
not an unfamiliar pattern in American movies, either—especially
Westerns.

The females in children's stories are no more exciting than the
insipid blondes of Victorian literature. Sleeping Beauty may be the
ultimate example of passivity, but Snow White and Cinderella didn't

do a lot more to shape their environments. The only exception that comes quickly to mind is much more recent. Ask any woman who is somewhere around thirty or a little older—regardless of her attitude toward "liberation"—whether she remembers Wonder Woman. I'll bet you your Batman and Robin poster that her eyes will light up with the pleasure of the memory.

It's interesting to recall that Wonder Woman was a conscious attempt by its creators to change the feminine image. All-America Comics, Inc., deliberately set out, or so they announced, to come up with a "female Superman" whose appearance would mark "the first time that daring, strength and ingenuity have been featured as womanly qualities." [3] They did this, they said, in spite of the fact that "women still have many problems and have not yet reached their fullest growth and development."

The presumption that in 1943 men didn't have problems and *had* reached their "fullest growth and development" is something of a frightening thought, but let that go. In any case, Wonder Woman, though she wasn't around for too long, did have a surprisingly heavy impact on a lot of young female minds. Mary Ritter Beard raises a literary eyebrow at the fact that WW appeared on the first cover "dressed in a scant bathing suit," but the important thing is that she *did* appear.

And disappeared. Friedan has noted about "women's magazine" fiction that the images of women were far stronger and more independent in the 1930s than in the 1950s (she gives many examples). Pauline Kael has made the same observation about movie heroines, and Marjorie U'Ren has pointed out the same difference in the images of female children between the early part of the century and now. Whatever may have gone before, however, there is certainly nothing there now that holds out any hope for the parent who would like to keep her or his kid from being conned into an unnatural, if widespread, role.

As recently as 1968, Jules Henry wrote a long essay for *The New York Review of Books* about the stereotypes, the assumptions and the unaccountable absences in American textbooks. He wrote about the false (or absent) images of blacks, of organized labor, of war, of the bomb, of economics, of politics. But he didn't say a word about gender.

He couldn't get away with it now—and if the women's liberation movement were to have no other effect but to make us look at the stereotypes in the books our kids read (including the ones they're forced to read), it would be worth everybody's trouble to date. Mary Ritchie Key sums up what has happened since Henry's essay:

During the last two years [she wrote in late 1971], over a dozen different studies have been made on children's books: picture books, early-childhood books, teen-age books, general library books, a series for minority groups, and California textbooks, which every child in California is exposed to. The remarkable thing about these studies is that, although they often make statements which are identical or similar and they reinforce the conclusions of one another, there appears to be no awareness between them of the other studies. They seem to have sprung up spontaneously across the nation, from student, mother, writer, professor, administrator, teacher and librarian.

Leah Heyn lists several ways in which these books are important to the development of children. They may not provide the child's ideas, but they certainly reinforce the ideas that come from other sources (including ideas which may be contrary to yours). They play a part in the child's ability to perceive the outside world. Obviously they provide a direction in which knowledge is likely to expand— that is, they channel the child's mind toward learning some things instead of others. And they bring to the child a large part of her or his picture of the possibilities for the future.

And while we're mostly concerned with the images of females, it's an essential part of the pattern that male stereotypes are just as fixed. The boys and the men in virtually all the books are aggressive. Virtually all of them are not only unemotional, but hold the expression of emotion in contempt. Rarely are they allowed to make normal mistakes. If you look at the pictures, you'll see that boys are almost always taller than any girl in the same scene.

Key herself is a linguist, which may be why she notices things about the girls and women in children's books that go deeper than the wearing of aprons. Our linguistic behavior, as she reminds us, is certainly learned—there's no controversy about that—and kids learn a lot of it from books. But there is "a pathetic lack of conversation with bright, adventurous females of any age. Rarely is there a give-and-take dialogue in which a female is shown to be capable of making a decision or where the input of the female is intelligent and useful information." And the result isn't only a lack of female models:

> Males who have grown up learning dialogues such as are in children's books today are not able to listen to a female in adult life. Males paralyze when a rare female makes a constructive suggestion. . . . There are no linguistic models in this early literature for females to take active parts in the dialogue nor for males to respond with dignified acceptance and a willingness to listen.

Virginia Kidd expanded on this point in her acid criticism of the Harper and Row Basic Reading Program, whose four- to eight-year-old readers are used in the California schools. Mark and Janet, the readers' version of Dick and Jane, have parents—parents who, Kidd says, "never quarrel, espouse political ideals, engage in artistic activities . . . , get sick, display mutual affection, or—most depressing of all—speak to each other."

In fact, in 410 pages of text, Mother has one line of dialogue—"I want a speedboat ride, Daddy"—and Daddy has one line of his own —"Look in the box, Mother."

In a newspaper story about Kidd's criticism, San Francisco reporter Michael Grieg quotes Lee Mahon, elementary educational officer for the San Francisco school system, about the teachers who are using these books: "I'm sure they'll point out the limits of the world of Mark and Janet." [4] I wish I were as sure as Lee Mahon is. I would have to be sure first that the teachers *see* the limits.

Irvin Child and his colleagues did their study way back in 1946. John Honigmann's book was published in 1967. In a passage based partly on the Child study, Honigmann writes:

> Central characters in the stories are male more than twice as often as they are female. Surely this confirms the reader's belief that one sex is more important than the other, even if that isn't the only way he [sic] finds it out. . . . Stories frequently differentiate male and female roles, just as our culture does. They generally leave female characters to display affiliation and nurturance and to flee danger; rarely do girls display traits of activity, aggression, achievement, or construction; seldom do they win recognition. In other words, girls are pictured as kind, timid, inactive, unambitious, and uncreative. . . . The school readers portray males as bearers of knowledge and wisdom, and also as the persons through whom knowledge reaches a child.

A more recent generalization (early 1970), from a newspaper interview with U'Ren, who studied California elementary school textbooks:

From the beginning, girls are discouraged from trying. They are given no interesting or imaginative or creative patterns to follow, save the basic mother-figure, and this is presented as uninteresting. . . .
The inventors, the scientists, the historic figures, the doctors, the athletes are all male. Girls are represented as having less strength of character, often collapsing in tears, or the butt of the joke, incapable of keeping a secret. Our primary textbooks say in effect that it is neither natural nor likely that a girl should achieve.[5]

Stinson Worley's study of basic readers, published in 1967, found that "there were twice as many stories reflecting male story situations as there were stories reflecting female story situations." The study concluded that "the heavy emphasis given male figures creates a distorted and perhaps harmful sex-role image for all readers."

Jamie Frisof's 1969 analysis of social studies textbooks for grades one to three found men shown or described in more than one hundred different jobs; women in fewer than thirty (this is backed up by a new and, I believe, completely separate study [6]). In the women's jobs shown, women are usually either serving or helping men; in any case the jobs are those traditionally associated with women. Beyond that, Frisof found that when women are shown at home, their role is downgraded. They are not shown teaching their children, disciplining them, handling money or even cooking anything complicated.[7] The books, Frisof writes, "do their part in preparing girls to accept unquestioningly their future as unimportant, nonproductive, nonadventurous, and unintelligent beings."

U'Ren took a similar look at the "mother-figure" in California textbooks used in the second through sixth grades:

She has no effect upon the world beyond her family, and even within the family her contribution is limited to that of housekeeper and cook. . . . She enters a scene only to place a cake on the table and then disappears. Or she plays foil to her husband by setting him up for his line. It is mother who asks, "What shall we do?" and by doing so invites a speech from father.

Next time you yell, "How come *I* have to decide everything?" remember those schoolbooks. That's your role, Father.

So if we get mad at those Saturday morning television commercials conditioning our kids into wanting low-nutrition cereals and undesirable toys, why don't we get mad at the whole structure of textbooks that condition them into white middle-class, noncontroversial masculine stereotypes? It's a lot more damaging than bad teeth. You can get false teeth.

But generalizing about the effects doesn't really convey the whole story. Let's look at some specifics from some textbooks, beginning with a gem found by Komisar. The book showed pictures of a number of workers and pictures of an equal number of tools. Problem: Match the worker with the tool. There was one woman in the group. Her "tool" was a shopping cart.

From a California reader by McCracken and Walcutt:

Bill said, "I will sit in front and steer the sled, Joan. You sit in the back so that you can hold on to me." [8]

From Kidd on those other California readers, referred to earlier:

Mark shows Janet his toys: parachute, rocket, space suit, helmet, gloves and boots. He declares himself Mark the astronaut. Then it is Janet's turn. She shows her toys: playhouse, chairs, curtains, dolls, buggy, doll bed, dishes.

Evertts and Van Roekel, whose *Crossroads* is part of the same Harper and Row Basic Reading Program, at least acknowledge the existence of Madame Curie; but U'Ren notes that the famous physicist is described primarily as her husband's helper in the book. "The illustration which accompanies this section," U'Ren goes on, "reinforces that view of her. It portrays Madame Curie peering mildly from around her husband's shoulder while he and another distinguished gentleman loom in the foreground engaged in serious dialogue." I hasten to add that the authors *may* not be responsible for the illustration.

In a group of books called *The Roberts English Series: A Linguistic Program,* which they studied in Books 3 through 8, Key and her colleagues found a somewhat subtler pattern in connection with the poetry that is prominently featured in the books:

Many of the poems are written with pronoun referent unspecified as to sex, e.g., "I, me, we, they." The pictures accompanying the poems,

103

however, with the exception of Book 3, are almost all male-dominated. In Book 4, 11 poems are illustrated thus, with none illustrated by a female or female-dominated picture.

One more example, which I found fascinating, has to do with *The Bank Street Readers*, created specifically for what we euphemistically call "the inner-city child." These books really drew the huzzahs when they came out. The kids in them lived in cities (not the familiar small-town, white-picket-fence, one-family-to-a-house world of the usual readers). They were multiracial. They wore realistic clothes.

But believe it or not, in the three books there is only one working mother. The best that can be said for her is that she is realistic, if hardly inspiring; she works in a cafeteria.

Most of the studies, whether they're of textbooks or of other children's books, have been unable to find any working mothers at all. Working *women,* yes. Working *mothers,* no. Eve Merriam did write a lovely book, *Mommies At Work,* but that was eleven years ago, and you can go quietly mad trying to find a copy.[9]

Working women are themselves extremely rare in textbooks, and not all that much more common in other children's books. This doesn't have much to do with the real world. "Of the 72 million women aged 16 and over in the population," writes Amundsen (using 1970 figures), "more than half had worked at one time or another during the previous year."

When they do appear in the books, they're in "women's jobs." For example, Heyn looked at a number of books having to do with health and medicine. In those books, the doctor is always male (and always white), the nurses and receptionists always female. The current rash of medical shows on television maintains this stereotype, by the way. There is a female doctor on some episodes of *Medical Center,* but she never touches a patient; she's a psychiatrist, and not incidentally a pretty one, too.[10]

As it happens, I was right in the middle of preparing this chapter when I read, in *Natural History,* an article by June Nash, an anthropologist studying the customs of Indian tin miners in Bolivia:

Finally a friend high in the governmental bureaucracy gave me permission to go into the mine. Once down on the lowest levels of San Jose mine, 340 meters below the ground, I asked my guide if I could stay with one of the work crews rather than tour the galleries as most visitors did. . . . The men let me try their machines so that I could get a sense of what it was like to hold a 160-pound machine vibrating in a yard-wide tunnel, or to use a mechanical shovel in a gallery where the temperature was 100°F.

Most women, I presume, don't particularly want to go clambering around Bolivian tin mines more than 1100 feet underground—but then most men don't, either (including many of the men who do it). But *she* wanted to; she found it exciting, besides its being an important part of what most of us would agree is important anthropological work.

The only way any girl in an American schoolroom will ever hear of Nash—of her courageous descent and her determined wrestling with a 160-pound machine—will be if an extremely unusual teacher happens to bring that issue of *Natural History* to class as a teaching aid. There are no such women, no such options, no such possibilities in school books. And there is little in the children's section of your neighborhood bookstore that is any better.

Alleen Nilsen reports on a course entitled "Writing for Children," in which the teacher gave the following sober, commercial advice:

The wise author writes about boys, thereby insuring himself [*sic*] a maximum audience, since only girls will read a book about a girl, but both boys and girls will read about a boy.

Nilsen also says that a prizewinning children's book, *Island of the Blue Dolphins,* was rejected by one publisher because the author wouldn't change the heroine to a hero. What makes that especially fascinating is that *Island of the Blue Dolphins* is based on a true story!

Many nonschool children's books are in school libraries or are used as supplemental reading in classrooms, assigned for "book reports," etc. Elizabeth Fisher, in *The New York Times Book Review,* reported her study by saying she had found "an almost incredible conspiracy of conditioning." Females appear in illustrations less than 30% of the time, and when they do appear they are shown only in relation to boys. They are sometimes sly but never active. "They walk, read, or dream. They seldom ride bicycles; if they do it, it is seated behind a boy. . . ."[11]

105

Nilsen's essay is partly a report of a study on the winners and runners-up for the Caldecott Award over the past twenty years. This is one of the two highest awards there are for children's books; it's given by the American Library Association for the most distinguished picture book. The study involved eighty books. A quarter of them had no females, or only token females; more significant, perhaps, the presence of females in the Caldecott books is diminishing steadily over the twenty-year period of the study.

The other big award is the Newbery Award. "Among the 49 Newbery Award winners of 1969," writes Key, "books about boys outnumbered books about girls some three to one."

There are less sweeping, but interesting, generalizations in particular studies. The Feminists on Children's Literature (FCL), in one of the most analytical and comprehensive of these studies, have a number of intriguing discoveries, including this one:

We are bitterly tired of seeing depictions of the woman as castrator. Even a well-known writer, whose portrayal of girls we frequently admire, slipped badly in some recent picture books. In one of these, the mother reproves her son for spilling the mud he is playing with—even though the scene is outdoors!

"Woman as castrator" may be a little strong (possibly it seems that way to me because I am tired of Freudian analogies), but whatever you call the pattern I can understand why women might well resent it. This group of critics, incidentally, join with U'Ren, Frisof and others in protesting the way in which even the traditional feminine role is presented. They agree that it is bad enough that all the women are Mommies, but that it is even worse that the Mommies in the books are all such insipid figures.

As the writing teacher hinted above, there are really two kinds of children's books: books for children and books for girls. People my age remember when there used to be a category that might be called "books for boys," but below the teenage level that category hardly exists anymore, with the possible exception of sports books. That is, publishers don't really want to publish books which are expected to exclude female readers.

Still, it's possible to find those novels which are particularly popular with boys, and that's what Diane Stavn did in her study. She

106

wanted to know what attitudes about girls and women appeared to be common in those books. It turns out to depend on whether the females have what we might call a "sexual" identity—which of course, for young males, includes mothers.

The girl friends and mothers are almost always unrealized or unpleasant characters—one-dimensional, idealized, insipid, bitchy, or castrating—while sexually neutral characters, such as little sisters and old ladies, are most often well conceived and likable.

I won't attempt to analyze that, but it is surely intriguing, if true. Especially if you have a son who likes to read.

Books for girls, on the other hand, are so common that publishers sometimes list them separately, and libraries (and library associations) often use the category on recommended-reading lists. It isn't really clear to me why these books-for-girls lists exist, but the FCL report doesn't like it. Such a listing, as the report quite accurately says, "provides boys with a list of books *not* to read, further polarizing the sexes." It is especially damaging, of course, if a book with a decent representation of a female is thus kept from male readers.

Both Key and the FCL note that this "girls' list" is heavily loaded with books about love, dating and romance. And, adds the latter, "there are the companion books about young girls with problems like shyness, overweight, glasses, acne, and so on, that are supposed to interfere with romance." If you have a daughter who prefers comic books, by the way, take a look at those some time. Key says of these romance books that "a female has no alternate life styles, but lives in a limited world with no control over her future." An additional fact about the females in those romance comic books is that they are also unutterably stupid.

We referred to the female's limited world, in a different context, before. The children's (and teenagers') books reinforce the idea that a boy's future is limitless in its forms and unpredictable, while a girl's is "written in the stars" at twelve. They reinforce the idea that a girl's future is marriage and motherhood, while marriage and fatherhood are to a boy so incidental that he never thinks of them when asked about his ambitions. "Boys, too, are involved in romance," the FCL report says, "but their books are about other things."

No wonder young girls become fascinated, almost obsessed, with their personal appearance. That is what heroines do, that is what they *must* do, to win the reward: happily ever after with the charming prince in the fairy tale, or just a dance with the basketball star in the book "especially for girls." Her diploma is to be printed on an apron.

I do not mention aprons lightly, for the apron is such an omnipresent fact in children's books that Nilsen refers to it as a "cult." Next time you're around a bunch of children's books, try counting the aprons; it'll surprise you. Writes Key:

Of 58 picture books which happened to be on a display cart of children's literature at Eastern Michigan University last year [1970], 21 had pictures of women wearing aprons. Even the animals wore aprons!— the mother alligator, mother rabbit, mother donkey and mother cat.

As I said, try it for yourself, especially among the books for the younger children. Especially try it on your kid's early-grade readers.

The "books for girls," like any formula books, have repetitive patterns, one of which is a form of what the FCL call The Cop-Out Book. Clara Kirchner's 1966 bibliography, *Behavior Patterns in Children's Books*,[12] has a whole section called "From Tomboy to Young Woman." One sample:

A Girl Can Dream by Betty Cavanna (Westminster, 1948): Loretta Larkin, tops in athletics but poor in social graces and jealous of a classmate who shines socially, finds out that being "just a girl" can be fun.

Well, maybe she'll get over it; that psychologist did say a few pages back that a woman who actually *does* something will usually be one who was a tomboy at some point in her life. The Feminists on Children's Literature, perhaps not incidentally, don't like the word "tomboy" too well. They ask reasonably, "Why can't a girl who prefers baseball to ballet simply be a girl who prefers baseball to ballet?"

In case you don't go to the nearest bookstore to check me out, here are some examples—*not* in the least untypical (though it's true a couple were chosen because they're real doozers).

From *I'm Glad I'm a Boy! I'm Glad I'm a Girl!* (1970) [13]: "Boys invent things. . . . Girls use what boys invent."

Some quotes that Stavn found in her study of books popular among boys, the age level here being about that of puberty:

Remember—she's a female, and full of tricks.

Men . . . liked to talk about women as though they had some sort of special malignant power, a witchlike ability to control men.

Polly . . . says, "I'm a witch . . . I was being nasty. . . . Girls just do those things, I guess."

If she [my mother] hadn't torpedoed my father's idea to buy a garage, he might not have taken off.

[A female] began to think she should run the show. That's where I had to straighten her out. And after I got her straightened out she seemed happier.

Key makes the point, by the way, that a great many males read quotations like these just "at the time of their lives when their thoughts of female relationships are predominant, and they are formulating ideas about the kind of woman they want as a partner." But let's not quit yet.

Mabel O'Donnell (the speaker is a boy): "Boy, this is going to be fun. . . . No girls can be in on this. Just boys."

Mae Knight Clark:

Peter said, "You can't do it, Babs. You will get scared if you do."
"No, I won't," said Babs.
"Yes, you will. You will get scared and cry."

A 1967 Newbery Award winner was Irene Hunt's *Up a Road Slowly*,[14] in which a *sympathetic* male character says gently, "Accept the fact that this is a man's world and learn how to play the game gracefully." A winner ten years earlier was Sorensen:

For the millionth time she was glad she wasn't a boy. It was all right for girls to be scared or silly or even ask dumb questions. Everybody just laughed and thought it was funny. But if anybody caught Joe asking a dumb question or even thought he was the littlest bit scared, he went red and purple and white. Daddy was even something like that, old as he was.

There is nothing in the book to tell the reader that there is anything wrong with the attitudes expressed in that passage.

One more. The FCL report found on the Child Study Association's "recommended" list a 1969 book by Honor Arundel titled *The Two Sisters*. In it, a young heroine tells her father that she may decide to give up a university scholarship. Her husband, it seems, has gone off to find a better job in another city—not a transfer, not even an existing job, just a search. The heroine's father, who is very much the male dispenser of wisdom of whom Honigmann wrote, answers her quietly:

Geoff's quite right to be ambitious and you're right not to stand in his way. A man who doesn't get a chance to fulfill his ambition makes a terrible husband.

End of book. Also end of heroine—who doesn't get a chance to finish her education, to fulfill *her* ambition, who indeed gives up her potential completely. But she is expected nonetheless to make a splendid wife. So it goes.

All of these studies may have their effect on the content of children's books. Key looks forward to a day when Bill won't steer the sled and tell Joan to hang on; Joan will take her turn at steering and say to Bill, "Hang on, 'cause we're going a new way!"

We can hope. But I'm afraid Joan is going to have to steer that sled clear around the schoolhouse. If she gets too close to it, the teacher's going to put Bill right back into the driver's seat again.

10

I N June, 1870, the French government's school inspector for the Bordeaux district filed his report, covering both religious and lay schools:

In the girls' schools as well as the boys', the education offers all the guarantees of morality which families could desire. . . . Both nuns and laity receive with deference and docility the instructions which are given them by the administration. As I always say, devotion and a sense of duty, generally stronger in persons of this sex, help to compensate for their weakness in other respects.[1]

School administrators haven't changed much in a hundred years. Take this simple observation of a schoolyard by Amundsen:

Watching the children play on the outside jungle gym, for instance, teachers would quickly interfere with a little girl having trouble in climbing up to the top: "Take it easy, dear—we'll help you down." But a boy trying the same daring feat would be cheered on: "That's the boy! You can make it if you want to!" Similarly, a girl acting aggressively would be put down for being bossy, while identical behavior in a boy would be dismissed with an easy-going shrug: "That's boys, you know."

Are the teachers in our schools deliberately instilling masculinism? Some are, no doubt, but not most. If you live in a masculinist culture, you become a masculinist without knowing it, and until you have learned to see it and thus to challenge it, you're naturally going to pass on your values.

Besides, teachers have to learn their jobs, too—and some of the things they're told as professionals slide by without challenge, become a part of what the teacher "knows," often without the young teacher-to-be ever realizing it. That's another benefit we all gain (well, all of our kids will, anyway) from the women's liberation movement: Those things *don't* always slide by without challenge any more.

Meredith Tax, for example, has a feminist friend who was studying education at Boston University, where the friend encountered a lecture on how children learn to read. There is of course some controversy about that, but the lecture was in the current eclectic mode— children should be taught differently, each according to the method most appropriate. What that turned out to mean, however, was not so harmless. Tax quotes the lecturer:

> Little boys learn by taking things apart; they like to know how things work. The way to teach them to read is to show them an object, like a toy truck, and teach them the names of its different parts. They learn best through tactile and mechanical tools, so that's how to teach them language. Little girls learn best by rote. They learn faster than boys for this reason. All you have to do is show them flashcards.

You will have noticed, of course, what looks like a distinction between the *analytical* and the *contextual,* and is certainly a distinction between exploratory and docile. You will also have noticed that the lecturer had never heard of Jo Freeman's Rule; to him all boys are exploratory, all girls are docile. And apparently, it had never occurred to him (until Tax's friend challenged him) that he was helping to manufacture the differences he was talking about—teaching his teachers-to-be to perpetuate a self-fulfilling prophecy. If girls are taught that way, girls *get* that way. Nor did he let the challenge deter him:

> The teacher admitted that the question might ultimately be one of socialization rather than nature, but "After all, you have to teach them the way they learn best, no matter what the cause is. And it makes your job easier—they're easier to teach."

Who says you "have to teach them the way they learn best"—if it turns them into something unnatural, something distorted, something

112

actually retarded in more important ways? Nobody pretends that teaching children is easy; that's hardly an excuse for shrugging off the chaining of their minds and the stunting of their development.

And don't think that pushing girls (and boys) into culturally shaped and sharply limiting gender roles doesn't retard them. Komisar found a study showing that girls were poorer than boys at mathematics, but they improved if the mathematics problems were posed in terms of cooking recipes—one of the few things they had been truly allowed to understand for themselves.[2]

The more or less affluent liberal, facing the problems of the school system, is likely to think wistfully of a private school, in which things will be done more sanely, and his (or her) daughter (or son) will be able to develop without the cultural pressures from "peers" who don't accept the same values. It won't work too well as far as gender roles are concerned, unless you find an extremely unusual school; I have been unable to find a reference to one. The famous Summerhill model certainly doesn't do it.

So we know that the schools don't break the roles. They may even push the roles that exist. But surely, if a parent or a pair of parents provides a set-breaking pattern at home, that's going to swing a lot of weight, isn't it? Answer: Yes, it is—perhaps more important than any other single thing. And the school isn't actually going to interfere, is it? I mean, women may be discriminated against, but if they fight hard enough they *can* do anything they want to, can't they?

That is a little more complicated.

Let's put it this way. Suppose you and your wife do the best possible job, even some sort of ideal job if we knew exactly what the "ideal" would be within the limits of the culture. Suppose, on top of that, that the heredity is good. Suppose that what you've got, there in the school system, is a bright, aggressive, ambitious daughter, combining the best of both gender roles—the analytic sharpness and eagerness we call "masculine," the intuitive sensitivity we call "feminine"—without any apparent strong anxieties or hangups.

Well, sure. She'll probably make it—for herself, anyway. She'll probably make an intelligent choice about what she wants to do with her life, come up with the energy to get it done, and do it well, without worrying about whether it fits a role or not. And she'll probably be a strong feminist besides, fighting in whatever way she can to free her less fortunate sisters.

But that's what happens when you ask theoretical questions.

Somewhere there may be such parents and such a child, but neither you nor I has ever laid eyes on them. The best we are likely to arrive at is a daughter who is a little closer to that model than most girls—and when that happens, what we do, fellow father, is take a good look at the school system and try not to break down in unmanly tears.

For what girls do (and, in the later adult world, what women do) is not only what they are allowed to do, in the sense that nobody forbids them. It is what they are *expected* to do, and what they are *encouraged* to do.[3] Schools would not accomplish nearly so much as they do (however much you may think that is) if they simply allowed children to learn. Children have to be encouraged to learn—and that encouragement, whether even the teacher is aware of it or not, is selectively given. Here is Figes:

> A lazy boy will be prodded into ambition and aggression, but a girl has to be quite exceptional, to have that natural hunger for knowledge, that burning passion which may lead to great achievement, because no external motivation is provided.

More than that. She has to have not only her own ambition, coming entirely from within herself, but she has to have it in such measure that, in contrast to the boy's, it can break through the prejudices and the expectations that she will meet almost every time she opens her mouth or puts a word on paper.[4]

Rosenthal and Jacobson have demonstrated, in a now famous study, that the expectations of teachers literally determine the achievement levels of pupils. They were working with ethnic minorities; they would tell a teacher that an upcoming group of blacks or *chicanos*—who in reality were quite "ordinary" pupils—was especially brilliant and outstanding. The teacher, believing this, would then treat them that way; and it turned out that the achievement the teachers expected was the achievement they got. No experiment was done differentiating girls from boys, but you can bet, given the mechanism demonstrated, that it would work the same way.[5]

Most girls, of course, do not bring to the classroom that "natural hunger for knowledge, that burning passion." Neither do most boys. Most girls, *un*like most boys, are not prodded into it. Rather, they are in a sense prodded out of it.

Then, conditioned into being relatively unambitious, they encounter the dream-version of marriage and motherhood in the ro-

114

mantic books and on the tube. Some pollster comes along and asks them whether they would prefer working or being married and having a family (a phony choice in real-life America anyway), and then takes the answers to prove that young women today "reject women's lib."

Somebody said to me dryly that getting pregnant is a hell of a lot easier than getting an A. So it is—which is why so many more people are able to do it. But it's more than that. To the unexceptional girl who is not burning with ambition, working is a pretty dreary business. We men all know that whether it's a huge capitalistic insurance office or a small bunch of radicals planning a revolution, we have the same name for what the females do: shit work.

I sometimes wonder whether any poll can really tell us how many defections from "male roles" there would be if boys, at fourteen or so, could actually face a realistic choice between (1) going out into a harsh and cruel world with only their own skills and talents to defend them and (2) living at someone else's expense in an atmosphere seen from that vantage point (via books, TV, etc.) as filled with love, romance, and really not very much work.

As it is—even knowing what we know about the realities of married life—it is not hard to understand that given what most women *do* when they work, they seize the chance to get married and quit. If we had their jobs, we'd seize the chance, too, if it ever came. In fact, that's one of the dreams of a lot of men, isn't it? Isn't that where we get the comic-strip stereotype of the worker walking in and punching the boss in the nose?

Of course there's a stereotype about women in the foregoing paragraph, too. Most working women *don't* seize the chance to get married and quit, either because the chance doesn't come or because they're already married. Turnover is actually less among female workers, as a matter of fact. The business about quitting and getting married is mostly an excuse for job discrimination, unsupported—actually contradicted—by facts.

The real difference is that the learned roles provide that it's "all right" for a man to support a woman, but not for a man to be supported by one. Unless, I should note, she's putting him through graduate school; then suddenly it *is* all right. You sort of wonder what kind of "natural difference" exists that isn't natural any more once the male is going to a certain kind of school.

As for girls learning the reality of what is before them, as opposed

115

to the comic-book and especially-for-girls image, our schools are terrified of the subject. The whole society is uptight, as we all know, about sex and sex roles; but the schools—perhaps because they have to deal with the most uptight of the parents as though they were truly representative, and the rest of us sit around and let it happen—are far worse than the society as a whole. My best witness, I think, is a Queens, New York, high school student of sixteen who got a rare chance to talk to a high-powered panel about her education.[6] She was particularly bitter on such an obviously important but (to the schools) frightening subject as contraception—and she's talking about New York City, not some conservative small town in Iowa:

> Because contraception is not included in the high school curriculum, I made a special request to my hygiene teacher that we discuss it. For one day, the teacher wrote on the blackboard all the methods that she knew.
> "What method would you recommend to a 16-year-old girl?" asked the students. "Sleep with your grandmother," she replied . . . one of the girls in my hygiene class had a baby approximately ten months later.

It is not so much the misinformation that troubles me. Schools hand out misinformation on all sorts of subjects all the time, just as they did when we went. What troubles me is that the schools can be so uptight about sex or anything relating to it that—for girls especially, but certainly for every student—indignity is piled upon insult for the slightest variation from the repressed norm, even if that variation is only an honest question about contraceptive methods.

And with that uptightness about sex goes a remarkable uptightness about any attempt to deviate from the culturally prescribed gender roles, especially for girls. There seems to be in a lot of Americans' minds some sort of idea that freeing female minds and personalities from the limits of those roles is connected somehow to promiscuity. In the narrower mind, there almost seems to be something *dirty* about any suggestion that a vagina does not necessarily imply an apron.

I said that I would not take up things like not wearing bras until late in the book; but there is obviously a connection that fits right here. One encounters references to those *indecent* women who don't wear bras. They weren't even invented all that long ago, but some people seem to regard them as being as vital to decency as was a covered knee in Victorian England.

116

And the schools are right there. An attorney announced a suit against the West Palm Beach, Florida, school system because, he said, any girl suspected of not wearing a bra is taken before the dean of girls and made to jump up and down. Too much bounce gets her sent home.[7]

In fairness, the superintendent of schools said that there was no such test, and I've never seen another report on it. But the point is that you believed it just now when you read it. You know that it's *possible,* that it is something a school *might* very well do, whether it happened in West Palm Beach or not. And in fact there doesn't seem to be any question that Sherry Platt was in fact kicked out of high school in Kent, Washington, a couple of months later for not wearing a bra—despite the fact that the Associated Press sent a picture of her, dressed in what she'd worn to school, all over the country, where it was printed in family newspapers everywhere without a murmur of complaint.[8]

In most schools, the roles are as restricted as the breasts, and long before high schools. By the seventh grade, according to one investigation reported by Komisar, girls and boys are already so used to their respective positions in life that they hardly notice it any more—and, what is even sorrier, most teachers don't notice it either. One did, and responded with some bitterness when she was asked whether girls run for school offices:

No, they don't. Most presidents of the student body are boys. Maybe the girls don't run because they think they're going to lose, but why are they going to lose, and why don't they take the chance anyway?

They are the secretaries. They have learned this at twelve and thirteen years old; so, by the time they are mature, why shouldn't they think of themselves as secretaries? And why do they make good secretaries? Because they have had the training from the time they were twelve! They have been trained to serve men.

The teacher said that she didn't think that boys took the good jobs —school and class officerships, editorial jobs on publications, etc.— away from girls. The girls just didn't try to get them. Another teacher (of "social studies") had her own disheartening story:

In one seventh-grade class we wrote our own constitution. Then we elected a government—and the president was a boy, the senators were

117

boys—one or two of the representatives were girls—but all the higher officers were boys. One of the girls typed it up! And this was a very bright class.

"Bright" doesn't do it. Given what we've done to our sons by then, a boy would have to be damned near unique even to notice. A girl, of course, has to be more than bright; she has to be a Magic Flautist. In San Francisco, in fact, the school system has actually written the Magic Flute Theory into the rules.

San Francisco has a high school, Lowell, which is where the smart kids get to go. You have to have a 3.0 average to get in. Or, rather, you used to have to have a 3.0 average to get in. Now, you have to have a 3.0 average to get in *if you're a boy*. If you're a girl, you have to have a 3.5 average. Too many smart girls.

The excuse, for those of you who like to collect bureaucratic explanations for things that seem obvious to the rest of us, is that there's a shortage of girls' locker space.[9]

We all know, I'm sure, what happens to girls and to boys after they get to high school. Girls take cooking. Boys take auto shop. Once in a very great while, somebody breaks the pattern, but to do so means going against the pressure of teachers, counselors, deans and (too often) fellow students, even if the parents aren't opposed. And the patterns just won't die.

Not in a high school but in a community college—Grayson County College in Denison, Texas—Carolyn Goodwin enrolled in a course in automobile mechanics. Her teacher, Walter Oyler, didn't seem to mind. And it turned out (as any idiot might have guessed) that there were a lot of girls and young women interested in the course, except that they had been afraid to take the first step.

The response? "We plan," Oyler said, "to offer a for-girls-only basic course in the spring." [10]

Why for girls only? So the boys won't see them in coveralls with their hands dirty? Or to keep them away from the nasty language a boy is likely to use when a lug wrench slips? What do you think females say when a lug wrench slips?

Closer to home (my home) is Dr. Paul Scholten, a physician who believes that Americans are nutritional idiots and ought to learn how to use some sense when they eat. He calls the average American meal a "culinary disaster," and insists that nutrition ought to be a required part of education. So what's his solution?

> Every high school girl should spend six to eight weeks in full time attendance in . . . a culinary and homemaking school, preparing for what will be the most important job in her life, preparing nutritious meals for herself and her family.[11]

Reporter Elizabeth Mehren appears from a newspaper account to have found that formulation just a wee bit masculinist—as do I. In any case, she pushed a little:

> Ideally, Dr. Scholten would extend his course to all students in the public school system. However, he hastened to add that "it should start out required for the girls, but should be an elective for boys in an all male class. That way it would not seem like a sissy thing to do."

It would not seem like a sissy thing to do if we broke down the whole basis for that stupid concept in the first place. It would seem like a routine thing to do, which is what it ought to be if it ought to be done at all.[12]

In New York City, reflecting and reinforcing those early divisions we discussed in previous chapters, the school system for years maintained a special high school, Stuyvesant, for students with exceptional talent in science and mathematics; and until 1969, Stuyvesant High was open only to boys. Alice di Rivera had to go to court to get into Stuyvesant and to get the benefit of its special courses and training.

Which may have done *her* some good, but doesn't seem to have done all that much for the handful of girls who followed her into Stuyvesant. Komisar quotes a male student about the girls: "They didn't give them shop courses there; they gave them a special arts program." Nice try, Alice.

Friedan's book appeared nine years ago, and she spent some space on the study by Macfarlane and Sontag, reported nine years before *that*. There it has lain for nearly two decades, apparently worrying educationalists (and parents, if they know about it) not at all.

A team of California psychologists who had been following the development of 140 bright youngsters noticed a sudden sharp drop in IQ curves in some of the teenage records. When they investigated this, they found that while most of the youngsters' curves remained at the same high level, year after year, those whose curves dropped were all girls. The drop had nothing to do with the physiological changes of adolescence; it was not found in all girls. But in the records of those girls whose intelligence dropped were found repeated statements to the effect that "it isn't too smart for a girl to be smart."

Measures of "intelligence" are of course imperfect (in fact, some of them are totally lousy), but they are quite good enough to make the general overall result accurate enough in the Macfarlane-Sontag study, or in distinguishing in a rough way who belongs in, say, the top 10%. We can trust the figures that tell us that in 1953, out of the top 40% in intelligence of all American high school graduates, only half went on to college. Of the half who did *not* go to college, two out of three were girls. Or we can take the state of Indiana in 1955, and look at only the top 10% of high school graduates. Of the boys, only 15% did not go on to college. Of the girls, 36% quit their education.[13]

So girls learn how to get along, how to avoid the pressures and the anxieties that go with trying to be what, deep down inside, they know that they are (at least until the schools and the parents and the rest of society convince them that that isn't what they are at all). Since we had all those figures from the 1950s, we might look at what that distinguished investigator, Mirra Komarovsky, thought was a "well-adjusted girl" at about the same time:

At the present historical moment, the best adjusted girl is probably one who is intelligent enough to do well in school but not so brilliant as to get all A's . . . capable but not in areas relatively new to women; able to stand on her own two feet and to earn a living, but not so good a living as to compete with men; capable of doing some job well (in case she doesn't marry, or otherwise has to work), but not so identified with a profession as to need it for her happiness.

Things haven't changed much in twenty years. That will still describe a well-adjusted girl or young woman. The trouble is that we aren't very careful about the words we use.

Psychologists and psychiatrists and particularly educators—especially educators—love that word, "adjusted." Not too many years

120

ago, in fact, "life adjustment" was loftily propounded to be the entire purpose of American public education, and a whole theory grew up around it (or at least, a whole lot of words grew up around it). But think a minute.

We take a guy who steals a car and we toss him into San Quentin or Joliet or Attica or somewhere. If he behaves himself, and goes docilely to his cell when he's supposed to, and doesn't make any trouble, and in general acts the "model prisoner," we say that he has *adjusted* to prison life. But we don't pretend that he is fulfilling his potential as a human being. We don't pretend that he is doing what he was born to do. We don't pretend that he is not in prison. In short, we say that he is *adjusted,* but we make no pretense of believing that he is free.

Remember that the next time someone tells you that you have a well-adjusted daughter.

We cannot leave the schoolhouse without a look out the window at the athletic field. I have Komisar to thank for the fact that I have a couple of figures for Syracuse, New York, but I don't think it will take you longer than about twenty-seven seconds to figure out that the proportions in your town are about the same.

It seems that a female teacher in Syracuse filed a job-discrimination lawsuit on the interesting ground that male teachers are the only ones paid for working in after-school extracurricular activities. The activities, of course, were athletic, and the male "teachers" were coaches.[14]

It isn't the lawsuit that's interesting. It's the fact that the Syracuse school system spent $90,000 a year for extracurricular athletics for boys—and $200 for girls.

All over America huge chunks of the school budget are being spent unfairly for the benefit (if that's what it is) of only half the student body—arbitrarily chosen on the ground of sex. Obviously I don't mean that girls should play football, although if that's what they want to do, it's okay with me. I do mean that if a school system is going to spend tens of thousands of dollars on extracurricular activities—whether they're athletic activities or anything else—there is something wrong with a system that routinely and without noticing it spends it all on the boys.

So now you know, and knowing, you are now responsible. So what can we do about it?

Well, obviously the biggest problem we face is the question of what we'll do to our daughter if in our zeal we turn her into something that her fellow students will regard as a kook. That's not all bad, of course. We want all of our children to be "exceptional," and to be exceptional, female or male, is to bring about a certain distance between you and the "others." If you are exceptional, you have to get used to the idea sooner or later.

But we don't want to put her into agony. The theoretical answer leaps to mind, and de Beauvoir, an admirer of Stendhal, thought of it too:

> No single educator could fashion a *female human being* today who would be the exact homologue of the *male human being;* if she is raised like a boy, the young girl feels she is an oddity and thereby she is given a new kind of sex specification. Stendhal understood this when he said: "The forest must be planted all at once."

Yes, of course. The forest must be planted all at once. But where —in the wilds of Alaska?

In the first place, if there is one thing we do *not* want it is females who are exact homologues of males. Males are, as we have noted and as we will note some more, just as screwed up as females are in this culture, only differently (and they get the best of the screwed-up result, of course). What we want is un-screwed-up people, and freedom from those deep-planted, seemingly "natural," almost unbreakably binding gender roles.

But even if we knew what that would mean, we are obviously not going to march downtown to the Board of Education tomorrow morning and change the entire structure of the educational system so that we can plant a new forest all at once. Most of you are not going to be convinced that it's that serious, even if you thought it were possible. The rest of you would have to contend with the fact that the culture simply disagrees with us at this point.

If you're affluent enough and live in the right place, you can perhaps get together with a few other people and start your own little forest, in the form of a private school in which the staff is chosen for its awareness of the problem and the whole structure of the institution is designed to break down gender roles. That's a lot better than making your daughter (or your son) carry the load alone in a school

122

full of kids who don't have her (or his) advantages at home, and full of teachers who think gender differences are "natural."

But it's a solution not available to most of us. We ought to work toward the day, certainly, when that forest will be planted, but we know realistically that our kids will be out of school by then and worrying about their kids.

So I can only suggest what amounts to guerrilla warfare—in a polite American P.T.A. kind of way, of course. Look at the books and then complain about them (I don't say complain "if you find anything" because there's no "if" involved). Listen carefully to what the kids are saying, and if it's masculinist and it's coming from the school, complain about it. Counter at home the nonsense that comes from the school on this subject—just as you do now on other subjects. And keep letting the kid alone and providing only love and a lot of stimuli.

Let us not, however—because they are ours—leave the subject of the conditioning of our children without just a few more words. It is worth it, because it is the one subject we must understand if any of the rest of women's liberation is to make sense.

11

THERE is one subject related to women's liberation about which I can write only at distant second hand: menstruation and the mental attitudes that go with it. I can to some extent identify with, say, a woman who is intelligent but intellectually frustrated, and who is trying to break out. I was a kid from a poor neighborhood, intelligent but intellectually frustrated by *class* stereotypes, who struggled to break out—and there are some parallels on the level of feelings. But I can have no emotional empathy with whatever feelings go along with menstruation.

I do know—because women are unanimous about this and because there are formal studies on the subject—that many women are frightened at the time of their first menstruations, and that many women feel, for a variety of reasons, that there is something distasteful, or impure, or (in the biblical sense) "unclean" about the whole thing.[1] From this, it seems to be true that a lot of women at first, and some for much of their lives, feel vaguely apologetic or guilty about the fact that they menstruate.

It's pretty well established that even today, an overwhelming majority of girls are psychologically and/or factually unprepared for the onset of menstruation. "Sex books" clinically and euphemistically tell them esoteric things about eggs and tubes—and sometimes their mothers do, too—but you'd be surprised how few are ever warned that they're going to *bleed*. The occurrence itself can be terrifying.

If we cannot imagine menstruation, we can at least imagine the horror of suddenly finding ourselves to be bleeding from the genitals. We can try to imagine how traumatic such an experience might be. De Beauvoir, however, perceived that this shock and uncertainty comes to females at the same time that the perception of future adulthood becomes a fact instead of a fantasy. Indeed, puberty is a part of that change in perception.

For boys, even though the pimply uncertainties of adolescence lie ahead in our culture, there is, as soon as the physical changes of puberty are understood, a quality about it of today-I-am-a-man. With that feeling comes a sense of the world's being out there to challenge and to conquer (and a sense of there being girls out there to "conquer," too).

But what comes to most girls is today-I-am-a-woman, which means even in our relatively enlightened culture (and it is relatively enlightened, if we stress the adverb) not worlds to conquer—though she may for a time think of boys that way—but the final admission that she is *not* male, that she does *not* have the choices, that where he sees freedom she sees a fence. As a child she could dream dreams in which the difference did not exist; newly a woman she cannot, any longer.

What de Beauvoir saw is that the menstruation hangup itself is associated with that other, cultural admission:

We are now acquainted with the dramatic conflict that harrows the adolescent girl at puberty: she cannot become "grown-up" without accepting her femininity; and she knows already that her sex condemns her to a mutilated and fixed existence, which she faces at this time under the form of an impure sickness and a vague guiltiness.

This is exactly the age at which it seems normal to be filled with hope, and eagerness, and the promise of tomorrow. This is exactly the age at which we first seriously consider independence and find it thrilling. But we do not find that "normal" because of some masculinist notion that it must be normal because males feel it. Not this time. We find it normal because it *is* normal—it is *human*. Girls feel it too.

But when we feel the thrust toward independence as exciting, many girls, possibly most girls, feel it as menacing—for by now they are thoroughly conditioned to dependence as their proper state. They are so thoroughly conditioned, in fact, that their thrust toward independence is often repressed by the girls themselves, because virtually every authority there is has told them overwhelmingly and unanimously and repeatedly that independence, and the desire for it, are "unnatural" in girls.

As she often does, de Beauvoir writes about this as though it were a conscious process—as though girls sit down and think these things out. They don't. Perhaps it was conscious in de Beauvoir herself, brilliant and analytical as she is. Still, if we allow for the fact that the ideas do not actually enter the consciousness of most girls, her description remains chillingly accurate:

It is a most unfortunate condition to be in, to feel oneself passive and dependent at the age of hope and ambition, at the age when the will to live and to make a place in the world is running strong. At just this conquering age, woman learns that for her there is to be no conquest, that she must disown herself, that her future depends on man's good pleasure. On the social as well as the sexual level new aspirations awake in her, only to remain unsatisfied; all her eagerness for action, whether physical or spiritual, is instantly thwarted. It is understandable that she can hardly regain her equilibrium. Her unstable temperament, her tears, her nervous crises, are less the consequence of physiological frailty than the evidence of her profound maladjustment.

A father, confronted with his daughter's emotional upheavals during this period, is likely to say, "Well, she's upset because she's starting to have periods." But that is simply mistaking a label for an explanation.

A novice in physics, asked why people don't fall off the side of the earth, is likely to answer, "Because of gravity." After a couple of years of college physics it may begin to dawn on her (or him) that "gravity" is not an explanation. It's just a name for the fact that people don't fall off the side of the earth. Even in mathematical terms, "gravity" is just a way of describing the phenomenon more precisely.

You are saying in effect that your daughter cries and has nervous crises because she is in a period of her life when girls cry and have nervous crises. That isn't much help. And it isn't much more help to say something about her hormones being "out of balance," whatever you may think that that means. There may be, almost certainly are, physiological effects on the emotions; there may also be, almost certainly are, emotional effects on the physiology. There are certainly strong cultural effects on both. Women in many other cultures do not go through the same kind of emotional crises at puberty.

Human beings have an astonishing ability to adapt. Most girls do just that. They accept, they "adjust." And once they have done so, there is almost a fierceness in the completeness with which they adopt the stereotyped role to which they have adapted. If that's how it is, they seem to say, then that's how it's going to be—all the way, and let there be no dissenters.[2] No women's liberationist will ever find among males a resistance any more determined than that which she can find in some "typical" sixteen- or seventeen-year-old American girls.

To anyone genuinely concerned with the idea that every human being ought to have a fair shot at developing her or his potential, no phenomenon of current American culture is more depressing. Not just American, of course, and in fact one of the most depressing examples is a lengthy description by Figes about a study of fourteen- and fifteen-year-old girls at a London grammar school.

The study was in 1968, and it was very simple. The psychologist simply asked the girls to write an essay. The subject was: "Today is my 80th birthday, and I look back to the time when I left high school." They were, of course, supposed to imagine their future lives and then write about them as though they were memories.

Figes doesn't say how many girls were involved, but it was obviously a sizable number. They were, she says, "girls of above average intelligence and with an urban background." They "certainly came from a working-class area with no tradition of 'professional' mothers," but on the other hand they had, compared with other girls, "a much longer tradition of two breadwinners in the family and the advantages this brings."

There was in the entire batch only one essay that did not follow the same monotonously bleak pattern—that one from a girl whose parents were divorced and who was convinced that marriage led to unhappiness. All the others had themselves married by twenty-three, an enormous majority by twenty. By twenty-five all of them

127

imagined themselves having started a family, which always ended with either two or three children (and almost all of which included twins).

The greatest expenditure of words in these descriptions of sixty-five years of future life was on the details (romantic, not sexual) of marriage and honeymoon. And "just as marriage and honeymoon figured disproportionately large in the description of the early years, so the marriage of children and the arrival of grandchildren seemed the only reality in later years—not what they themselves could actually be doing."

Many thought of future education, but only as something they would use during the year or two before marriage ("the time for fun, travel and adventure"—and apparently the *only* time) and possibly for a year or two after. The possibility of part-time work after the children were grown did come up, but always, curiously, as a temporary measure until about the age of forty-five, at which time almost all the girls "thought they would become what they called 'an ordinary housewife.'"

"The total aggregate of years worked," Figes goes on, "even after specialized training, tended to be at most only about ten years between the ages of fifteen and eighty!" Among those who seemed to think more seriously in terms of possible work, nearly all decided that they would be schoolteachers.

"Teaching hours suited both of us," wrote one girl, "as I was always back home before five o'clock to do the housework and cook a meal." This was the kind of factor mentioned by several girls who had chosen teaching as a profession, particularly the fact that one could be home at the same time as one's school-age children. But none of the girls doubted that they would be doing housework.

None of them had any picture of *herself* doing *anything*. These kids didn't see themselves, in the future, as people at all! The vision is one of robots, or of faithful servants who never go off duty. There is not an individual image in the lot. And this is a vision held precisely at the "age of hope and ambition, at the age when the will to live and to make a place in the world is running strong."

If they do not rush at fourteen and fifteen to adopt this "feminine" view of themselves, then what will happen to the only tomorrow

128

they can foresee? The males on whom their whole future being is focused will not approve—and if they do not approve, the whole thing falls apart. The girls accept and adapt to this, but they are still torn; and being torn, they band together against any among them who seems to have a different view. Jo Freeman describes it as a form of scapegoating:

Teenage girls are particularly vicious in the scapegoat game. This is the time of life when women are told they must compete the hardest for the spoils (i.e., men) which society allows. They must assert their femininity or see it denied. They are very unsure of themselves and adopt the rigidity that goes with uncertainty. They are hard on their competitors and even harder on those who decline to compete. Those of their peers who do not share their concerns and practice the arts of charming men are excluded from most social groupings.[3]

Judith Wells, in her moving and perceptive account of the effects of all this on her own development, points out that training as an intellectual provides no liberation in itself. The Daddy's-little-girl syndrome simply shifts itself to other males in any case, and intellectuality only changes the forms it takes:

I was unable to work when my boyfriend was around and felt guilty over surpassing male friends and my father in intellectual achievements; but I also knew I had to accomplish something to get masculine approval. The only activity this ambivalence brought on was diarrhea.

Notice what the psychologist calls the "double bind," [4] known to the rest of us as being damned if you do and damned if you don't. And don't forget to add in the fact that in this culture, when a woman in that position exhibits symptoms of distress, our usual reaction is to reply that there's something wrong with *her*. If we're psychiatrists we set about "adjusting" her to her femininity (i.e., her prison). If we're just ordinary guys like you and me we say that her trouble comes from trying to do something "unnatural."

A girl (intellectually ambitious or not) must be extremely unusual to rebel at all as a teenager and at least fairly unusual to rebel ever. If she does, she will almost certainly find that rebellion, especially with regard to her dealings with males, can come only accompanied

—for a long time, anyway—by anxiety and fear. This is the subject on which Wells' honesty seems to me most moving:

> I have found that . . . my rebellion against my Daddies has its own peculiar Little Girl cyclic rhythm: compliancy toward a man—simmering hate—explosion of outrage—anxiety over having stepped over the line— fear of reprisal—compliancy toward a man—and the cycle begins again.

This comes about, Wells feels, because the only identity many girls and women have at all comes from a man—originally Daddy, later other Daddies. The girl or woman who rebels faces the (more or less unconscious) problem that if she "destroys" her current Daddy, she may destroy herself. I admit that it all sounds a little mystical in spots, but Wells' description of what *happens,* quoted above, will sound familiar to any of you who has ever had any sort of sustained relationship with a woman who is not yet totally molded into shape by the pressures of the culture.[5]

Meanwhile, back at the high school, there are boys there, too, with their own "masculinity" problems. I have taken a couple of swings at psychiatrists in general, but it is their theories and their therapies I don't like. Their perceptions, especially their perceptions of personal problems, are often so clear as to be almost frightening in themselves. Edrita Fried, for example:

> Many American men, fearful of and awed by real women—that is to say mature women—prefer the child-girl. They are greatly attracted to young girls, though they usually do not carry their sexual desire to the point of action. Even more often, American men are enamored of the "boy-girl"—slim, casual in manner, and dressed in modified male outfits. She acts like a pal, is young and seemingly ageless. Once more the impact of the grown woman is avoided.[6]

I am among those who argue, with that superb novelist John D. MacDonald, that the ready eye of the middle-aged male for the passing young thing is often something other than "the erotic daydreams of traditional lust," being sometimes more of an "aesthetic pleasure of looking upon pleasing line and graceful move." [7] In any case I feel no need to apologize personally, or to regard myself as a male chauvinist pig, because I enjoy the sights on a sunny stroll near the campus during a Berkeley spring.

But there is certainly a difference between enjoying the probably

130

harmless pleasure of watching all the girls go by—of course we are in a sense seeing them as objects, the same sense in which we see a painting or a sunset as an object, but we do not pretend to ourselves that that is *all* they are—and the inability to deal as adults with adult women. And that problem, I'm sure you'll agree, an awful lot of us have.

You look for hope, and you can find it. *The New York Times* found some in the Future Homemakers of America (can you imagine a nationwide organization of teenage boys called the Future Bread-winners of America, focused entirely on their family role?). There are 600,000 girls in the organization, and there was a convention —of delegates, I presume—in New York a couple of years ago. "These girls want to be homemakers," the *Times* reported, but "they also believe they won't feel fulfilled as women unless they also have careers." [8]

And then there is a more recent and more comprehensive study, run by Gilbert Youth Research for the Institute of Life Insurance, in which 3000 people between fourteen and twenty-five were inter-viewed.[9] This study got a lot of publicity, and while we're at it we might note that much of the reporting was obviously done under the delusion that in a poll, the biggest number is the only important one. *The Berkeley Gazette,* for instance:

Asked to choose a life style "most appealing" to them, more than 42 per cent of the young women picked the "average" homemaker image, living a "pressure-free life, attending to family interests."

And later:

The survey . . . suggests that the impact of the current feminist movement . . . has yet to be gauged.

But let's take a closer look. Two paragraphs *after* the story gives us that 42% figure, we find this:

The prospect of becoming a "successful" career-woman-with-family appealed to *only* [my emphasis] 26 per cent of the young women, while another 14 per cent would choose to be "single-with-good-job."

Twenty-six per cent plus 14% equals 40%, which is practically the same thing as 42%. In other words, an equal number of the

131

girls questioned would prefer a future that *breaks* the image of the "average homemaker . . . attending to family interests."

But what girls *want* may still have little to do with what they are convinced is going to be true whether they want it or not.[10] Even at fourteen, girls know that their future is probably going to be dependent on men, and much more than is true of boys, they are concerned about their security. Forty-four per cent of the females in the same study said they were "very concerned" about their "future financial security." On a question asking for reactions to three statements about life insurance (the point of the whole poll, obviously), two of three females thought that "everybody should have it," as against only half the males.[11]

Remember the salesman's wife who reacted so strongly when her husband decided to play the guitar?

The culture may be changing, slowly, but it has a long way to go. The overriding masculinism is still there. If the teenage girl does go on to college, she will find that she is urged, more or less subtly, into disciplines "suitable" for women. Nutrition, lower-level teaching and a few other areas are woman's work at the college level. The arts, the humanities and the social sciences are okay, but she is likely to get into a little trouble if she expects to achieve on the same level as the men. A list of the female engineering students wouldn't use up the inside of a matchbook.[12]

It's still true, though, that even if she's bright, she is much more likely than her male classmate *not* to go to college; and anyway, not everybody is the sort of A student about whom such measurements are usually made. Which brings us back to her having to learn to be a miniature Schnauzer. Just at the time of her life when she should be able to see herself as the *subject,* the actor in her own adulthood, she is simultaneously required to become an *object,* something to be seen and experienced by others. It is not completely accidental, you know, that I referred to the male eye for the passing young *thing*.

In fact, the tensions we have spoken of earlier in this chapter all revolve around this cultural requirement for self-objectification on the part of the female. The "scapegoating" among teenagers of which Freeman wrote turns precisely on the process of becoming an object; it is the girl who refuses to do it, or who simply isn't competent at it, or who simply doesn't make too good an object for physical reasons, who draws the scorn of her contemporaries.

132

Objectifying themselves is what the English girls were doing in projecting their lives forward. It is her conflict between awareness of herself as subject and past approval as Daddy's object that Wells is writing about. When de Beauvoir deplores the fence built around girls just at the "age of hope and ambition," she is talking about the need for the girl to become object, a need with which boys don't concern themselves.[13]

And it is this conflict which is at the root of women's liberation, for not only does the entire feminine role in our culture depend on it—the entire masculine role depends on it, too. In truth, if you understand what is meant by man as subject and woman as object, then all you need to become a feminist is the conviction that it is somehow unnecessary and unfair that it should be that way. That—and possibly one other thing.

Possibly you also need to understand that most women don't know these things either, in the sense of being conscious of them in so many words. *They* think in *our* terms, *they* live by *our* values; and most of them are just as convinced as we are that those terms and values are "normal" and "natural" ones. That is itself a part of their self-objectification, their adaptation, their adjustment to prison life—so complete that they can argue vehemently about how much they enjoy their prison.

It is not surprising that they do so. Freedom hurts. It will hurt your daughter, if she tries to free herself from the determined effort to convince her that she is an object first and a person second, if at all.

Psychiatrists will tell her she's sick. Teachers and girl friends will tell her she's unfeminine and can't get a man that way. Someone is sure to tell her that she'd make a lousy mother. The entire commercial advertising culture is specifically directed toward her existence as an object, and to selling her all the things that go with her objectification, from mascara to acrylic floor polish. It is no wonder that girls are afraid to be free, and that women passionately defend their own deformity. Friedan, using one of my favorite metaphors in all of women's liberation literature, described the situation exactly and I can do no better than to quote it all:

How did Chinese women, after having their feet bound for many generations, finally discover they could run? The first women whose feet

133

were unbound must have felt such pain that some were afraid to stand, let alone to walk or run. The more they walked, the less their feet hurt. But what would have happened if, before a single generation of Chinese girls had grown up with unbound feet, doctors, hoping to save them pain and distress, told them to bind their feet again? And teachers told them that walking with bound feet was feminine, the only way a woman could walk if she wanted a man to love her? And scholars told them that they would be better mothers if they could not walk too far away from their children? And peddlers, discovering that women who could not walk bought more trinkets, spread fables of the dangers of running and the bliss of being bound? Would many little Chinese girls, then, grow up wanting to have their feet securely bound, never tempted to walk or run?

She's your daughter. They're her feet. You want them bound or unbound?

INTERLUDE

◆

The Feminist Consciousness

12

So now you know how it happens—or at least you know as much about it as I do and am able to jam into this much space. With minor differences, how it is happening now is how it has happened in the past, to you and me and our friends, but especially (and more repressively) to women.

I had thought, at this point, to devote some space to the result of all this—a fuller description of the masculinist culture in which we live. But I suspect, now, that having got this far you already know what I would say. If you want the facts—about job discrimination, about the double standard in the home, about how objectification affects women's sex lives—then you will find them, with surprisingly little disagreement, in Merriam and Friedan, Millett and Greer, Morgan and Amundsen and Figes. Their philosophies, their proposed solutions, differ somewhat; their perceptions differ hardly at all.

My hope is that you will be able to read them now with less hostility, less defensiveness; for what I hope is happening is that your feminist consciousness is developing. That phrase may still carry a little disturbing overtone. What *man* wants to have a *feminist* consciousness? There is just a little shade of softness in the expression, the tiniest suggestion of a requirement that we surrender some-how a bit of masculinity.

Yes, there is. My first impatient reaction to that realization is to snap at you to quit being so egocentric—nobody else is worried about your masculinity, why are you so worried about it? A bad way to communicate. My second reaction is to use a kind of abstract reason: Male and female we can say are absolute characteristics, but masculine and feminine are relative—all men have a little femininity, all women a little masculinity; let's just accept that and go on from there.

Not so good either. You concede that intellectually, but you don't really believe it. Besides, you probably suspect that even calling some characteristics "masculine" and some "feminine" won't stand up, and you don't want to be left adrift without any comfortable concepts to build your life on. It's genuinely an anxious feeling even to begin taking down those blocks, no matter how badly they're piled.

So you leave me with the necessity of hoping that you are really trying, that you do really want to understand and to break whatever sets you can, and that you're willing to try to do it with just plain effort. On that presumption, I'll simply describe a feminist consciousness, and leave it to you to try to develop one. I will simply add, in case the phrase really does bother you, that if you change your consciousness so that you are increasingly aware of racism, and if you're white, the new consciousness does not make you any more black than you were before.

If you have a feminist consciousness, then you can see the things you have been looking at all this time without seeing them. That's really all there is to it. You notice, when you go to work, where the women are and where the men are (and you notice how the men dress, and think about why, and how the women dress, and think about why). You notice that Bill always drives the sled and Joan always rides behind. You hear yourself calling the "girls" at the office "sweetie," and you wince, and pretty soon you stop doing it.

You hear jokes and light conversation differently. A friendly and well-intended joke about women doesn't hit your ear the same way. Where you used to wonder impatiently why "those women don't have a sense of humor" about some "women's lib" jokes, you now

138

begin to hear what they hear, and you don't think it's funny either. You wonder why the other guys don't hear the hidden insult that is becoming obvious to you.

You notice television commercials. Oh, boy, do you! Of course you know that you can't put together a message to sell a product, given only a minute to do it in, without relying on *some* stereotypes—a guy with a hard hat is a blue-collar worker, a man behind a desk wearing a white coat is a doctor. But you know, too, that using a stereotype tends to reinforce it, which is why advertising messages now scrupulously avoid using stereotypes about ethnic minorities. Or at least try.

I watch television a lot—I'm not too fussy about it, and it's a way of relaxing—and as I sit here I can think of only three commercials I've seen on national television during the months I've been working on this book that seem to try in any way to break the two great female stereotypes of the culture: women as pre-marriage sexy object, and woman as contented middle-class housewife-and-mother. Even making some of them black doesn't change it.

I've seen a Tiparillo commercial explicitly referring to women's liberation. I've seen a Camaro commercial involving an independent (wealthy) young woman who flies her own plane on business trips (but there does seem to be something of a "castrator" image implied in that one). And I've seen an ambiguous Clairol commercial: On the one hand it tells a woman that dyeing her hair will let her be who she really is, a dubious proposition; on the other, it shows a woman with a husband and child, obviously past her early twenties, graduating in a cap and gown, and finishing the commercial by putting the cap on the head of her daughter in an obvious promise for the future. Certainly better than the usual does-she-or-doesn't-she, with its thinly disguised *double-entendre*.

But once you begin to develop your feminist consciousness, you will immediately realize that there are a number of fields in which that woman could not be graduating, because you will be thinking about things like the fact that part-time study, combining even shared child care with academic work, is impossible in those fields. Medicine, for instance. The schools are not set up for it and will not as a rule make allowances. They are masculinist organizations, run on the assumption, conscious or not, that doctors are men. Women

139

who want to enter them must adopt to some extent the life rules of men.[1]

You will recognize, as Jo Freeman does, that there are some things about women that we cannot even determine, because the standards of "normal" measurement are in fact masculinist:

Achievement motivation in male college sophomores has been studied extensively. In women it has barely been looked at. The reason for this is that women didn't fit the model social scientists set up to explain achievement in men.[2]

The phrase "feminist consciousness" comes to me from Van Allen, who used it in a paper about the political roles and activities of women in eastern Nigeria. Those women, she argues, have been largely invisible in the writings of historians and anthropologists, except when they acted politically in such a way as to force administrators and, ultimately, writers to notice them. And even then, nothing was learned:

Their brief "visibility" was not enough really to shake any assumptions. Their behavior was simply seen as aberrant. When they returned to "normal," they were once again invisible.
To have a "feminist" consciousness means that one *notices* that invisibility. One *wonders* where the women are—in life and in print. To have a sexist consciousness means, among other things, that one does *not* notice the invisibility, because the assumptions which support sexism are norms below the level of consciousness [her emphases].

It seems to me that a feminist consciousness would also have to mean, not only wondering about what *isn't* there, but seeing the distortions and the stereotypes that *are* there—seeing them, that is, for what they are. Once you have it, you will spot the things that irritate women—and you will be different now from most men, because you will find that they irritate you too. You will be insulted that so much of the world takes it for granted that you are still content in the role into which you have been conned—just as movement women are insulted for the same reason. You will start to see what those stereotypes of women imply about you, and you won't like it.

Of course you have to know when it's a stereotype and when it's not. That should be easier now when it's about women in general, but we still have the women's liberation movement itself to deal with.

You will have no trouble, now, with the news story that described a women's liberation convention in England as a "militant hen party"; that probably annoys you already somewhat more than it did before you started reading, because you can feel the sneering condescension of which you yourself used to be guilty.[3] But when your feminist consciousness is really clicking away, almost every newspaper or magazine or television reference to women's liberation will grab your attention and raise your adrenalin.

The stereotypes about the women's movement are of course familiar enough. The trick is to know what's real and what isn't; and it's hardly our fault if we don't know, since most of our information comes to us precisely through those stereotyped views—as held by reporters and editors and columnists as well as those who have their own axes to grind. And without a feminist consciousness, we aren't aware of how comforting it is to our own psyches to believe those stereotypes.

We are more comfortable, for instance, with a group of young women from New York who call themselves "Pussycats," and who were quoted in a newspaper as hostile to women's liberation:

Why, the poor querulous creatures. They're mostly obese and have skin problems. They're afraid they'll never get a man to love them. That's why they have razor blades sticking out of their elbows . . . they try to look like men and act like men.[4]

San Francisco socialite Louise Rohner Athearn told a reporter, "So many of the women in Women's Lib would rather be men. This overt hostility, this masculinity is offensive to most women." [5] An interview with the vice-president of the National Organization of Women produced this gem of stereotyping by *Women's Wear Daily*:

She is hardly typical of today's feminist heavy. Bella Abzug, Betty Friedan and Fannie Lou Hamer, for example, are buxom women with biceps and bullhorn voices. . . .
Blonde, svelte Brenda, on the other hand. . . .[6]

The interviewer also said that Brenda, who is Brenda Feigen Fasteau, was not "anti-male as many of her counterparts are."

Now, in fact, most of the women in the liberation movement are not obese, do not have skin problems, are not "afraid they'll never get a man," do not try to look like men, do not try to act like men, do not want to be men, are not "buxom women with biceps and bullhorn voices," and are not anti-male. Truly, the more you learn about the movement the sillier some of the stereotypes get. Komisar whimsically dissected the most frequently heard canards:

Critics say they are unsexed women who really want to be men— though that hardly accounts for the demand for the right to abortion. Opponents claim that they are probably ugly old maids who cannot get a husband—though that hardly explains the demand for universal child care. They say that a woman's true vocation is as mother and home- maker—yet they ignore the fact that 40 percent of all mothers work. They talk about the need for special laws to protect women workers— yet they do not say a word about the kind of protection women need and do not have—the right to maternity leave and protection against being fired for pregnancy and childbirth. They insist that men really have a harder time while women lounge around at home, going to mu- seums and beauty salons in their hours of spare time—yet they are quick to decline any suggestion that they trade places.

But the stereotypes keep coming. "The women's lib extremists," says Morton Hunt, "make such an issue of hatred for men, marriage and mothering that they don't offer women liberation at all—just a way of cutting off many things that are gratifying to many women." [7]

I will leave you to decide whether his unconscious choice of phrases there at the end betrays his concern.

But despite the fact that *Newsweek* thinks that Hunt is some sort of expert on sex roles (I have never met or read a woman who agrees with that assessment), his overall statement is hogwash. Read everything listed in the Bibliography, and you will find one short essay on the "issue of hatred for men," and two people who discuss the possible liberating effects of extrauterine pregnancies at some time in the future. There are, it's true, a lot of different views about marriage, and many women who think the institution as we know it ought to be abolished; but they don't hate it, they analyze it.

Kearon's essay, on hating men, is actually (in my opinion, of course) worthy of serious reading by men; it has to do in part with the ways in which a masculinist culture prevents women from giving

142

vent to any real hatreds they may feel. But it's also interesting because Kearon makes it clear that women at movement gatherings are *not* man-haters, whether they *should* be or not:

> We have been unable to get out from under their [men's] definition. I've been at meetings where women actually left because they thought that "man-haters" were on the loose. One woman talked to me in awe and disgust about a woman who she felt had made an anti-male statement at a meeting.

Most women in the movement do not even reach that stage of sophisticated concern on the subject. Barbara Burris writes in weary wryness, "We, as women, do not want males to feel guilty. We don't care about guilt; what we want is change." Carol Hanisch [8] talks about her difficulty with doctrinaire Marxists: "If we don't blame the capitalist system for everything, they think we hate men. . . . They are so concerned that we think men are *the* enemy that they can't hear anything else we say." And an anonymous writer, in a witty piece about her own staircase wisdom, comes up with the answer she says she should have given when accused of manhating:

> When a man says that, it's a self-defense tactic—trying to put feminists into a hate bag, the way whites do to black militants. When a woman says it, it's usually because she doesn't see her own oppression.[9]

More than two years ago in *The New York Times,* Deirdre Carmody, covering a National Organization of Women convention in Illinois, wrote a long story in which she patiently described the women's movement (not only NOW) and quietly took apart a great many stereotypes about it—a truly remarkable reporting job given the space.[10] "On the whole," she wrote, "women in the movement are not anti-male and want to create an equal partnership with the other sex." But alas, looking at the newspapers since then (and despite the fact that newsmen all over America read the *Times*), she might as well have been writing in the sand on an uninhabited beach.

So we have Abram Kardiner—"their most conspicuous feature is self-hatred. . . . They think it's a curse to be female and have exaggerated opinions about the merits of being a male"—and Senator Jennings Randolph of West Virginia—"the small band of bra-less bubbleheads"—and the furtively anonymous editorial writer of *The San Francisco Chronicle*—"shrill harridans of the sweatshirted extreme left." [11]

These things get started, and then the rest of us read them, and, having read a dozen or two of them, begin to think that we *know* something about it, not realizing that all we have done is absorb the same stereotype over and over again. A feminist consciousness, if it does nothing else, enables you to break this pattern, because you at least know what you don't know.

Columnist Harriet Van Horne, regularly read, provides a sometimes startling example of the debilitating effect of stereotypes. With one or two exceptions (she is a strong defender of traditional marriage), she embraces virtually all the ideas of the women's liberation movement. She praises Millett, criticizes Cellestine Ware while agreeing with almost everything in Ware's book except a couple of phrases, and deplores protest against the Miss America contest while agreeing with the point of the protest.[12] Yet at the same time, she persists in perpetuating in the minds of her readers an almost cartoon stereotype of the movement itself:

I am only sorry that so many of the liberators—with their karate lessons and ritual bra burnings—have been so militant, filled with contempt for their own sex.[13]

Now, with the women's liberation movement running things, the revolution is a bit less delicate. Karate lessons, separate bank accounts and a single standard of heigh-ho permissiveness—that's the way the girls are fighting back today.[14]

In one column, she dumps on the "New Woman" partly because she wears "enough beads, chains, amulets (and eyelashes) to outfit a road company of 'Kismet,' " and partly because "she is picketing beauty contests and throwing her bra and girdle into a huge bonfire." [15] The idea that a woman who would burn a bra (assuming that there were such a woman) would probably not be the same woman who would wear false eyelashes does not seem to have occurred to her. For one thing, she'd singe the eyelashes.

So why pick on Harriet Van Horne? Well, first of all because as columnists go, she's pretty good—certainly much better on the problems of women than most columnists, female or male. I don't know what she has against karate (maybe she doesn't know what's been happening with the rape statistics), or where she got the idea that women's liberationists are "permissive," but it seems clear to me that a woman who is herself sharp and alert has been blocked off by stereotypes from seeing a movement that should be important to her—and that as a result, those stereotypes are being passed on to thousands of other people (mostly women) who have even fewer sources of genuine information than she has.

In other words, all that she lacks is a feminist consciousness. It may be odd in someone who seems to have understood Millett so well, but it's true all the same, and that's really why I picked on her: to demonstrate that you can come part way without developing one, but then you hang up, right there.

If you really want to tangle with a stereotype about the women's liberation movement, though, I'll give you the big one. De Beauvoir's is certainly the earliest book that we can relate to the current movement, and the stereotype started that early, as Figes reminds us:

In her autobiography Simone de Beauvoir records that when she published *The Second Sex,* among the vituperations heaped upon her head by the press and private individuals were many suggestions that what was really "wrong" with her was that she had never been properly fucked.

That idea—that and the related idea that "they're all lesbians," which is also nonsense—is perhaps the most recurrent of all stereotypes. Dudar wrote in *Newsweek* that this is "an obsessive male view—what I have to call the Big Bang theory of women's liberation. Men seem transfixed by the notion that all any of these women need is really swell copulation." And our friend Harriet Van Horne wrote, "My feeling about the liberation ladies is that they've been scarred and wounded by consorting with the wrong men." [16]

The whole idea is not only inaccurate but grossly insulting. It is masculinist in so many different ways at once that it is probably impossible to sort them out. It assumes, to take just one insult, that women are too dumb to recognize sexual frustration in themselves, while men are smart enough to recognize it in the women—even if they have never met the women! It implies, to take another, that the speaker is of course the ideal provider of just the therapy required (that's doubly bemusing because the remark often comes from men whose sexual experience is a lot more limited than they like to admit). But most of all it is insulting—as a feminist consciousness quickly makes clear—because it assumes that that is *all* that women are *for,* that once their lives are "adjusted" with relation to men they will have nothing to complain about.

Now let me wander for a moment, and partially exempt from that criticism the Van Horne quotation of two paragraphs back. Substitute "women" for the condescending "ladies," and change one other word so that it says, "*some* liberation women," and I find her statement not all that debatable. In fact, I know for sure that there are women in the movement who would agree with it—if you take it away from the Big Bang context—as a literal statement of fact about themselves.

For there is one thing we're likely to forget (perhaps it comes easier to me because I am both in my forties and, as a journalist, somewhat history-oriented). Many of the women in the movement are quite young. Some of them are both young and brilliant; when you break the shackles, when you taste the excitement that comes with realizing that you're not a weirdo after all just because you have brains and don't want to be a Schnauzer, you want to share that excitement—and one of the things you do is write.

But at twenty or twenty-two few women in our culture have had a varied sexual experience; nor is that experience likely in most cases to include any of those men who have achieved a little maturity in their own lives. The movement *does,* then, give rise to some rather absurd generalizations about men, and indeed in all women's liberation literature that is the one subject about which most women write badly.

One of the few sensible things in Mailer's "Prisoner of Sex" is an appeal to movement women who write. They argue that there are many complexities about women which men don't understand. Mailer asks them to see that men, too, are complex, sometimes in ways that women don't understand. It's not a completely valid request; in order to survive, women have to know more about us than we have to know about them. But taken as a more or less urbane comment on the positiveness of some younger women, it's fair enough.

Even de Beauvoir says that only women can see a man as "virile, charming, seductive, tender, cruel." No male movie fan can do anything with that claim except shrug it off. John Wayne in one way, the younger Charles Boyer in another, are obviously virile, and men can easily see them as virile. Cary Grant is charming. And so on.[17]

Not that we are only perceptive about men in the movies. We see those characteristics quite well in each other, and they aren't all that different in meaning, either. True, some of us may repress to varying extents the implications of seeing each other as "virile," but you're reading a book by yourself now; you can acknowledge to yourself that you admire some other men for what are partially sexual reasons.

Ellen Willis writes that "one reason men don't take us seriously is that they are not physically afraid of us." [18] I am a great admirer of Willis, but the sentence is just plain wrong. I take a lot of men seriously of whom I am not physically afraid. There are many men whom I cannot take seriously at all, in any way whatever, though I'm sure that in any physical situation they could clobber me. Of course, if all she means is that I take seriously, in the middle of an argument, the possibility that some men can hurt me, she's right— but it does not make me treat them any more respectfully before or after.

Shulamith Firestone says that men think that "to express tenderness to a woman is to acknowledge her equality." She also says, "Men walk about in a state of constant sexual excitement." Of course any sentence is "out of context," but I don't think I'm being unfairly selective. Among young and less brilliant women, who write for the plethora of tossed-together newspapers and newsletters that flood the movement, there are a great many statements far more absurd than any quoted. Some of those writings are outpourings of personal testimony (important in the movement for other reasons, as we will see shortly), and in those writings particularly an older reader does get the feeling that some of the writers have had especially bad luck with a very few very immature men and are unfairly generalizing from those experiences.

All this, however, besides being partly self-indulgence, is by way of saying that you don't have to agree with every feminist in the world in order to have a feminist consciousness. You don't have to agree that you are some kind of pig. You don't have to become a crusader for extrauterine pregnancy. You don't, to put it more abstractly, have to surrender your critical intelligence. You do, of course, have to face the fact of your own masculinism and recognize the structural masculinism of the culture; but past that point you couldn't agree with *all* of women's liberation no matter how hard you tried.

Women new to the movement are apt, for a brief period, to be both personally euphoric and extremely sensitive to any criticism of the movement, especially criticism from a man. But once that point is past—and it does pass—I have never met a woman in the movement who was not willing to listen to serious criticism, sometimes heavy criticism, from a man, if the man was clearly himself trying to break the masculinist assumptions, if he is showing some sign of an embryonic feminist consciousness.

You will often get screaming arguments—for you are both dealing with the most difficult human process there is, the process of unlearning what you had thought was truth. You are both facing, and trying to free, repressions that have been there since before you could talk. The emotion pours out. But next day or the day after, even after the screaming, both of your intelligences are at work again, and both have a little new material to work on. Believe me— they *don't* want to castrate you.

Please don't misunderstand me. I don't mean that you should develop a feminist consciousness *like mine*. A feminist consciousness is not a thing, like a purple chair. You don't either have one or not have one.

It is simply a name for the ability to break the masculinist cultural sets—and that is something that you do to greater or lesser degree, each person in a different way at a different time. It grows, once it's started—but it may start anywhere, and it may grow in any of a number of directions. Even a fairly well-developed one does not always prepare you for the next area of growth; a new kind of masculinism keeps surprising you in an unexpected place.

Women will help you, once you begin. But it is well to remember that they are not always right, either. As with any other subject— racism, civil liberties, starvation in Bangladesh—the person who is already deeply involved in the movement can, and sometimes does, use your own guilt against you.

Once you make that first concession—"Yes, I have been wrong; I should have paid more attention to this question; I recognize my ignorance, but I want to do better"—then, reasonably enough, you probably feel a little bad about not having recognized it before. Immediately at that point, anyone who seems to be in the movement can hit you with almost anything (quite sincerely, of course), and tell you that *that* is what you have to do to assuage your guilt and purge your soul. Wash the dishes. Quit your job. Contribute money for a lawsuit. Join a commune. Struggle with your brothers. Anything.

It may be the right thing, or *a* right thing among many, or it may not. But imagine that you have just, for the first time, heard about the people starving in Bangladesh. Someone who has been in the Feed Bangladesh Movement for the last six months or a year starts to talk to you and assures you authoritatively that what you must do, to assuage your guilt, is mail immediately to an address in Dacca six boxes of Rice Krispies.

It's not exactly *wrong*. But it's not exactly *right,* either. A feminist consciousness does not require you to give up your capacity to recognize that for you, there may be better ways. Nor does it keep you from an intelligent search for those ways that best fit your life and needs.

What you do have to guard against is a strong tendency that is not particularly male; it happens to anyone who is trying to change her or his mind about a subject, when the existing "set" is already comfortable. It is in this case a tendency to think you're developing a feminist consciousness, when what you're actually developing is a new and more sophisticated set of masculinist defenses. This is, for instance, what happens when a husband agrees that he ought to "help with" the dishes—instead of seeing that the dishes are a dirty, rotten job that nobody wants to do, but a job that is as much his concern as hers.

Possibly I am hypersensitive to how women are treated in newspapers and magazines, because of my own profession. But it is truly frustrating, once a little of that feminist consciousness starts to develop, to read such a remarkably moving and thoughtful piece of

149

journalism as Dudar's, and then to find accompanying it (and presumably written by someone else) four "profiles" of prominent feminists—including "pretty, blond Leslye Russell" and "tall, elegantly feline Ti-Grace Atkinson."

In *California Living,* a San Francisco newspaper supplement, Tom Emch wrote an article about a woman who wrote a novel. He met her in a "darkened . . . apartment illuminated chiefly by her large green eyes." He quotes her about her book—"It's about the whole ambience I was involved in [she had been a model] and the men who didn't want to meet us on a human level"—and then he says, "Translated, that means the book is about sex." She is then described as "unexpectedly articulate" (did he expect an inarticulate novelist?), and we are told that her bookcase contains "surprises"— books by Kierkegaard, Graves, Waugh, Woolf, Lawrence and others.

It's true, the worst examples of this are receiving a little resistance within my profession. A *San Francisco Chronicle* editorial on women, consisting almost entirely of gratuitous "humorous" remarks on the level of Rastus-and-Mandy jokes, drew an indignant letter from twenty-nine members of the *Chronicle* staff, which they insisted, successfully, that the paper publish. Fourteen of the twenty-nine signers were men.[20]

Finally, as your feminist consciousness grows, do not let the fact that I'm being a nice guy about all this make you think that *all* the masculinism in the culture is simply the result of conditioning. I am, after all, trying in part to give you, personally, an out—to give you a chance to say, okay, I'm sorry, I didn't know, I was conditioned into it, but I'm trying.

There are, however, masculinists who are quite conscious and deliberate about it. A lot of them make a buck, or quite a few bucks, at it. Cosmetics manufacturers want no part of women's liberation—even as they scramble to demonstrate on the tube that three different kinds of eye makeup are necessary to give females the "natural look." The guys who construct the masculinist television ads for almost everything know perfectly well what they're doing, and they are usually guys. It is the male fantasy into which they play, even if the ad is directed at women who have internalized that fantasy. Some men really *have* earned the title, "male chauvinist pig."

150

A memo on women's liberation, from Hugh Hefner to his editor, the late A. C. Spectorsky:

These chicks are our natural enemy. . . . It is time to do battle with them. . . . What I want is a devastating piece that takes the militant feminists apart. [They are] unalterably opposed to the romantic boy-girl society that Playboy promotes. . . . Let's get to it and let's make it a real winner.[21]

The article that resulted from that memo, which was published as some sort of "objective" assessment of women's liberation, was written by the man *Newsweek* called an "expert"—Morton Hunt.[22] Most of it was about a women's absurdist-theater group in New York that is peripheral to the movement and that may have had as many as a dozen members at the time.

I could have begun this book, obviously, with the promise of the title: a description of the women's liberation movement itself. I didn't do that because I am quite serious about feminist consciousness. I think I had to get this far first, because otherwise there would have been too much for most of you to resist. Unless at least a few of the blocks on the top of the pile are jarred loose a little, none of it can make sense at all.

As it is, no one with any sense would expect miracles. I'll say it again: No little light is going to go on over your head; you are not going to feel the sudden overwhelming impact of conversion like Whittaker Chambers staring at his daughter's ear and becoming a Catholic. But at least there is a chance, if you are really trying to understand. Let us, as the masculine metaphor has it, take a stab at it.

PART THREE

The Women's
Liberation
Movement, and
About Time

13

THIS may come as a shock to you, but Betty Friedan didn't start the women's liberation movement. Not even its current (say, post-1960) manifestation. Of course, she has never claimed that she did, but a lot of other people have made the claim on her behalf.

Different people have said other equally simplistic things. Firestone and some others describe the movement as entirely a product of the civil rights movement, on the one hand, and the anti-war movement on the other. Like the statement about Friedan, Firestone's has at least a glancing contact with the truth. One weird article has it all growing out of the formation in Washington of a group called Women Strike for Peace.[1]

Social phenomena of this importance do not spring to life from a single book or as offshoots of a single more-or-less-related cause. In a sense it can almost be said that they tend to spring to life when their time has come—that (for example) there would have been a best-selling middle-class book on the subject in 1963 or 1964 whether Friedan had written hers or not.

The Second Sex we have had in English since 1953, though it is probably more significant that the paperback edition first appeared in 1961. You will recall that the civil rights movement was already stirring then, and there was much rhetoric of freedom abroad in the land. There was also, on campuses, much attention to the existentialists, and de Beauvoir was already known as an associate of Camus and Sartre—so that any book by her, inexpensively available, would have achieved some circulation.

During these years, Eve Merriam published most of what became *After Nora Slammed the Door*—and while it's true that it has unaccountably disappeared, it certainly didn't go unread at the time. Marya Mannes, too, was already battering at the cultural fences that surround the woman of talent. And the growing interest in the rights of blacks may have sent a few people back to Myrdal's *American Dilemma*—complete with its Appendix on women.

There were important stirrings in other, more esoteric areas as well; look at the dates on some of the more scientific-sounding items in the Bibliography. In January, 1963, the University of California Medical Center held a full-week symposium on *The Potential of Women*. I covered that symposium for *The Nation*; Judith was with me, and tells me that to some extent at least she dates her own feminist consciousness from that gathering. The printed record of the papers and discussions (listed in the Bibliography under Farber and Wilson) is still a primary source for the women's liberation movement.

It is difficult to remember this after nearly ten years, but all of this predated Friedan. It also preceded the anti-war movement, and preceded most of the participation by young whites in the civil rights movement in the South. It preceded, too, the Free Speech Movement of late 1964, which was not the beginning of the American "student movement" but was probably the event that gave it its greatest impetus.

This is not to devalue Friedan, whose book was of enormous importance. It is merely to point out that her book did not arise out of a masculinist vacuum. Nor is it fair to say, as some young women now do, that it is "merely" a "liberal" book, concerned only with the struggle by traditional political means for the legal rights of women. The book goes much deeper than that. For some years afterward there were only the three books—de Beauvoir, Merriam and Friedan—that truly tried, for a general readership, to explore the effects of a masculinist culture on the individual psyches of women.

In 1966, Friedan and some other women founded the still extant and still growing National Organization of Women. By and large,

156

this was and is an organization of middle-class women, often professionals, usually well educated, and including a number of women over thirty-five (though I know of no breakdown, and I'm sure the majority are younger). It also has a handful of male members.

In the meantime, however, there came into being among the young what eventually had to be called simply The Movement. There was a somewhat earlier (pre-Vietnam) peace movement; there was the civil rights movement; there was the later anti-war movement; there was the ongoing student movement spreading from the FSM. Increasingly from about 1960 onward, these movements appeared and merged and grew somewhat more radical, somewhat less enchanted with the possibilities for working within the system, somewhat more perceptive of the system's hypocrisies and inner contradictions.

By 1965 it was The Movement. It was (and is) not necessarily revolutionary, though revolutionary rhetoric is common to all shades of opinion and revolutionary models—Cuba, China, Algeria—are often invoked. It ranges in fact from what might be called the left-liberal (who does not believe in the system as does, say, a Young Democrat, but who believes either that it is the only workable route as of now for any change at all, or that it at least ought to be made use of) to anywhere that you might think of as being to the left of that position.

In the years since, The Movement has had many subgroups, a few of them formally organized, most of them amorphous. "Movement people" have been "community organizers," attempting to organize the people of a particular neighborhood in their common anti-system interests. Others have stayed in college and in graduate school, attempting to turn their particular disciplines away from Establishment-determined directions. Some have worked in electoral politics, in major or "minor" parties. Some, of course, divide their time among different activities.

Many have been protestors—marching and picketing to dramatize opposition and dissent. A smaller number are civil disobeyers—nonviolent lawbreakers. A very, very tiny number, played up in the press partly because their activities are sometimes dangerous but much more because they make more dramatic copy, believe in the direct application of physical violence, though almost always against property, not people (a much-overlooked distinction).

157

In 1967 and 1968, women in The Movement began to realize that they were not much better off "in the revolution" than they would have been in an insurance office, with their leisure time spent in "body shop" bars. They were still doing the shit work, and they were still regarded primarily as typists and mimeographers by day and bed partners by night. When the "heavy" decisions were made, men made them. The women began to stir, restively.

This didn't just happen any more than Friedan's book did. In the first place, the civil rights movement had brought to the fore, at least among the college-trained who were accustomed to theorizing about what they saw, the concept of *racism* as distinguished from simple *bigotry*—the idea that racism is something built into the culture. As Firestone noted in a quotation we used earlier, it was difficult for many women, once they had reached this concept, not to draw the parallel.

Also, those young white women who went to the South learned quickly, if they did not already know, that being female is a lot different from being male. The overriding Southern male concern (black and white) with stereotypes of black man–white woman relationships could rarely be forgotten by a white woman living and working and fighting by choice with blacks.

On another level, Friedan *did* exist by now, along with Merriam and de Beauvoir, and Farber and Wilson had been published, and those ideas were still circulating and being discussed and refined, at least among the middle class—from which most white members of The Movement came.

One version has it that Jo Freeman founded the first women's liberation group in Chicago in 1968. This is more of the American journalist's tendency to turn complex events into simple ones; in any case the date is at least a year too late. Another, similar approach gives a Berkeley group the credit for first using the expression, Women's Liberation Front (wherever it came from, it was obviously based on the National Liberation Front of South Vietnam, and the previous uses of "liberation front" by independence movements elsewhere). There was for a short time a group in Berkeley that formally called itself that, but it may not have invented the term.

In any case, "women's liberation" arose out of The Movement, separately from the formation of NOW by women whose identities, if not their concerns, were more "Establishment." It was, at first, rather badly treated. The Movement—whose male leaders have always tended to pride themselves on their relative political sophistication and have tended to sneer at, for example, the Communist Party as "naive" and "simplistic"—took a very long time to arrive at the understanding of the issue that existed in the CP in the 1930s (where the phrase "male chauvinism" came from).[2]

By and large, The Movement's males tended to agree that yes, women are discriminated against, and yes, they should have a voice. What they did *not* agree to was the idea that the "woman problem" has its own identity, like the "race problem" or the "anti-war effort." They were willing that there should be a "women's caucus" in each movement activity, but they were not willing to say that women's liberation should *be* a movement activity.

In a broader sense it is a disagreement that goes on among movement women today. Some older writers, including writers as different from each other as de Beauvoir and Elisabeth Mann Borgese, seem to feel that there is some natural affinity between femaleness and collectivity (Borgese), or between feminism and socialism (de Beauvoir). Others, like Persis Hunt—who tells some interesting stories of masculinism in the Paris Commune—are not so sure.

Within the women's movement as it exists today, there is of course wider disagreement. Friedan, even in 1963, was annoyed with women who accept their feminine role as a part of their struggle for another, perhaps also desirable, goal:

It is, perhaps, a step in the right direction when a woman protests nuclear testing under the banner of "Women Strike for Peace." But why does the professional illustrator who heads the movement say she is "just a housewife," and her followers insist that once the testing stops, they will stay happily at home with their children?

Today's version is the house sign or bumper strip that reads, "Another Mother for Peace," or the woman who studiedly pushes a baby in a stroller along the route of a peace march.

Among the radical segments of the movement, however, the argument continues to be (in simplified form): Which is more important, women's liberation or the struggle against capitalism? The answer per se may not concern you—so maybe you *like* capitalism (somebody must)—but it's important to know that the argument exists, because of the ways in which information reaches us all.

"Women's liberation" is no longer solely a radical movement. It is *one* movement, but it confuses us because it is a movement with many positions within it. The press, therefore, is likely to quote an article, or a speech, or a book by a women's liberationist and give the impression that the quotation sets forth the position of the women's movement.

Thus you may hear this from Joan Jordan:

The first essential to solving women's problems, if one is not naive, is to win a society that poses all questions for rational solution. That means the elimination of capitalism. . . .[3]

Or, more directly, this from Nancy Mann:

If you can't get along with your lover you can get out of bed. But what do you do when your country's fucking you over?

On the other hand, you may read Carol Hanisch:

I don't want to work for worker control of factories if women will still end up doing the housework.[4]

Or the more sedate words of Anne Koedt:

We do not believe that capitalism, or any other economic system, is the cause of female oppression, nor do we believe that female oppression will disappear as a result of purely economic revolution.[5]

The most positive "anti-political" statements are those of Firestone, who spreads italics all over the place in a display of her unfortunate tendency, in the midst of stimulating argument, suddenly to lay claim to absolute truth:

The failure of the Russian Revolution is directly traceable to the failure of its attempts to eliminate the family and sexual repression. This failure, in turn, . . . was caused by the limitations of a male-biased revolutionary analysis based on economic class alone. . . . *By the same token, all socialist revolutions to date have been or will be failures for precisely these reasons.*

I guess you'd have to say from a Left point of view that the Russian Revolution has failed all right, but one might be inclined to think that several factors could have been involved. And I wish I could be as sure as she is about what's going to happen tomorrow, much less about why.

But while this argument, and some of the other arguments I've mentioned, have assumed importance within the movement, they also illustrate something else: the movement's phenomenal growth. If we take 1968 as a beginning year (Koedt's *Notes from the Third Year* is copyrighted in 1971), it has been a truly amazing surge. Four years ago almost nothing was written; today one person can barely attempt to read any sizable proportion of it. Four years ago even the idea that such a movement might exist was outside the imaginations of all of us; today there is hardly one of us who could escape it if we would. In those four years have sprung up "women's studies" programs on campuses all across the country, women's caucuses or committees on the status of women in an enormous variety of professional and other organizations, a burst of political activity that has pushed the Equal Rights Amendment through the Congress in the forty-seventh successive year of its introduction.

Of course, with this growth there comes argument. We are dealing with the first of the Chinese girls to have their feet unbound, and it is hardly surprising if neither they nor we have any idea what they ought to look like when they walk naturally and well.

And if women's liberation still somehow bothers you, don't rush to take comfort in the fact of disagreement. This is, at the moment, the most prominent defensive position to which the fearful are retreating; it takes the form of assuming that there are two, and only two, "branches" to the women's movement, and that they are opposed. The trick is to support the least threatening one—or, as it is usually stated by whoever is being quoted in the papers, "I'm for equal pay for equal work, but I don't go along with the radical bra-burners."

I may have made it sound, by picking up one thread from Friedan and another from the anti-war and civil rights movements, that that's how it is—but it isn't. The disagreement about capitalism divides political radicals within the women's movement, but does not even concern other large segments. NOW is usually referred to as "respectable," but it was NOW that desegregated McSorley's Old Ale House in New York City.

Willis, who defines a "radical" change as one that the system

161

cannot accommodate and remain the same system, points out that repealing abortion laws is not by that definition radical, but that radical women favor the repeal all the same. "We must admit," she says, "that we will often have more in common with reformist women's organizations like NOW . . . than with radical men." [6]

The unity of the women's liberation movement—and it is *all* the women's liberation movement, as much as some people, especially men, may want to cut out "women's rights" into a separate corral—is much more important than any differences that may come up. Intuitively, we know that it is a single movement, which is why a single phrase has come to stand for it.

What are different are only methods of attack, and the significance of the difference is no greater than if you and I were moving on a target of some sort, and you were to say, "You take that side and I'll take this side." We're simply going at the same enemy by different routes. Even the abstract theoretical differences within the movement don't change this; you may not even agree on who the enemy is, but you know he's over *there* somewhere, and that's the direction in which you have to move.[7]

And so there are women, and groups of women, who pursue a legal attack—an assault on discriminatory laws, an attempt to broaden existing legal interpretations to include women, the breaching of any number of exclusionary walls from the right to attend a class to the right to become a jockey. There are women, and groups of women, whose approach is organizational—whose primary effort is directed toward contacting other women and spreading the feminist consciousness.

There are women, and groups of women, whose approach is political in the broader sense—who are trying to change the structure of power. There are women, and groups of women, who are devoted to analysis—to refining their perception of the problems, to examining the previously unexamined in our culture with the hope that a greater understanding of our social interrelationships will result.

There are women, and groups of women, who are trying to bring new insights about the nature of culture into special areas—sociologists, for example, who are concerned both with discrimination against women in the profession of sociology and with hidden masculinist assumptions within the *content* of the discipline.[8] There

162

are women, and groups of women, as we have seen, who are concerned with trying to change the conditioning processes of our culture—by studying children's books, or by monitoring television, or by trying to influence writing and publishing through activity in the Authors' Guild.

There is NOW and there are Marxist groups and there is a group called The Feminists and there is another group called The Radical Feminists (both of the last two quite influential) and there is Bread and Roses and there are the Redstockings and there are all kinds of others, including one group rather cutely called Radicalesbians. There are groups that come and go before anyone can learn their names, and there are groups that are local where you live, if you live in any town larger or less remote than Post Creek, Montana.

They are all "women's liberation," not only because all of us who are not a part of the movement lump them together, but because they belong together. They are, despite any differences I have described or will describe, much closer to each other than they are to us.

If you remember the civil rights movement in the 1960s, then you can draw still another analogy. No one then confused the NAACP with SNCC, or CORE with the Black Muslims, or the Urban League with the Southern Christian Leadership Conference. It was quite possible to understand their differences. No one thought that Elijah Muhammad spoke for Martin Luther King. But no one doubted for a moment, either, that there was *one* movement, with one overall goal regardless of arguments about its definition; and no one doubted that they were closer to each other than to any group of whites.

One reason that we have some difficulty in understanding all of this—aside from the recurrent pattern of simplistic distortions in the press—is that there is a strong sentiment within the women's movement against hierarchy. Many of the women, particularly those who came from or are associated with the anti-war movement, are suspicious of individual leaders, of "spokeswomen"—who tend, as happened in the civil rights movement, to become "stars."[9]

"We must fight," says Germaine Greer of all people, "against the tendency to form a feminist elite, or a masculine-type hierarchy of authority in our own political structures" (in the same paragraph she refers to an extremely odd entity, "the matriarchal principle of fraternity"). Nancy Ferro and her sisters, dealing especially with the problem of contact with reporters, put it more completely:

> We are attempting to build, within our movement, non-exploitative ways of relating to one another based on trust and concern rather than political expediency. We have serious personal/political intentions in breaking down hierarchical and elitist structures, and for experimenting with leaderless groups and collective decision making. In dealing with the media these revolutionary principles and practices are destroyed. The media works to create leaders, it knows no way of relating to us on our own terms. Being interviewed and presented as a leader is a real ego trip —the media brings out the most counter-revolutionary traits in people. Elitism, dissension and division are the ultimate results.

One would think that among three writers—at least one of whom I know to be an accomplished professional—there would be one who knows that "media" is a plural noun; but I have quoted the passage as printed. Both syntax and New Left rhetoric aside, however, the point of the above passage is a crucial one in understanding women's liberation.

It isn't that all women agree with it. Leslye Russell is quoted by Dudar as saying that the movement "isn't really organized," that "there must be . . . some kind of structure." Clearly, NOW has spokeswomen. And Atkinson seems to regard herself as a leader when she says in the same issue of *Newsweek* that carries Dudar, "It's easy to mobilize women, but once we mobilize them, we don't want to lead them over a cliff."

It's also true that while the media do tend to create leaders, saying so doesn't solve the problems of even the most conscientious reporter. She or he has to talk to someone, and if it's television, that someone has to be on camera.[10] The words that that someone uses have to be her own. Two or three women appearing together may help on one occasion to mitigate the star syndrome, but it is an idea more suited to the discussion format or the lengthy interview than to daily news.

Even then, the problem of spokeswomen is not solved for either side. A good reporter will want to be fair; but she (or he) knows that in any group there are some people relatively less articulate, some relatively less informed, some relatively less quick, and a few outright dimwits. Simply sending up a team instead of an individual, or rotating spokeswoman duties throughout the group, is more likely to result in inaccurate coverage.

Then, too, a reporter, especially a print reporter, depends on being able to trust individuals. If I need a fact about the practice of medicine, there is a doctor whom I call because I know he'll give it to me straight and I can trust him. His name may never appear, but I could not function without a network of such personal contacts —and it means talking to the same person every time.

New ideas, however, create new forms, and so we must understand the passage and its implications. Only when we understand why the argument is made can we avoid the simple oppression of pretending that it can't be dealt with.

What almost all women in the movement are trying to do is to examine not only their personal lives, and the obvious social discriminations and oppressions, but the institutions of the culture. They are hunting out the structural masculinism wherever they can find it. And some of them, at least, believe that the way in which organizations are usually put together in our culture is itself masculinist. Some of them believe that concern with gratifying the individual ego (being a "star") is a masculinist concern. And—since they can all see that some women in any group will be better at some things and will know it—it is a genuine and an enormous psychological effort to try to break those cultural patterns and to set up new ones.

Of course a few women will see masculinism where none exists. And of course, in this particular case, the concept blurs off into some general concepts of the political Left. But neither of those things is important. What's important is the determination of women who are willing so completely to examine the social bases of their lives and their activities.

Even the "small group," the "consciousness-raising session," in which we can now find middle-class women who have discovered the beginnings of their selves, but whose political ideas are no more radical than those of, say, William Proxmire, derives in part from the Left; there is a connection with similar practices, engaged in by both sexes, in China. Again, however, that isn't what is important to us.

What is important is what those women *do* in those sessions.

14

SCRATCH a woman," says Jo Freeman, "and you'll find a feminist."

Not quite. Conditioning being what it is, and the resultant resistance by a lot of women being what *it* is, the "scratching" is sometimes more like scraping the semi-permanent inch-thick layer of white makeup off the face of the aging Elizabeth I. All the same, she's under there. Even that woman you know, who is so absolutely perfectly contented with her feminine role and who thinks women's libbers are all fat grubby crazies, might surprise herself if she were to spend a few sessions in a consciousness-raising group.

We are still ridden—the culture is still ridden—with the idea that if you can't adjust to the way things are, there must be something wrong with *you*. Women, as should be clear by now, are doubly ridden ("Psychologists cannot fix the world," says Greer, "so they fix women"). Besides keeping us all isolated from each other to some extent—if it's something wrong with *me,* there's no point in my talking to *you* about it—it keeps us from looking at our society as squarely as we might.[1]

Women can break this as individuals, to some extent, and a few do. These women tend, oddly, to be somewhat unsympathetic to women's liberation. I did it, they seem to say to other women, why can't you? The accompanying implication is that another woman could do it, too, if she were smart enough or strong enough or ambitious enough—which brings that other woman back to the idea that there is something wrong with *her,* when all that is wrong is that she cannot play a magic flute (or nobody needs a flute player right now). The successful woman of this sort lacks a feminist consciousness; having made it through the interstices of institutionalized masculinism, she insists that no such thing exists.

But once a woman starts to crack the pancake makeup of her conditioning—once she has a glimmer of that terrible and wonderful and fascinating fact that she might yet indeed have a self, and that it is not her fault that she craves one—it comes quickly. That is the beginning of what "consciousness-raising" is about. The first consciousness-raising session on record in the current feminist literature happened accidentally, and was recorded by Friedan:

> On an April morning in 1959, I heard a mother of four, having coffee with four other mothers in a suburban development fifteen miles from New York, say in a tone of quiet desperation, "the problem." And the others knew, without words, that she was not talking about a problem with her husband, or her children, or her home. Suddenly they realized they all shared the same problem, the problem that has no name. They began, hesitantly, to talk about it. Later, after they had picked up their children at nursery school and taken them home to nap, two of the women cried, in sheer relief, just to know they were not alone.

Remember Steinem's astonished discovery, quoted earlier? "Women *understand.*"

Never mind what the problem was (or is). It was a common male reaction at the time Friedan's book was published to say that "the problem that has no name" was simply boredom. None of us, of course, bothered to notice—since we do not in fact notice what women say—that no *woman,* possibly excepting a handful of Old Left types, thought for a minute that the problem was boredom. Women, at least middle-class women, knew perfectly well what the problem was, even if they couldn't name it.

But set that aside for the moment. The point in my quoting that passage is in the final phrase. Its intensity of meaning is lost in the writing, but I certainly cannot convey it any better: Just to know they were not alone.

167

If this is all really new to you, you cannot conceive of the extent to which that discovery affects women in this culture. Over and over again, in writing and in conversation, it turns up as the first and—even after months of attending "small groups"—the overwhelmingly most important personal reaction to consciousness-raising: the simple realization by a woman that she is not different from other women, that they feel the secret inner things that she feels.

This is one of the things that men most resent, one of the things that makes us most hostile, when "our" women become involved in women's liberation. We think of ourselves as being—and some of us really are—loving and gentle and understanding. We want, of course, to be loved in return, and often we are certain that we are. It is a karate chop to the ego when the woman goes off to a session with a few other women, whom she may not have known nearly so long or so well, and returns full of joy because she has been understood—understood, she may even say, for the first time in her life.

It is threatening. Our status, as lovers and understanders and providers (as substitute fathers, perhaps), is threatened. The one who has given us her love now seems to love someone else in a way we cannot share, and there is an inner terror that we may suddenly find ourselves alone. We feel that something is being asked that we cannot give, we discover that she has a need that we cannot meet. And to top off all this, it comes about precisely through a movement that is critical of males in general—and we are males.

Of course we are hostile and defensive; and in our hostility and defensiveness we do and say things—whether angrily, or mockingly, or in what we see as "serious discussion"—that simply confirm what she has just heard at her small-group meeting about the hostility and defensiveness of men. Like it or not, there are only two ways out of this for a man. The woman, once she has begun, cannot go back; it is impossible. So either the separation grows, or you, too, try to learn.

The small group has of course come some distance from the accidental occurrence described by Friedan. A lot of trial and error has gone into it (it's not unusual for a women's liberationist to belong to several small groups serially, and some have been at it for years); some people, like Kathie Sarachild, have even tried to set up formal outlines for consciousness-raising.[2] For the most part, though, small

168

groups aren't conducted all that formally. Mostly they have only a few simple things in common.

Usually the same group of women meets regularly, with men excluded.

Although new members may join one at a time and individuals drop out, the group usually tries to maintain a continuing identity (most women seem to feel that three is too few and nine too many; within those limits there are differences of opinion about size). Maintaining the same group gets rid of the need to go over the same ground repeatedly, and enables the members to come to know each other as individuals. This in turn does more than make it possible to understand each other despite the difficulty of phrasing ideas that are coming to consciousness for the first time. It also means that they become aware of each other's patterns of evasion, so that they can push each other to be honest.

As a rule, women, once they *do* know each other and once they have committed themselves to honesty, quickly learn to pick out those occasions on which a member blames masculinism (or society, or "her" man) for something that is her fault. Often that fault is her own unwillingness to stand by her beliefs, to assert her own equal existence.

Women also try to be sharply critical of each other in cases where one woman tries to "dominate" a meeting or to force her ideas or interpretations on the others instead of simply subjecting those thoughts to mutual examination. I say "try" because this practice has a double purpose. Besides preventing domination, it helps all of the women to break the culturally conditioned pattern that says women are "nice" to each other. One of the things the sessions try to overcome is women's difficulty in criticizing each other face-to-face.

They meet regularly, for the most part, for mutual convenience, but there is another reason for that, too. We do not for the most part realize that almost every demand on a woman's time is either a male demand (*he* has to go to a meeting, and who's going to take care of the kid?) or more subtly a masculinist demand (some activities are regarded by women as more important than others because men so regard them). It's okay for a bunch of women to get together and talk so long as there's nothing more important to do. The regular meeting date and time helps to condition (or, perhaps, uncondition) women so that they regard their own affairs as just as important as ours.

They exclude men because they must. Men will not let them talk, and if they do get a word in, men do not listen.

I said that flatly, in simple declarative form, because it is flatly true. The exceptions are so few, so rare, that they are truly negligible in this culture. You can test it yourself, quite easily, if you can somehow get yourself into (or arrange) the right situation. It requires only a group of congenial men and, among the women, one or two whom you know to be reasonably well-informed and knowledgeable. Start a conversation—on politics, say—and then simply detach your mind a little, sit back, and watch.

If the men are polite (and often they are surprisingly impolite), they will stop talking when the women speak. But if the woman speaking says anything that contributes to the conversation—if she introduces a new idea, or raises a serious question about something one of the men has said—the conversation will pick up, as soon as she has finished, almost as though she had not in fact spoken at all. The men will almost literally not *hear* her. And if you watch them, you will see that they are talking to each other, exactly as though she were not there.

It is astonishing how often this is true. No one has been more guilty of it than I, and I have had my own tendencies in this direction called sharply and regularly to my attention for more than ten years (I have a loud voice anyway, and grew up in an Azorian Portuguese family in which the loudest voice usually "won" the argument).

If it is not true, if a woman or women *are* admitted to a conversation on any subject of male importance, then a subsidiary phenomenon will take the place of simply ignoring the women. It is, more precisely, the pattern that leads women to exclude men from women's liberation groups; and you can watch it happening, too, even in the politest of circles. Men express opinions to each other, listen to each other's opinions, reason with each other to some extent; but they *explain* to women. Many men will let "their" women finish, and then turn to the group and repeat the statement or argument, restating it in an "explanatory" way ("*I* have learned to

170

understand what this strange creature means, you see, and I will translate").

As I said, you can see these patterns for yourself, if you are willing to detach yourself from a group conversation a few times and watch. They are of course reinforced when the men go to one side of the room, or into a different room, and separate themselves from the "girl talk." You can see these patterns, and a moment's thought will show you an exact parallel. There is another group of humans who are treated exactly the same way in serious conversations. We are sometimes polite and listen, we sometimes explain to them, we sometimes explain "ours" to other people, but we go on talking to each other. And sometimes we send them out of the room.

I am of course referring to children. And in serious conversations the pattern is exactly the same. Men have serious conversations. Women are children.

The frustrations of intelligent women who have lived through such scenes dozens or even hundreds of times are among the first frustrations that burst out in consciousness-raising groups.[3] There is no "girl talk" in the small group.

Feminists detest that phrase, by the way—"girl talk"—but I must say that I have never understood why. It's precisely accurate. A "girl" is an immature female, and "girl talk" describes conversation on the level of females who have not developed, or have not been allowed to develop, into mature women. Whether the females are fifteen or forty-five, the subject matter is the same; only the perspective differs. It is of course insulting to grown women when a national television show is called *Girl Talk,* or when a man who is otherwise as perceptive as Bobby Troup writes a condescending song by that title; but the insult is in the suggestion that women are capable of nothing else, not in the description of what some females sometimes do.[4]

The small group is not "therapy," either, and calling it that is a good way to get into a sizzler of a fight. A reflection of the indignation comes through from Hanisch:

The very word "therapy" is obviously a misnomer if carried to its logical conclusion. Therapy assumes that someone is sick and that there is a cure, e.g., a personal solution. I am greatly offended that I or any other woman is thought to *need* therapy in the first place. Women are messed over, not messed up! We need to change the objective conditions, not adjust to them.[5]

So what do they talk about? About their lives. About their perceptions of the world. About why *they* think things are as they are, how *they* think things might have gotten that way—free from having it explained to them by males in what, as they painfully work out for themselves in the group, are masculinist terms. They describe things that have happened to them, and tell how they felt at the time—and as often as not discover to their surprise that other women have had similar things happen and felt the same way.

What is really hard for us to grasp—so fully do we live in our culture—is the extent to which women are conditioned to feel that certain attitudes and expectations and feelings are *normal* for women. Since we believe the same things, and since we can't feel like women, we spend our lives acting as though they're true. Women, also, spend their lives acting as though those things are true—but almost every woman, inside herself, knows that they are not in fact true of *her*.

She believes, though, that those attitudes and expectations and feelings *are* the attitudes and expectations and feelings of other women, and that she is unusual and very likely somehow weird. She is convinced that if she says out loud what she really feels, people will think that she's crazy (I am *not* exaggerating). In the small group, she determines, or she is coaxed, to say one or two of them out loud—and she finds that she is not crazy. Delighted—truly astonished—cries of recognition, and of joy in that recognition, are common in small groups. So is the phenomenon described in that accidental meeting of Friedan's—the rush of relieved tears.

For that feeling of difference, of wrongness—that feeling that *other* women really believe and feel the things they're "supposed to," and that I am the different one, the weird one—brings a load of guilt with it, and a heavy burden of self-doubt. Even the woman who has accepted (as she sees it) her difference and is in there fighting for her opportunities is frequently assailed with doubts and anxieties, the fear that possibly it *is* therapy she needs.

In the group, as Anita Micossi writes, "the self-hatred that comes with failure and disappointment is hurled outward in a liberating catharsis . . . converts often remark on their 'new

172

strength,' an exhilarating feeling of 'wholeness' or 'a great sense of myself and my potential.' " There are a hundred quotations in the literature on the order of, "Talking with other women made me realize that it wasn't me personally, but me as a woman." [6]

Treated as an equal (very possibly for the first time in her life), the woman gains self-confidence. Treated as an equal by other women who obviously care about her on a deep and satisfying level, the woman gains not only a new self-esteem but a new esteem for other women. Several have said that they now *like women* for the first time ever. The conditioned feeling that other women are competitors in the dog show passes, and they begin to become "sisters."

There is astonishment. "I was amazed," Steinem wrote, "at the simplicity and obviousness of a realization that made sense, at last, of my life experience: I couldn't figure out why I hadn't seen it before." [7] Another woman, calling herself only Barbara, came to the small group from a bout with psychotherapy, and reported her early reactions:

I got into the women's movement and began to see that other women were also called crazy. The relief at finding I was not alone was incredible. I was stunned. Here were women who were strong. And what's more, they were smart and had ideas about how things ought to be. It had been very effective in therapy calling me different than my sisters, trying to make me believe that I could find an individual solution without changing the external . . . conditions. It had effectively separated me from my sisters and even made me start to hate them. It put me in the position of not being able to identify with other women.

Where the dots are, I took a word out of the above quotation, because I didn't want to interrupt your train of thought with a jarring word—especially one that tends to turn the phrase into a cliché. The word is "political," and we have to take at least a brief look at it, because women's liberationists keep using it. They don't all mean the same thing all the time, of course; but they don't mean what we're likely to mean either. Obviously it has nothing to do with who runs for Congress; slightly less obviously, it does not refer to what political thinkers have meant in the past by "the class struggle" or "the power elite" or "the system."

We could use those terms, of course, by changing their application a little. Men and women are in some senses "classes." Men are certainly the "power elite" relatively to women (and of course some men are more elite than others). It is a male, or at least a masculinist, system. And in a very vague way these are the things that are meant when women's liberation speaks of its struggle as political.

Millett called her book *Sexual Politics,* and one portion of it is devoted almost entirely to examining the ways in which the conditions that oppress women are "political." In a somewhat different way, Amundsen does the same thing. I will simply sneak out of it by quoting a generalization from Pam Allen:

> After sharing, we *know* that women suffer at the hands of a male-supremacist society and that this male supremacy intrudes into every sphere of our existence, controlling the ways in which we are allowed to make our living and the ways in which we find fulfillment in personal relationships. We know that our most secret, our most private problems are grounded in the way women are treated, in the way women are allowed to live.

If the realization that she is not alone is the most important thing that happens to a woman in a small group on a *personal* basis, the most important thing that happens to her as one of a number of women is the realization that is in Allen's last sentence. Those private, personal feelings, which she finds are not unique to her, turn out instead to be political—to be rooted in the way the society is put together.

There is no use in being afraid of the word, or in thinking that its use makes the whole thing into a Communist plot or some sort of New Left nonsense. As a rule, small groups do not have leaders, and their members come from backgrounds too many and too varied for us to assume that their conclusions are somehow manipulated. There is no way—even with some common reading matter—that so many groups could arrive at almost the same conclusion, starting with nothing but the personal lives and educations of their members, unless that conclusion had some solid basis in fact.

A woman feels personally oppressed, personally frustrated. She takes her oppression and frustration into the group, as do the other members. They look not at what is "wrong" with *them,* but at what has happened *to* them. And they arrive almost inevitably at a political definition: The society *is* masculinist, it *is* oppressive, and

174

it, not the individual woman's psyche or her adjustment, must be changed.

I have made it seem as though this is all an exhilarating and a joyful experience. It seems that way because that is often the first stage; the first discovery, the feeling of breaking out of isolation, the realization that she is not alone, the recognition of sisterhood—that *is* exhilarating and joyful. But that is not all there is to it.

Particularly among women who are what we loosely call intellectuals, or those who have achieved some success in generally male fields, there may be feelings of anxiety. It comes not so much from assessment of their own positions as from their having learned, more than most women do, to think analytically about what is happening to them. Dudar learned this not from joining a small group but from her journalistic investigation of the movement:

One of the rare and real rewards of reporting is learning about yourself. Grateful though I am for the education, it hasn't done much for the mental stress. Women's lib questions everything; and while intellectually I approve of that, emotionally I am unstrung by a lot of it.

"Unstrung" happens to some women. Downright goddamned good and mad happens to a lot of others.

I hope that *you* get bitterly angry when you discover that you've been conned into something. I know that I do, and if you do too, you will be better able to understand me and better able to understand women who have the same reaction. Certainly neither you nor I has ever had anyone try to con him, in effect, out of his entire life, his entire being, as women are conned by this culture.

"Conned" is the word. Conditioning is, after all, a form of conning; it doesn't matter that we can't find anyone to put in jail for it. Television advertising, with its stereotypes, is a con and everyone knows it. Certainly *Playboy* and *Cosmopolitan* are cons (actor Burt Reynolds, who posed for a "nude" foldout in *Cosmopolitan*—as a put-down, he insists, of *Playboy*—told an interviewer, "The philosophies of Hugh Hefner and Helen Gurley Brown are those of paper-doll cut-outs" [8]). What happens to women when they find that the whole culture has conned them must be something like what you and I feel when we discover that we've been conned on some smaller basis.

And so now, with (I hope) my feminist consciousness beginning to bud, I find that I, too, am angry about being conned into a "masculine role," even though it is a better role. I read complacent statements, especially statements by apparently complacent women, referring to women's liberationists as "angry" or "bitter"; and I respond out of my own anger, "Why the hell shouldn't they be angry and bitter?" In fact, I am surprised that so many women's liberationists seem able to retain any equilibrium at all; I suppose it's that or go mad like a subculture of female Lenny Bruces.

Susi Kaplow has written an essay taking a careful look at this anger—for it is something that many women in the movement go through and can then come to look back at, although it never completely goes away. She describes the initial realizations about the masculinism in the culture as coming haltingly at first, after which they "begin to hit you like a relentless sledge hammer, driving the anger deeper and deeper into your consciousness with every blow."

I am reminded that there is a book called *Black Rage*, and I wonder whether some female psychiatrist will overcome her fascination with masochism enough someday to write *Female Rage*, for it is surely there to write about. It seethes or it explodes, and neither is completely satisfying. It builds, for instance, in the "Daddy's little girl" of Judith Wells' essay:

> Because the Little Girl has suffocated her own desires so completely in favor of her Daddies, her potential for rage is volcanic once she questions the belief that "Father knows best." Yet for myself and probably for most Little Girls, each explosion is followed less by a sense of triumph than by anxiety and fear of reprisal.

Women don't break their conditioning—despite the artwork on some women's liberation posters and the metaphors sometimes used in argument—in one clean action, like breaking shackles. A woman chips away at it; the understanding grows; the rage grows. But the doubts don't all go away just like that—they keep creeping back. The desire for male approval lurks waiting to make itself felt ("Now that my rage has exploded, will he reject me, deny me his approval?"). The cultural assumptions she has so far overlooked suddenly confront her as new frustrations. And if she loves a man, she still loves him.

Besides, there are of course too many targets for the rage. For a while she seems to stay angry all the time—angry at "the system," angry at her parents, angry at schools, angry at newspapers, angry at television, angry at you if you happen to be around, angry often

176

at things that seem to you trivial and that sometimes (not always) are.

If we judge women's liberation by a particular opinion which may be shared by only a few, as we noted before, we will misunderstand. In the same way, we will badly misunderstand the movement if we happen to run into a woman while she is in this common initial stage of anger, and think that that is what women's liberationists "are like." It would be easy for anyone, female or male, to be turned off by the whole idea if it seemed to put women permanently into the constantly angry state about which Kaplow (addressing herself to women) is writing:

> This is an uncomfortable period to live through. You are raw with an anger that seems to have a mind and will of its own. Your friends, most of whom disagree with you, find you strident and difficult. And you become all the more so because you fear that they are right, that you're crazy after all. You yourself get tired of this anger—it's exhausting to be furious all the time—which won't even let you watch a movie or have a conversation in peace.

But here again, the small group becomes important. That "fear that they are right, that you're crazy after all" is taken back to the group, which probably contains one or more women who have been through the same thing. No, the woman finds out once again, she *is* seeing what's there, the emperor *doesn't* have any clothes, her anger is justifiable, she is *not* crazy.

She goes back, too, when she is sure she is right but feels weak, when the struggle for selfhood saps her strength, when the incredibly mighty undertow of her conditioning threatens to pull her under. Maybe she loves a man, but for the moment cannot take the strain of continuing to stand up to him and be herself. Maybe she isn't so sure she loves him, but has no place to go and no way to get there if she did. Maybe she can't quit her job and can't stand the place she works because of its masculinism—anything that can happen to a newly awakened woman may be happening.

What she finds—and it is another crucial term within the movement—is support. She gains back a little strength, the strength to believe in herself, to stand up for herself one more time, to resist that powerful pull to go back to being Daddy's little girl or the well-behaved miniature-Schnauzer-with-a-mop. She gains from the group a little more trust in her own perceptions. She is reinforced in her new understanding that she is as important, as a separate individual, as a man, the man, any man.

Because here, while she is seized with this new rage and this new vision, is right where we screw up again. "It must be wrong," we say. "Look what it's doing to you." Or we say, "There, there, dear, it's all right." Or we say, "Well, look it isn't *me*." Or we say, "For Christ's sake, people are starving in Bangladesh and you're worried about our housework." As though it were the housework she's worried about. Or we say plaintively, "All *right,* dear, but what is it you want me to do? Just make a reasonable suggestion." Or we say, "Oh, come on, it's only a television commercial."

Make up your own. With one minor variation, I've used every one of the responses above, and never once insincerely. We should put ourselves on tape at times like that. Come back later and listen, and you can hear your own desperation, your own fear.

So we say these uneasy things back, and she tries, but she can't make us see that they are all just that much more masculinism—and there is nothing else she can do but go back again to the group for support (because she still wants our approval, that hasn't all disappeared overnight, and maybe she loves us, too), and we are that much more jealous of the group, and around and around it goes and will keep going—spiraling outward so that the distances are greater —unless we break the pattern. As I said, she can't go backward now.

Small groups do other things for particular people. It's even tempting to suggest, on the strength of the Lucille Iverson interview cited in the Bibliography, that they might even be the answer to a part of the drug problem. They certainly helped "Susan," the interviewee:

I felt so good after going to the group that I cut down on drugs—from two or three times a day to two or three times a week. I felt a release— buoyant. Before, I hardly related to anyone. But in the group you get a lot of attention—you feel important, you matter.

When I went to a clinic, I was told that they have so little success with women addicts—far less than with men—that they almost believe it's physiological. But I don't think so.

You feel important. You matter. You don't have to be an addict, if you're female, to find that an unusual circumstance. Outside women's liberation, women are *not* important and they *don't* matter.

Oh, in a few places, maybe—the theater needs actresses, and as a consequence some actresses may sometimes be treated as individual human beings. A handful of women attain that status in a few other fields. But not nearly so many as take drugs.

Some women have written that the small group in particular, and women's liberation in general, broke them of a kind of elitism. Women who have been politically active, especially, share with their male colleagues the feeling that they are either more intelligent or more knowledgeable than most other people, or both. The movement turns their heads around, and they come to feel that they have more in common with other women, regardless of education or experience, than they had thought—that the similarities are more important than the differences.[9]

The "awakening" experience doesn't have to come through a small group, of course—particularly if the woman in question is already given to intellectual, analytic activity. But it isn't likely to come without contact with the women's movement in some way.

As noted, it happened to Dudar when she got the assignment to "cover" women's liberation for *Newsweek*. Already an accomplished and successful reporter, convinced of the reality of her own emancipation, she approached the assignment, she says, with some ambivalence:

I suppose the ambivalence lasted through the first 57½ minutes of my first interview. Halfway through an initial talk with Lindsy Van Gelder, a friend and colleague, she said almost as a footnote that a lot of women who felt established in male-dominated fields resented the liberation movement because their solitude gave them a sense of superiority.

I came home that night with the first of many anxiety-produced pains in the stomach and head.

Elsewhere she describes what happened to her professional detachment:

I came to this story with a smug certainty of my ability to keep a respectable distance between me and any subject I reported on. The complacency shriveled and died the afternoon I found myself offering a string of fearful obscenities to a stunned male colleague who had "only" made a casual remark along the lines of "just-like-a-woman."

There's that volcanic rage, there's the anxiety, there's the pervasive effect of the feminist consciousness, once budded (note

179

the careful quotation marks around "only"; very few men would have put them there, but of course they belong there).

Many feminists would like to get every woman in the country into a small group for at least a couple of go-rounds; if that woman you're currently identifying yourself with isn't into it yet, she very well may be before you know it. It might be well to note, then, that not all groups always work out too well.

The most common failing, as you might guess, is that the people just don't get along. Sometimes this is simple personality clash. Sometimes women with more experience in the movement tend to lecture newcomers rather than sharing with them or supporting them; sometimes, too, they become impatient with the "slowness" of neophytes. Women's liberation helps a lot of women and helps them a lot, but it's no panacea for personal traits and it doesn't raise IQs.

Sometimes women with different theories—on marriage or on capitalism or whatever—will spend so much time arguing with each other that the rest of the group falls apart. Sometimes one woman, convinced that *she* has *the* answer, stifles discussion. Groups have broken up because members insisted on talking about lesbianism, and because members insisted on not talking about lesbianism.

A surprising number of groups, though, get past most of these hangups. There are other problems in the small-group operation that are a little more widespread.

It is not easy for any woman in this culture to tell *anyone* how she really feels about anything inside herself. She is trained, in general, not to do so. She is trained to distrust other women to some extent and to see them as competitors. She is trained, too, to distrust her own thinking, to have little confidence in her ability to use her own mind and to arrive at her own conclusions; she is likely to be especially distrustful of her conclusions if they are all unorthodox.

Once in a group, as these things begin to slip away, she begins to trust her sisters; in addition, they provide her with help and support. Understandably, she is reluctant to risk their disapproval—and consequently reluctant, sometimes, to criticize a sister's ideas and approaches, or to suggest alternatives or even variations. If this hesitancy affects several women in the group, the group bogs down. Honesty, both intellectual and emotional, is necessary to its function.

Pam Allen, who discusses this problem briefly, also discusses the related problem of maintaining individual strength in a group situation:

> It is a temptation to transfer our identities onto the group, to let our thinking be determined by group consensus rather than doing it ourselves. [But] we believe that our hope lies in developing as individuals who understand themselves, their own needs, the workings of our society, and the needs of others. Thus we try to resist the temptation to submerge our individuality in the group and struggle instead to make contact with our feelings and thoughts. Freedom is frightening and difficult to use.

Also related, but also different, is what we might call the problem of depth, which derives from the fact that we can't magically plant Stendhal's forest all at once. We can never get rid of *all* the masculinism in the culture, or *all* the masculinism in our conditioning. Nor can a woman get rid of all of *her* conditioning or escape the culture.

That, in turn, means that as the group goes on, there is always one more level to deal with—both in examining the culture and in the self-examination, helped by the group, that each woman performs. There is always a deeper fracture to be mended, always a more subtle relationship to be probed. For many women, even partially liberated women, the pain at some point is too great.

One of the principal concerns of women in small groups, as we have still to discuss in a little more detail, is the question of sexuality: briefly, the distinction between the "sex role" imposed by the culture and the adult woman's own sex drives and desires. It is a major effort for many women even to find out for themselves what the demands of their own sexuality are. And men know enough about sex hangups to see that the functioning of some groups might well come to a halt right there. If we were trying to talk as openly as we could to each other, most of us can feel intuitively that there is a point at which each of us might very well stick.

Finally, there is the simple tendency of some small groups to turn into nothing but gripe sessions, not all that different from a group of suburban housewives around morning coffee complaining about last night's particular set of husbandly insensitivities. That happens much less often than you'd think, but it does happen.

Which reminds me. There is one uneasy question to which every husband and boyfriend seems to want the answer, especially if he has honestly given something of himself to the relationship—if he has made himself, as lovers do, truly vulnerable to the beloved. He wants to know: Does she talk about me?

You bet your John Wayne cowboy hat she does.

How could she not? If the personal is political (to borrow Hanisch's title), then the political is also personal; she can arrive at an understanding of structure only through her own experience, and you are—at the moment anyway—her experience. The more honestly she tries to deal with her own overall oppression, the more honest she has to be about her feelings toward you and her perceptions of you.

At first she is likely to dwell on your good points. It's a standard gag in women's liberation that every woman in it lives with the only real male feminist in the world. This goes away, as the mutual use of honesty within the group builds mutual trust and as she learns to detect the structural reality that underlies even *your* easy-going manner. But if you have anything halfway decent going, even in terms of the unliberated masculinist world, I wouldn't worry too much.

Figure that she will tell them a little more about you than she admits to you. Figure that she will tell you a little more about them than she admits to them. Beyond that, forget it. She may be the only one in the world you have ever told about the thing you have for wearing purple over-the-knee socks to bed—but if you have told her, then you already know how trustworthy she is. She won't discuss that—or she would have told somebody anyway, without a women's liberation movement. The women's movement does not turn trustworthy people into untrustworthy people.

As for your minor foibles, stop gnawing at the pedestal of your ego. They've heard it all before; you're not so unique either. And you're not that important to anyone except (maybe) her. If it still bothers you, try working on not giving her so many things to complain about. The biggest effect on you will be her demand that you try to attain, within your relationship, something like half the honesty she has learned to expect from her group. Worry about that instead of what she says when you're not there.

The small group can, theoretically, go on forever, if the members continue to struggle for honesty and openness, and if they go on being willing to peel off one more layer of the problem. But it is not women's liberation. Getting together and boosting each other,

182

raising each other's consciousness so that each member can then go out into the world alone and do her thing in a male world, is not the idea at all. The idea is to do something together about changing the roles so that the world is less masculine.

This can be done in little ways—as demonstrated in Berkeley and environs by a group called The Women's Defense League.[10] This is simply a group of women which comes to the support of other women who would under "normal" circumstances be physically trapped in a male world. In one case a woman living in a Berkeley apartment had a male guest who refused to move out. Instead of calling the cops, she called her sisters—who came and moved him out (he may have been inhibited a little by our male I-won't-hit-a-woman thing, but if so, it was a good thing for him; there were thirty of them). One of the women involved described another League "case":

> We called the police in San Francisco, after a Pinkerton guard who lived upstairs in a two-family building persisted in harassing the woman living downstairs. The police labelled it a "private matter," said they wouldn't interfere except that if either of the parties called again they would arrest both.

Other women took turns, in groups of two or three, staying with the lone woman in the downstairs unit.

Most men, you'll admit, hardly ever think of problems like these; but most women, even if they've never been in such situations, will feel an immediate identification with the fears, the helplessness, that the two women felt. The solution is unusual; the problems are far too common, and they exist partly *because* their conditioning isolates women from each other. Believe me, if every woman over twenty in an American city had ten other women she could call on in a time of need, there would be a lot of changes in our culture very soon.

The Women's Defense League, of course, is not a program for women's liberation; it is simply an incidental, if happy, result of its existence. But as we have seen, there are women, and groups of women, pursuing all sorts of attacks and approaches, inside the system and out, focusing on broad theory or on specific problems in specific places, dealing with media problems or organizing new communications systems.

183

The one thing that they are *not* doing is trying to make it "on their own"—a process that requires submitting to male judgments, accepting structurally masculinist conditions for accomplishment, and learning to play a magic flute. The one thing they *are* all doing, whatever their other fields of endeavor, is always, always reaching out to still more women. They are indeed the direct descendants of another feminist, as roundly excoriated in her day as any of today's radicals, but honored now on a fifty-cent stamp—Lucy Stone:

In education, in marriage, in everything, disappointment is the lot of women. It shall be the business of my life to deepen this disappointment in every woman's heart until she bows down to it no longer.[11]

15
▼

THE women's liberation movement thinks, talks, analyzes, organizes and acts. Virtually none of this comes to public attention except the acts, and only certain acts at that.

As with other "movements," including the labor movement, not everybody is in on all the acts, most "members" don't even know about them, and by no means does everybody approve of them. Some one group, with perhaps as few as a dozen members, may be entirely responsible. The press, however, reports those acts it *does* report as acts of "the women's liberation movement." This confuses a lot of people.

The acts the press reports are of two kinds. It reports legal actions if they border on the sniggery-sexy (the "bounce test" story on Florida high school girls) or if they seem to be of genuine importance, especially locally (some lawsuits by such organizations as NOW or, increasingly, the American Civil Liberties Union). And it reports the far-out, dramatic protests, such as the desegregation of an all-male bar in New York City (it was done in San Francisco, too, but nobody cared that much, there were no incidents, it wasn't a bar where newsmen go, and it had no national coverage), or the famous Miss America protest at which bras weren't burned, but the whole country got the idea that they were.

It is tempting to say that by fastening on these stories, the press gives the rest of the nation the impression that women's liberation is concerned with the trivial. I am resisting the temptation because, as Komisar said in another context, people said the same thing when black students began lunch-counter sit-ins; and also because one feminist wrote that when she hears the word "trivial," she knows she's getting close to something important.

Komisar's statement had to do with desegregating a previously all-male "executive flight" on an eastern airline; she then quotes a law student, Jan Goodman, on the clear legal/moral question involved:

What is at issue is the indignity and humiliation to a class of people who can be excluded from public places by a male dominated society that can enforce its personal prejudices through law.

Is any woman truly humiliated, does any real live woman's dignity really suffer, if she can't take an executive flight or have a beer at McSorley's? Yes. Not every woman's; not even most women's—just as not every black, perhaps not most blacks in Greenville, South Carolina, wanted to eat at that lunch counter, had ever thought of eating at that lunch counter. But their dignity was *involved*. And for *some* women, it is humiliating to know that you can be arbitrarily excluded from anywhere—a feeling they can feel even if they don't like beer.

So it is not really trivial.

Under our system, if the law is itself illegal (i.e., unconstitutional, as discriminatory laws are), you have to have a particular case with which to demonstrate it. If you want to eliminate the practice of arbitrary exclusion of women from public facilities, you have to have a particular public facility for a test—say, a bar.

The "trivial" action is also a demonstration, both literally and in the current media sense. It is a symbolic act, serving notice that there is a group of women no longer willing to tolerate discrimination; it also and simply calls attention to the fact that discrimination exists. Of course it may not be *discrimination* as such that the demonstrator wants to combat; she (or they) may wish to call attention to the masculinist nature of a phenomenon where it may not have occurred to you before.

186

The problem is not that desegregating a flight or a bar or pro-testing the Miss America contest is itself trivial. The problem is that it is *reported* as trivial. It turns up in the paper, sometimes even with pictures, or on television; but the almost always male reporter never bothers to explain any of this. What the nation sees is a tiny handful of obviously kooky women with nothing better to do.

One result is that everyone knows the epithet "bra-burners," but not one person in a thousand could even tell you when or where the bras were *reported* burned, or why they were supposed to have been burned, or much of anything else about it. The answer you will most often get is that it has something to do with some sort of sexual freedom *à la* Hugh Hefner, which is very close to an exact opposite of what it did mean. And everyone knows about bars, regards it as a trivial question, and snorts that equal pay for equal work is more important.

See it all as one movement; try to understand every action, even if you disagree with its effectiveness, as a question of tactics, not con-tent; recognize that if it seems trivial in the press treatment, you are probably not getting anything like the whole story; remember that a few women in a particular protest are not "the women's liberation movement," or the "radical bra-burners," or any other stereotype. There: You're partly liberated already.

It is of course not trivial at all to protest the Miss America contest —tactics aside. If you have ever seen it, in person or on television, and if you have enough taste to distinguish The Rolling Stones from Lawrence Welk, then you know that it is a beauty contest pure and simple. The "talent" portion of the contest exhibits slightly less talent than you would find at a third-grade music recital.[1]

It is an upgraded and stylized slave market, and nothing more. Beauty *means,* in that context, meeting masculinist cultural stan-dards; it means being at best an idealized version of what men want to possess (not "love" or even "know," but "possess"). And since men cannot possibly know anything else about the contestant except that she meets those standards (and perhaps that she knows the lyrics to "Oh, Promise Me"), it is clearly a meat march.

Or, to revert to an earlier metaphor, it is a dog show in which the miniature Schnauzers are rated on conformation, carriage and mark-ings, with a few points thrown in if they are clever enough to sit up and bark for a biscuit.

Of course it is an insult to women. It presents things which purport to be women but which are not people. They are not even sex objects. They are display objects.[2] I have no objection—on the contrary—to looking at women I find physically attractive. I have an extremely strong objection to their being treated as though that peripheral fact about them is the only definition, the only identity, that they have. I have a vehemently strong objection to a culture in which that is what a good many young women are taught to want to be.

Obviously I didn't think that way twenty years ago. I would be grateful to women's liberation on a personal basis if the movement had done nothing for me except to show me how insultingly depersonalizing is the bathing-beauty image. But in fact, women's liberation is bringing a new view of all sorts of things, and the feminist consciousness, once working, can pick out almost any aspect of our culture and dissect it.

Since we are talking of dissection, take medicine. There is not yet a lot of material available, but I understand that various studies of the treatment of women by doctors are under way. Doctors are not really very good on the subject, you know, and never have been (in 1878, *The British Medical Journal* announced that "it is an undoubted fact that meat spoils when touched by menstruating women"[3]).

The material that is available ranges from grievances about condescending treatment[4] to a double standard toward female complaints to downright sadism. Four women students were suspended from American University in 1971 because they staged a sit-in—to demand gynecological health care in the campus infirmary.[5] Women are organizing a program of direct complaint to gynecologists about their treatment (an extremely frequent complaint is the use of a cold speculum—an instrument used to dilate the uterus; the speculum can easily be warmed if the doctor is considerate enough).[6] A woman wrote in one feminist publication:

A woman often can get *no* gynecological treatment without answering moral, marital and sexual questions irrelevant to her medical problem. We are made to feel embarrassed and even guilty about our medical conditions. In no other medical branch is this generally true. No one asks questions about your morality when you break a leg.[7]

I have before me a clipping, recording an interview with a Canadian gynecologist, W. Gifford-Jones, who it seems wrote a book

188

called *On Being a Woman* [8] and who was subsequently interviewed. "Unless it is a real emergency matter, I refuse to see a patient who comes into my office with her hair in curlers and in sloppy dress," he says.[9] And I say, Just who the hell does he think he is? It is difficult sometimes to hold back that phrase, "male chauvinist pig."

But if you think it's all about curlers and embarrassing questions, you're wrong. This one is from a medical publication:

> The charge that male doctors harbor an underlying sadism against women is increasingly being heard. . . . A discussion took place among surgeons on attitudes toward orchiectomy (removal of the testicle) and oophorectomy (removal of the ovary), and it was agreed that surgeons rarely hesitate to remove an ovary but think twice about removing a testicle. The doctors readily admitted that such a sex-oriented viewpoint arises from the fact that most surgeons are male. Said one of them wryly, "No ovary is good enough to leave in, and no testicle is bad enough to take out." [10]

Is that serious enough for you?

As I said, medicine is only an example. Women's liberation, and the feminist consciousness that is resulting, have changed our perception of a number of American institutions; it would be possible to compile another book simply by listing several cultural institutions at random and then investigating the impact of the women's movement on each.

You are not likely ever to think of prostitution in the same way again, for instance, if you will take the trouble to read Kearon and Mehrhof, the remarkable piece by Coleman, and especially Susan Brownmiller's "Speaking Out on Prostitution." Brownmiller has perhaps the finest talent in the entire movement for using the technique of reversal, which she applies to many subjects besides prostitution. I may not have the quotation exactly right, but I remember one instance well. She and another woman were appearing with Hugh Hefner on *The Dick Cavett Show,* and she listened incredulously as Hefner said that *Playboy* is not guilty of exploiting women.

"Mr. Hefner," she said acidly, "when you are willing to come out here in skin-tight clothing with two bunny ears on your head and a big piece of cotton attached to your fanny, then you can tell me that you don't exploit women."

In 1971, a committee of the New York State Legislature held a hearing on "Prostitution as a Victimless Crime"—despite protests from a number of "respectable" women. A women's liberation group, including Brownmiller, then took over the hearing and insisted on testifying; Brownmiller's article is actually a transcription of her testimony, which is filled with compassion but also with the same kind of quick insight—like that directed at Judge Morris Schwalb, who, she said,

> began to hold prostitutes in his court without bail after he got some complaints from friends of his who were in town for a Bar Association hearing. They claimed that they were actually being harassed by women on the street. Well, if Judge Schwalb were to put on a skirt and walk down 42nd Street, or even Fifth Avenue, any afternoon, despite his hairy legs, I think he would begin to understand for the first time in his life what street harassment is all about.[11]

It is enough of a demand on you to ask you even to begin, in the course of reading one book, to nourish a feminist consciousness. I shall not ask you to try to identify with a female prostitute. But you may be able to understand a little about why feminists, including some who are fairly strict about their own sex lives, are able to do so.[12]

"Politically and sexually the hooker is at the mercy of masculine overlords," writes Coleman—and demonstrates it for several paragraphs. She says also of the prostitutes she interviewed:

> That some of them honestly believed prostitution offered them more personal freedom than did working as a nine-to-five drudge in a department store is eloquent testimony to the degree to which women lack control over the forces that shape their opportunities and their lives.

Brownmiller is even more direct. Reminding the legislators that she is white, middle class and ambitious (she could have added that she has achieved some professional success), she said that she found it easy to identify "with either the call girl or the street hustler," and that she could tell them why in one sentence. "I've been working to support myself in the city for fifteen years," she went on, "and I've had more offers to sell my body for money than I have had to be an executive."

For a last word on prostitution as a "victimless crime," and on the question whether it is in fact a masculinist institution, I give you de Beauvoir, complete with her italics:

Around the turn of the century the police found two little girls of twelve and thirteen in a brothel; testifying at the trial, the girls referred to their clients, who were men of importance, and one of the girls was about to give a name. The judge stopped her at once: *"You must not befoul the name of a respectable man!"*

From prostitution it is an easy verbal step to abortion, an extremely important issue in all segments of the women's liberation movement. Abortion, however, is already one of the most widely and (recently) most openly debated subjects in the country. There isn't much to add here.

Obviously the only tenable feminist position is that it is her body and what she does with it is her business. Like any other minor medical procedure, abortion should be readily available to any woman, regardless of ability to pay (the argument by some feminists that it should be free confuses two issues—that of abortion and that of the cost of medical care).

If a woman wants to delegate her decision about her own body to a religious authority, that, too, is her business. My own opinion is that neither she, nor that or any other authority, has a right to dictate to *other* women about *their* bodies. Certainly a legislature has none. Beyond that, I can only quote for your study a sentence by attorney Florynce Kennedy: "If men got pregnant, abortion would be a sacrament." [13]

Social issues like prostitution and abortion aside, however, one of the major concerns of the women's liberation movement is the overall question of sexuality, including the sexuality of the "liberated" woman herself. A great deal of small-group time is devoted to this question, and a lot of the movement's "internal" literature is concerned with it in one way or another. The specific concerns range from use of The Pill and the question of wearing bras through the meaning of "orgasm" to the nature of marriage and finally to the implications of lesbianism.

But in a very real way they are all the same question.

191

16

▼

LIKE us, women cannot escape their culture and cannot fully escape their conditioning. That is as true about sex as it is about anything else. By the time she reaches the age at which women's liberation is apt to begin to affect her, a woman already has some sexual existence. There are things she likes to do, things she wants to do, things she does not want to do without.

We are not at all accustomed to thinking about sex this way—and it is a pretty difficult thing to do at first—but there is a genuinely *political* question about whether any of those things are things she *ought* to do.

Of course you don't want to think about politics while your erection is waiting. It is not suggested that you should—at least not by me. But none of us really believes that sex is all that simple, and it isn't as much strain as it might seem to think of it as political. Politics, in this sense, is simply a question of power—although it may be a subtle question of power in some cases. Possibly it will help if you follow Dudar as she came to understand the political definition of rape:

> Rape becomes political if you accept the premise that women are a class, probably the original oppressed class of human history; that their oppression is a conscious expression of the male need to dominate; and that a sexual attack is a display of power allowed by a "sexist" society.

The tricky words are "conscious"—I don't think it has to be conscious to be political—and "allowed." I think it would be enough to

192

say that a sexual attack is a display of power *in* a "sexist" society.[1] At any rate, those changes will suit our purposes and save us a long and abstract discussion.

You will note, in passing, that if rape can be called a political act, then obviously karate lessons for women are a political act—analogous, say, to military training for the defense of an oppressed ethnic minority. That's all I have to say about karate; I don't think men are hung up on the idea that some women are learning to defend themselves, although a lot of non-movement women seem to be.[2]

And if rape can be called political, then virtually all sexual relations between men and women in this culture can be called political. They are all based on a power relationship between the two sexes. It may be subtle, but it winds up being a relationship in which men define, and women conform or suffer.

Before I go on: I can sense a stiffening resistance here, and I sympathize with it to some extent. It has to do with a basic liberal concept of sex relations which has to do with consenting adults. Look, you say, she likes to do thus-and-so, and I like to do thus-and-so, and we enjoy it together, and why don't you take your politics and get the hell out of our bedroom (if it's something you do in a bedroom)?

Yes. Fine. No one, least of all me, wants to interfere in a relationship between (or among) consenting adults. If they are consenting *adults*. But a lot of women don't think they are.

Men define the accepted sexual practices (not just the ones in the bedroom), and women conform to that definition. When women come to the liberation movement, that is almost always the first form of oppression that they are able to identify. It goes back to the adolescent beginnings of their being turned into dog-show contestants instead of adults—and back beyond that [3]; it comes up to the realization that what they do with much of their lives is shuffle.

"Shuffle" is another women's liberation term derived by analogy from the black struggle. It means "to behave in the manner expected of you by the master class." It means that she looks up interestedly while you prattle about your golf score or your last exam, smiles when *you* think something is amusing, giggles softly instead of guffawing out loud, eats daintily in a restaurant so other men won't think your girl friend is a stevedore—and so on and so on, and if you don't think it's ninety per cent of some young women's lives, you just don't look around you.

It is this *political* oppression—this requirement *by the culture* that she submit to our definition of a proper sexual relationship and guide her behavior according to our standards—against which most women first rebel. In its more abstract form, it says that men are active and women are passive, that men do and women are done to, that men are "naturally" dominant (even the standard man-on-top position is "standard" only in Western culture).

Most men in this culture never question this pattern, and neither do most women so far. I'll bet a couple of pennies that you never thought of it as *continually* and *inherently* a dominance-submission relationship, much less a political one. But, whether the women or the men in the culture know it or not, there is a difference between their and your perception of it. They can get through a change in the dominance-submission situation without cracking up. It is not at all certain that you can.

I don't mean that no men can; some can and obviously do, at least to enough of an extent to make a genuine difference. A. H. Maslow, one of the better psychiatrists, said of "love in healthy people" that characteristically, "they have made no really sharp differentiation between the role and personalities of the two sexes. That is, they did not assume that the female was passive and the male active . . . " They could, he said, "be both passive and active lovers," and if you think that's easy, imagine yourself simply being made love *to,* without ever making *any* move to take over or direct the operation.[4]

Atkinson has been known to overstate things, but it's interesting to compare Maslow's observation about healthy lovers with one of hers:

I believe that the sex *roles* both male and female must be destroyed, not the individuals who happen to possess either a penis or a vagina, or both, or neither. But many men I have spoken with see little to choose between the positions and feel that without the role they'd just as soon die.[5]

This conflict between possibility and actuality, and the importance for the women's movement of this whole dominance-submission view of sex with its concomitant shuffling and repression of female individuality, is widely enough described in the women's liberation literature. What is *not* there is much information about men, which sent me looking.

It turns out that we come out looking pretty misshapen ourselves. In 1963, for instance (coincidentally the year of Friedan), Edwards and Masters came very close to describing a cultural condition as an inescapable one:

Feminine equality may only be achieved by masculine abdication and at the price of masculine subjugation. The sexual consequences of the subjugation by the "equal" female are well defined and have often been described: the male, in varying ways and degrees, is "unmanned." It would seem that a great many men, and quite likely the majority of men, are able to function at peak level sexually only with women who are submissive and who willingly accept, or skillfully pretend to accept, the domination of the male.

You almost have to be a grammarian to read that correctly; the meaning of the first sentence depends on its saying "may," not "can." That is, they aren't saying that it has to be that way—only that it apparently is. And what it means is tough for us to take. It means that most of us can't make it with a full-grown, adult woman.

I am messing about with your very secret concerns, in some cases concerns you don't even know are buried down there; and I know it. If I can learn nothing else from all this studying of women's liberation, I want at least to try to show the compassion and understanding that the movement women have learned to show their sisters. But I must learn also their honesty; and you *have* to go along with me here, for it is right here that we find out whether your intelligence and your openness (and your courage) are a match for all that sick conditioning.

Go back another six years, to 1957 and the Murtagh-Harris study on prostitution. Why, they asked, do men patronize prostitutes? Traditionally, because their wives are repressed and unresponsive; but no more (and this was fifteen years ago, remember). "Increasingly," the authors say, "the men who require the services of prostitutes say that they have wives who are *too* responsive and demanding. In effect, the pressure of having to please has become too great; the men 'cop out.' " And they quote a New York prostitute:

It burns them up not to be lords and masters in their own beds, and so they try to make believe they are in ours.

So (if these studies are accurate) we cannot deal with adult women, and we cannot meet the demands of women who are fully sexed. Not, one presumes, because we are physically unable (the

195

human race got here somehow), but because the cultural conditioning is so strong that many of us cannot function, or cannot function well, if we do not dominate.

There's nothing odd, by the way, about the idea of cultural surroundings affecting physical performance. Some men cannot urinate if anyone else is watching. We do not, in our culture, copulate on the sidewalk; if you were to try it (and simply hope that no one would call the cops), your fear and embarrassment might well render you impotent. To say that a change in deeply conditioned roles might have a similar effect is not to make a statement that is any different in kind.

It appears to be true from several studies that during the past decade or two, women's sexual demands, or their willingness to admit them, have risen to the point where men—not women as in the stereotype of the Victorian era—are the ones who feel that demands are being made on them. This in turn seems to be taken by many men as an implied criticism of, or threat to, their potency.[6]

Brenton interviewed an astonishing number of psychiatrists, psychologists and other authorities, and he set it out quite frankly:

One of the recurrent themes the experts I interviewed voiced time and again was the reluctance (or inability) of many American husbands to accept any sexual condition other than male control and male supremacy. They function perfectly well within the limits defined by the sexual stereotypes of masculinity and femininity. But if their wives, perhaps carried away during a moment of passion, take some of the sexual initiative, they become offended.

He went on to quote a middle-class wife: "I want to please my husband. I want to make him feel comfortable. But sometimes I feel like I'm having to walk on eggshells." Another woman was being treated for frigidity—and her quotation illustrates not only the point here but the way in which women are treated as sick because of what is done *to* them: "You know, I don't trust my husband. I'm afraid to let myself go. If I did, I don't really think he could take it."

William Hartman and Marilyn Fithian, a few years ago, did a study on women who couldn't reach orgasm. They found along the way a number of cases in which, when the women broke through and *did* attain orgasm, the men became impotent.[7] Figes cites a 1963 study showing that "happiness" in marriage "was related to the wife's ability to perceive her husband's expectations." It had nothing to do with the husband's perceiving the wife's expectations.[8]

It is unpleasant to find that we are yo-yos on the end of a string of conditioning. It is worse to find that we are such irrational yo-yos that we oppress the people we truly, if imperfectly, love. It makes the ego groggy to think that our sexual prowess—in which so much of our emotional investment is placed, on which so much of our fragile self-evaluation depends—fades away when we try to make it with a mature woman.

This seems to be the most obvious reason why so many of us resist so strongly the ideas of women's liberation. The woman who has been touched by the movement can no longer live with this cultural dominance-submission pattern, this connection in our heads between politics and potency. "Once a woman becomes aware of the nature of the traditional role," writes Micossi,

she cannot act as before. And this is a painful jolt for the converted woman. The extent to which our lives are played out through sex roles is considerable. And when a woman invalidates those roles for herself she becomes disoriented, and normal interaction is disrupted.

"I can't kid myself any more," says Wells. "I know my own sexual desires." But it is enormously difficult for her. She is *willing* to be subject rather than object, she is willing to take an equal role; but she still wants sex with a man, and the conditioning is still strong. There is embarrassment "when I want to be sexually aggressive or state my desires straight out." She will not shuffle—she will not engage in that grotesque parody of a girl-child's behavior that the Harriet Van Hornes and the Abigail Van Burens seem to think is "femininity"— and she cannot yet without embarrassment be adult.

This is of course only partly within herself; for sex with a man must be with a real, live human being, not an abstract construct. And he is likely, as we have just seen, to be terrified by the adult woman. That woman, Wells continues, "is discouraged subtly (a male's slightly chilly response to her phone call) and not so subtly (his impotence when she asks him to bed) when she is sexually aggressive."

She will not shuffle, and there are no men with whom she can be adult—or if there are, they are so widely distributed that the odds are overwhelming that she has never met one. Nor does she want to reverse positions in the dominance-submission game; her new understanding is not merely that she always loses, it is that the game is destructive in the first place and shouldn't be played at all. It is only the still dominance-oriented male (or the still submission-oriented female) who accuses her of "wanting to be a man." That is the last thing she wants!

And so, not outright perhaps but in some subtle way, she may at first reject sex entirely, or seem to. She is in the position of refusing to play in the only game in town, and comforts herself by saying that the whole thing is a shuck. In the small group she is critical of her sisters who "compromise their principles" by continuing to live with or regularly to have sex with a man, despite his masculinist imperfections. Depending on the depth and nature of her conditioning, the previously taboo idea of lesbianism may begin to tease the back of her mind. If she does deal with a man, she is feisty, on edge, alert to the slightest manifestation of masculinism, insulted at an offer to light a cigarette or open a door (why do women never notice that men sometimes light each other's cigarettes?), ready to see dominance in every remark and gesture.

If the man is you, you may make that same stereotyping mistake here. You may think that she is what women in women's liberation *are,* that to be in women's liberation means that she will always and inevitably take offense at everything and be unable to engage in any conversation.

You are wrong on two grounds. The first is that for most women that emotional state is a stage that softens, although of course neither the perception nor a substratum of indignation can ever go away entirely, and shouldn't. The second is that you are likely to forget that she is after all *right.*

There probably is masculinist content in almost everything you do or say. If you forget that, then when she is willing to make some allowances, you won't notice it; you'll keep seeing her as "picking on every little thing," and being defensive about it. If on the other hand your feminist consciousness grows even a little, then there will be fewer and fewer times when she jumps on you, more times when she quietly calls your attention to something in a spirit of mutual friendliness, and an increasing number of times when you will get indignant

198

together (or laugh together) at a shared perception of the masculinism you have overcome.

For she will come to see that she cannot deny her sexuality (and I need hardly add that if *you* are struggling in the meantime, that is going to benefit you). "True sexual maturity," said de Beauvoir, "is to be found only in the woman who fully accepts carnality in sex desire and pleasure." That is not, however, all that she needs to know. Very likely she knew she was "carnal" before the whole problem came up.

Remember that she has learned to see sexual roles, to see the whole dominance-submission sexual game, as political. Acknowledging her own carnality, she must now ask herself whether any given sexual relationship involves a betrayal of her political principles, a political betrayal of her sisters. She may face a very real conflict between what she *likes* to do and what she thinks, politically, that she *ought* to do.

If she is in women's liberation, she is always—*always*—responsible to her sisters. Probably she continues to meet with them, and they are not all in exactly the same place; they are different individuals with different ideas, and there is no one "correct" path of development. They may criticize her decision to remain with a man or to move in with one; if she tells them of the details of her sexual feelings, they may be convinced that she is reverting to a submissive position and offer criticism. She must be sure enough of herself to be able to assure *them* that that is not the case. That is what is meant by "coming to terms with her own sexuality."

I read an essay (it is lost and I cannot cite it) by a woman, long in the movement, who liked *fellatio*. She enjoyed it, as indeed many women seem to. She mentioned this in her small group and was pounced on by every other woman there, all of them arguing quite reasonably, if vehemently, that the act is *inherently* submissive. She assured them that she had no intention of submitting to anyone, that in fact she intended to do a little initiating. She also told them that it had taken a considerable effort for her to overcome her own conditioning, and to admit to herself that she actually liked it—for as common as the act is in America, the usual role-playing version is that the woman consents to do it to please the man, that he "makes" her do it or anyway "gets her to" do it. Eventually, that particular woman quit her group, although she remained active in women's liberation.

She had, she felt, come to terms with her own sexuality. It was true that many *men* still saw it as an act of submission, but, she said, she did her best to make her feelings about that clear; if they still didn't understand, she wasn't going to give up her pleasure just because they had hangups.

It makes a good illustration of the point, even if it is an unusual one. In most cases, of course, the conflict is not so dramatic (nor so titillating). She may simply have to deal with the fact that she really is more comfortable on the bottom. In still more cases the conflict has nothing to do with particular acts at all, but with a whole attitude toward sexuality in general, her own in particular, and the need to reconcile those attitudes with the immediate realities of a masculine culture and with the principles of women's liberation.

If you're waiting for me to tell you what a "liberated" view of sexuality is for a woman, you're waiting in vain. Every woman is different. Many settle for the best they can do with a man (there is nothing in all of this that says of a woman that she can't go on loving the same man she loved before), and try to move him toward a greater feminist consciousness while trying simultaneously to retain that precious core of individual integrity that almost every man tries to some extent to dominate.

In the long run, of course, the only answer is to change the game. Anne Koedt's interview with a woman who has turned to another woman for love yielded this gentle and important reply to a question:

At a certain point, I think, you realize that the final qualification is not being male or female, but whether they've joined the middle. That is—whether they have started from the male or the female side—they've gone toward the center where they are working toward combining the healthy aspects of so-called male and female characteristics. That's where I want to go and that's what I'm beginning to realize I respond to in other people.[9]

17

WHICH is not, by any means, all that there is to the subject of sex.

Unless you have spent the last five years on Bouvet Island, you must know that there is this thing in the women's liberation movement about orgasms. Since almost none of us know what the conversation is really about, we tend either to make fun of it—a rather obvious defensive move—or to slough it off as relatively unimportant, "trivial."

I suspect that one of the reasons is our fear that it will all turn out to mean that we are lousy lovers, a thought none of us likes. Let me relieve your mind. We are of course involved—that dominance-submission pattern, with its side effect that the woman does not really regard herself as a sexual equal, is very much in the way of her using what women's liberation has taught her about orgasms—but we are not the whole focus of the discussion. So rest your ego. If there is a man central to the issue, it is Sigmund Freud.

Space demands superficiality here. Lydon's article is a good popular treatment of the subject,[1] Anne Koedt's "The Myth of the Vaginal Orgasm" is the most precise and complete. By all means read both; in the meantime I'll try to convey the general idea.

In Freud's defense it should probably be said that he put forth a theory, to be tested in the future, and not a dictum (he particularly hoped, he said, that female analysts would pursue it). It became very nearly Holy Writ, however, and like other Freudian concepts it has trickled down through popular culture to become, in somewhat distorted and diluted form, an influence on almost all our thinking about sex, even if we've never heard of Freud and don't know a complex from a comptometer.

We don't need an illustrated sex lecture at this point, I hope, so I'll just assume that you know what a clitoris is, what a vagina is, and where they are, more or less, relative to each other. To a lot of women, an orgasm achieved by direct stimulation of the clitoris feels different from an orgasm reached through penetration of the vagina by a penis (the direct one, some women say, is more intense and less diffuse; and some say it's more satisfying, but that brings in psychological factors). From that fact, Freud concluded that there must be two kinds of female orgasms: clitoral and vaginal.

Given the knowledge of the late nineteenth century, it was a reasonable enough assumption; but the good doctor went on to spin quite a theory out of all this. The center of sexuality for a young girl, he decided, is the clitoris (which is what one would stimulate in masturbation). When she is mature, her center of sexuality shifts to the vagina. An "immature" woman is a "clitorid" or "clitoroid" personality.

With your newborn feminist consciousness perking away, you can already glimpse what he's done here. He has taken male concepts and applied them to females. Conventionally, boys masturbate at first, when they are still what he would have called "psychosexually immature," and then they "grow out of it" and become men, who take their sexual pleasure more maturely through intercourse with women (actually, of course, most of us never completely give up masturbation, whether we admit it to each other or not, but that wouldn't in itself invalidate his theory). Freud simply lifted this idea and applied it to women.

So if you're a woman, and sexual intercourse doesn't bring you to vaginal orgasm, there's something wrong with you. You may be able to make it by stimulation of the clitoris, but that leaves you immature, incomplete, un-grown-up, unresponsive, hung up. Off to the shrink for "frigidity."

An interesting word: We think of it as meaning "unable to achieve orgasm," but we define it in practice as meaning "unable to achieve vaginal orgasm." This distinction has made a lot of psychiatrists rich. And it has done terrible things to American women, as only a few feminists are really beginning to realize. For startlingly few women reach orgasm, or reach it often, via "normal" sexual intercourse. One 1944 study found that if vaginal orgasm is used as the measure, between 70 and 80% of American women are frigid.[2]

I know a woman who has no such trouble at all. She can have a climax clitorally or vaginally and sometimes from stimulation even less direct. She has also been in several small groups. And she has told me that whenever, in discussing orgasm, she tells the group that she makes it almost every time she is with a man, the rest of the group almost invariably regards her as some sort of freak.

Now think about *us* for a minute. We have been taught that we are not "performing" right if the woman doesn't reach orgasm. If she doesn't make it, and admits it, all sorts of insecurities creep out of us from just under the surface. Is something wrong with *me*? Am I inadequate? A lot of us immediately go off on a long guilt trip, with genuine fear just underlying the guilt.

No woman wants to put up with this; it isn't worth it. Besides, she "knows" that *she's* the one who's inadequate, immature, unresponsive, frigid. Beyond that, they love us, or at least like us well enough to get into the bed in the first place. They want to please us, not hurt us.

So they fake.

I don't mean that they don't enjoy sex; there is a lot to enjoy besides the orgasm, and that may be even more true for women than for men. If they don't have an orgasm, they are for the most part resigned to that fact, even though despair may underlie the resignation (and there are some who simply don't know what they're missing). They take what pleasure there is, and enjoy it.

But they don't want to fake. They want to reach a sexual climax just as much as we do. They are likely to feel that they are not really women, because that "mature" vaginal orgasm isn't there. And there is more to the two-orgasm theory.

If the vaginal orgasm is the true, mature orgasm, then it means that to be mature and sexual a woman must have a man. Anybody can toy with a clitoris, but only a man has a penis that will penetrate a vagina. Regardless of the pleasure that can come from clitoral stimulation, mature pleasure can come only heterosexually.

The man, at the same time, is not going to get the same kicks by stimulating a woman's clitoris; he wants his penis in and surrounded by the vagina. The idea that her proper orgasm is vaginal, not clitoral, serves *us* pretty well. It also works out, as I trust is obvious, that as long as this theory is in force, women need men more than men need women.

But along came Masters and Johnson.

There is something about the Masters and Johnson image of wired-up sex that turns a lot of us (female and male) off. The idea of going to bed with a woman, a camera, a tape recorder and a tangle of wires just doesn't do it somehow. But we have to guard against the idea that because we don't like the practice, there is necessarily anything wrong with the findings. And understanding those findings— one of them in particular—is necessary to understanding the whole question of women's liberation and sexuality.

All female orgasms are clitoral in origin.

The clitoris doesn't have to be touched directly; there can be indirect frictional stimulation from the penis, there are neural connections, and there are also conditioned psychological factors (just as there are in male orgasms). But anatomically, it all comes back to the clitoris, whose sole function, in fact, appears to be sexual pleasure.

The overwhelming importance of this finding is that it turns what has been seen as a psychological problem—there is something wrong with the individual woman's head—into a physiological problem. And a physiological problem can be dealt with outside the head, in the outer world.

Consider the fact that the Western "missionary position" is *not* the sexual position most widely used by the human race. Consider the fact that the physical relationship of clitoris and vagina is not a thing precisely and mathematically fixed—distances may be different, neural connections may vary slightly. Consider the fact that there is a considerable variation in the size of the clitoris. Consider the fact that when *we* think the vaginal orgasm is a real and separate thing, even the most considerate of us is going to try to stimulate the vagina, and generally to ignore the clitoris, during intercourse. You can see all sorts of differences.

It turns out that, female and male, we are simply doing it wrong. We are tied into doing it wrong by the myth of the vaginal orgasm, by our tendency to concentrate on orgasms instead of overall sexual pleasure in the first place, by our dominance-submission role-playing, and by the whole masculinist structure that has the woman misinformed about her own sexuality. If we are equals in bed, and if she knows that all orgasms are clitoral, then all she has to do is say, "No, not that way, *this* way." And if we can get over being threatened, if we can shake the idea that we have to dominate in order to fuck, we can make it together.

This realization about the nature of orgasm, passed from woman to woman through the women's liberation movement, has probably brought on more rushing tears of sheer relief than any of us could imagine. Women are truly oppressed by this conviction that there is something individually wrong with their sexual functioning. You only have to see once the change in a woman when she realizes that in bed as in the world, it is not something wrong with her but something wrong with what the society has done to her. You will very quickly knock off this nonsense about feminists being "anti-male" or "wanting to be men."

Why hasn't all of this spread like wildfire through the female consciousness, regardless of any movement for "liberation"? I can't answer that, but it's obvious that a masculinist society, peopled with men like you and me who beneath our bravado are terrified for our sexual identities and afraid that we can't make it with adult women, is going to have a little trouble with the clitoris as the seat of female sexuality. That means, you see, that they don't need us after all. Koedt's essay puts it this way (her italics):

Men fear that they will become sexually expendable if the clitoris is substituted for the vagina as the center of pleasure for women. Actually this has a great deal of validity if one considers *only* the anatomy. The position of the penis inside the vagina, while perfect for reproduction, does not necessarily stimulate an orgasm for women because the clitoris is located externally and higher up. Women must rely upon indirect stimulation in the "normal" position.

Lesbian sexuality could make an excellent case, based upon anatomical data, for the extinction of the male organ [did that hurt?]. Albert Ellis says something to the effect that a man without a penis can make a woman an excellent lover.

Hold on a minute here. Does this mean we're unnecessary?

The women's liberation movement, as I have been trying to assure you from the beginning, is not out to get rid of you. Women *like* going to bed with men. If they can straighten out the orgasm problem, they'll like it even more. Susan Lydon is every bit as much a feminist as Anne Koedt; let her reassure you:

> A difference remains in the *subjective* experience of orgasm during intercourse and orgasm apart from intercourse. In the complex of emotional factors affecting feminine sexuality, there is a whole panoply of pleasures: the pleasure of being penetrated and filled by a man, the pleasure of sexual communication, the pleasure of affording a man his orgasm, the erotic pleasure that exists even when sex is not terminated by orgasmic release.

Each woman must still deal with the extent to which these pleasures come from within herself, and the extent to which they involve her conditioned submission. But none is submissive per se; there are a lot of pleasures in sex besides the orgasm.

And that goes for you, too, incidentally. It would be a great idea if all of us could get rid of this conviction that the only purpose of sex is to finish doing it. That idea itself has had some strange effects on some women's perceptions of their own sexuality—they measure themselves sexually entirely by their orgasms, or, worse, by ours—and it hasn't done our perceptions much good either. Brenton says it explicitly:

> There has come into being a sort of sexual standard which defines female sexual satisfaction solely in terms of the orgasm—not only the orgasm, but the orgasm every time; not only the orgasm every time, but the orgasm attained solely via coitus; not only the orgasm reached every time strictly during coitus itself, but an explosive kind of orgasm closely approximating the male's; and not only an explosive orgasm achieved directly as a result of intercourse on every occasion that intercourse takes place, but this selfsame orgasm achieved simultaneously with the man's climax.

That's asking rather a lot of the poor woman, isn't it? But it is indeed a common picture in our culture of what a woman's sex experience ought to be—enough so that some women, if it doesn't happen that way, are off forthwith to the shrink at fifty bucks a go-round. Never mind what that silly concept does to you, and to your idea of

206

what sex is about; never mind that if it doesn't happen, your insecurities are likely to suggest to you that it's your fault, that you're a lousy lover. Think instead of what it does to a woman's head.

Her sexuality is defined in terms of something that happens to *men.* To the extent to which she believes in the above formulation, she judges both herself and her partner by it. If it doesn't happen just that way, the insecurities start to gnaw at *her.*

So it is not nonsense, it is not a trivial matter, when the women's movement insists on stressing the clitoral nature of all female orgasm. It is directly linked to extremely deep fears and insecurities in virtually *all* American women, whether they're in women's liberation or not and even whether they know it or not. And incidentally, understanding this question makes ludicrous the ignorant male's contemptuous joke that all they need is a good fuck. Most of us don't even know what that would be in the first place; and if we think *we're* good, it may have a lot to do with how often we've been successfully fooled.

Sex is not an orgasm contest. It is an act of love. There are no mechanical limits on love.

One of the things that gets very confused in our conversations about sex is that we use the same word for two phenomena so different that they are related only in a structural sense, like men and siamangs. A male orgasm and a female orgasm are two completely different things. They start differently, they do different things to the body, their duration is different, and they end differently. When we learn what an "orgasm" is in *us,* and then apply the same word to a sexual experience that a woman has, we are very, very likely to mislead ourselves. You are not both working toward the same end, one for you and one for her; you are moving toward two different things, and it doesn't make it any less fun to know that.

It is only one of many cases in which men and women use the same word and mean different things. One of my favorites is "femininity," for which I can perceive, though I probably can't explain, at least three separate meanings, one male and two female.

What "straight" women seem to mean when they say that women's liberationists lose (or are in danger of losing) their femininity is that they let their hair hang down, wear pants and don't shuffle. Dear Abby and Van Horne and the others seem to be saying, "Look, dear, you can be a success (like me) and *still* get a man, you can get equal pay for equal work and still smell nice." They would of course deny it, but now that you know about the conditioning process you can see that they are confusing femininity with adolescence, or perhaps infantilism. They will concede discrimination, and applaud accomplishment; but they don't want the roles attacked, they don't want to look at the structural masculinism in the society.[3]

It is in that sense that women in the movement often say that femininity is exactly what they want to lose.

The trouble with this concept of "femininity," especially when it is embraced by women with some access to communication media, is that it gets turned around. A women's liberationist is *defined as* a woman who fits this picture. Even Mary Ellen Leary, whom I have known for years as an outstanding reporter who hates stereotypes as much as she hates clichés, let slip in a recent article a reference to "articulate, aggressive feminists in their patched jeans and granny glasses." And in turn, the press tends to treat any *other* feminist as a non-feminist: "Although she agrees with many of the ideas of women's liberation, Jane Smith wears her hair neatly styled and is given to wearing smart dresses." You will recall "blonde, svelte Brenda," who is "not anti-male."

We suffer from this, and so do other straight women. All of us get our ideas from the people who write things like that; and when they refer to lost femininity we think that we know what they mean. But we don't. You and I—however masculinist we are or are not—could not stand on, say, Telegraph Avenue in Berkeley, watching women pass with their hair hanging down and trousers covering their legs, walking by with no trace of shuffle in their manner, and say with any honesty that we think they have lost their femininity. That isn't what *we* mean by it.

We mean something more like, "We are afraid that you will turn out to look and act like butch lesbians." Our fear that free women will lose their femininity is something more like an old-fashioned stereotyped prejudice against blacks: When we first come to know a real one, we begin by saying something like "Oh, well, *he's* different," and only after some continuing contact do we finally realize that we had the stereotype wrong all the time.

It is true that there are masculinists among us who think, for example, that women should decorate offices rather than be comfortable in them, and who therefore insist on something called "feminine" dress (usually something women were wearing by choice five years ago). That is, I think, a leftover concept; it is changing and will change more—and at least we can say that the same men require some standard of dress for male employees as well, even if we know it isn't quite the same thing.[4]

When we are dealing as individuals with individual women, however, we do not confuse femininity, as we use the word, with a lack of intelligence or even with a devotion to shuffling. Many of us know women who have attained some success in the world, who seem to meet men most of the time on fairly equal terms, who hold their own in intelligent conversations, and who are in no danger whatever, as we see them, of losing their femininity. And it does not depend for us, either, on miniskirts or makeup or perfume.

If I can define it at all, it means perhaps a lack of a harshness we tolerate in ourselves; there is a gentleness that seems to go more often with being female and that we call "femininity" even though we would never dream of applying the same word to precisely the same gentleness when we find it in another man. A man who displays some of what we call femininity we might call gentle. A man who displays what the Dear Abbys mean by femininity we would call effeminate.[5]

Women in the liberation movement have to deal with both of these definitions (if a woman is young enough she is very likely to get one from her mother and one from her father), but they are slowly evolving still another, and it is causing them some trouble.

It comes from the admirable idea that to be liberated ought not to mean that a woman takes on the undesirable characteristics of a man. If a woman tends to become dominant in a group, if she begins to explain instead of discussing, if she seems to place the satisfaction of her own ego above the good of a group, she is apt to be accused by her sisters of being unwomanly, or masculine, or (increasingly) unfeminine.

In this usage, to be unfeminine means to adopt masculine characteristics, to switch roles rather than working to abolish them, and to lose track of one's basic sense of the sisterhood of women. It is a little startling to realize that this is a concept within women's liberation; it goes so much against the stereotype. But it's true. The problem is that there are several traps in it, and I have known of cases in which women fell into them.

One is that it is easy to slip from the perception that it is a structurally masculinist society (unarguable) into the idea that all of the society's standards are masculinist (questionable)—and therefore it is masculinist to attempt to meet any of them.

It may sound silly to men, but I have heard the argument that women (publishing a feminist newspaper, to take an example in my own field) don't have to worry about writing well or clearly, or how they spell, or how the paper is laid out, because those things are all masculinist standards. I have heard the argument that it doesn't matter whether you learn anything in a university, because the idea that you *should* learn is a masculinist value in a masculinist society.

There is of course a tiny grain of truth under all that hogwash. Many standards, academic or professional or whatever, are masculinist; that is, there is such a thing as a standard that exists because when it grew into place no one had to meet it but men, and that remains now as a barrier to women. An example might be a requirement that a graduate program at a university has to be finished in a given number of years—based on the idea that all students would be full-time males, not leaving any leeway for the idea that a woman, possibly even a mother, might want that training.

But that does not alter the fact that if you want to read Hesiod (or Sappho) in the original, you will damned well have to learn to decline Greek verbs, and you will have to learn to do it right, no matter what a medical examination may find between your legs. To call a woman unfeminine, or to trash her for betraying her sisters, because she decides to learn to decline Greek verbs (or to lay out a newspaper so that it can be read, or to nail rafters straight on a house frame) is preposterous.

There is a more sophisticated form of the same trap: Wanting to learn Greek at all is a masculinist trip, it says. You want to learn Greek, sister, only because a masculinist culture taught you to want to learn Greek. You should learn to change your wants, so that you will want to do something that *women* would want to do.

Like what? Everything you can think of is a product of your culture, or you couldn't think of it at all. In practice, the argument usually turns out to mean that you should devote your life to organizing women—which seems as though it would ultimately be as self-defeating as the argument itself is illogical.

Akin to all of this is still another trap in the way some feminists look at femininity: It is the idea, prevalent in some groups, that a woman who aspires to excellence in any field is a "male achiever." It derives from the suspicion of "stars," or spokespeople, but it is not the same thing at all. In this version, the aspiration is masculinist, and if the woman is good at what she does, and knows that she's good at what she does, and doesn't try to hide it from her sisters or from anyone else, then she is masculinist.

This seems an odd position for a women's liberationist to take. If she hides her abilities, she's shuffling; if she doesn't hide them, she's a male achiever. It also reminds me starkly of Adler's dictum that little girls who like to climb trees must be imitating males, ignoring the idea that maybe they just like to climb trees. If you say that a little girl who explores and achieves is imitating men, any women's liberationist will climb all over you. If one of their grown sisters does the same thing, some of them climb all over her.

It is of course possible, especially when working with a group, for a woman to do something in an *unsisterly* way; but that is merely applying movement rhetoric to an ordinary human phenomenon—it has no special meaning. We could as well call it simply discourteous or thoughtless or (if it deserves it) rude. Certainly no one who by the grace of God or the luck of the roll is a little more gifted than her or his colleagues is thereby given a license to be arrogant and overbearing about it. But a little more drive, a little more aggressiveness of personality, even a little more certainty on some point of disagreement, doesn't make a woman masculinist.

The tendency (particularly among the humorless) to blame everything on masculinism sometimes goes far enough to an extreme to ruin what would otherwise be a perfectly good argument. This happens, for instance, when some women voice reservations about birth-control pills. A few women, noting (correctly) that pills make women responsible for contraception, argue that it is a sign of the masculinism of Western society that women have *always* had that responsibility. It all sounds a little silly to any male who recalls struggling with condoms before the days of diaphragms.

The controversy over The Pill, also very much a part of women's liberation, comes in two parts. One part is medical, and revolves around the question whether the things are safe or not. I have pored over eye-blurring masses of statistics about this question; my inexpert opinion, based only on some experience as a science writer and possibly biased by masculinism, is: I don't know, but I think they're reasonably safe for most women, with sufficient medical checking in advance by a doctor who knows what to look for. Beyond that it would take a chapter in itself.

It must be added, before gliding on, that in women's liberation there are skilled groups who have done quite a bit of research on this and who think that pills are decidedly *not* safe. And it is certainly true that The Pill has a variety of side effects about which women in America were *not* told until well after the thing was widely used— and some side effects which were not even discovered until then.

The other controversy, therefore, can be dramatized this way: If men instead of women took The Pill, would it have been approved for use and gained such widespread acceptance without a lot more checking than it actually got?

It takes a lot of forms, this contention. One form says that if chemistry were not a field so heavily dominated by males, the research would not have been concentrated on a pill for *women* to take. This may be true; it would not necessarily imply a plot by male chemists, only their existence in a masculinist society and the unconscious tendency to act in their own interest. Firestone turns it around by suggesting that if there were more women in science, there would be much more research on an oral contraceptive for males.

One thing I *do* know about all this is that there is a tendency in all of the physical sciences to pursue the lines of research that are already opened up, rather than to open up new ones (which takes a great deal more talent and is a lot less likely to bring the scientist a research grant). Once research was begun on female hormones as a route to contraception, that had its own self-perpetuating effect. It's at least possible that all we need is one breakthrough by one sharp chemist on an approach to a pill for men.

Other women have been known to grow indignant over the fact that in late 1969 and early 1970, a Senate committee held hearings on possible dangers from The Pill—and invited *no* women to testify. A group of Washington, D.C., feminists went into the hearing

212

and testified anyway.[6] One of the women who was present raised another interesting question that might not have occurred to you or me:

Doubts arise if [sic] it is really concern over the welfare of the American woman that brought about these hearings, or if it is more the concern over the new freedom and cultural changes that the pill offered to women: is it really medical concern that fights the big pill producers, or is it the societal value system represented through the churches and other groups?

Looking toward the long run, Firestone at least is unworried, since "present oral contraception is at only a primitive (faulty) stage, only one of many types of fertility control now under experiment." And Ruth Dixon reminds women (and us) that the switch from condoms and then diaphragms to The Pill gives women a method they may use, not only without disturbing "the spontaneity of the sexual act" but without their partner's knowledge. This means, she continues, "that women are for the first time truly able to control their own bodies in a *private* way, whether their mates agree or not."

But of course it does women no good to control their bodies if they find it necessary to shape those bodies to someone else's mold —and we are back at "sex objects" again. Let us finish the subject off once and for all.

The important word, wherever our attention may at first be directed, is "object." The phrase "sex object" does not refer (except when it is used by a humorless New Convert who likes to throw phrases around) to a woman who is attractive to men (or to one man) and who is sometimes willing, out of free choice, to dress or act accordingly. Nor does it mean "sex symbol," like Marilyn Monroe, which is something else.[7]

If you're old enough to have diagrammed sentences in school you'll get it right away. A sentence has a subject—the word that names the *actor*—and sometimes it has an object—the word that names the thing *acted upon*. Never mind the pun.

We have already been as clear as we're ever going to get about the fact that the sexual standards are male, and the women are trained to fit them. Men are themselves manipulable, of course (by fashion designers, for instance, who may decide that boobs are *in* this year), but the idea doesn't change. If men are manipulated, they are

213

manipulated into thinking that something is attractive, so that the women will then accept it in order to *be* attractive.

But don't men also want to look sexy to women?

There's a difference. Men want to look sexy to women *along the way*—along the way to whatever else they're doing with their lives. Women, for the most part, have to attract men, or they *have* no lives. "It is not by increasing her worth as a human being," says de Beauvoir, "that she will gain value in men's eyes; it is rather by modeling herself upon their dreams." See any issue of *Playboy*.

If you really want to understand the difference, you have only to imagine a couple married for six months or so, getting ready to go out. If she says more or less casually, "I don't think that shirt's very sexy," there is at least an even chance that he will smile indulgently and wear it anyway. The other chance is that he will smile indulgently and change it. But if *he* says more or less casually, "That dress doesn't turn me on much"—well, you know, don't you? There goes the evening.

To "model herself upon their dreams," what a woman has to do is literally to turn herself into an object, and she may just as literally torture her body to do it: unnatural spiked heels, unnaturally cinched-in waists, unnaturally girdled buttocks, breasts thrust unnaturally up and out, hair unnaturally curled (or unnaturally uncurled, sometimes even ironed on an ironing board), face unnaturally coated and colored, armpits unnaturally shaved—all are things women in our memories have had to do so that we would say that they are fulfilling their "natural" role.

I don't have anything against any of those activities per se except possibly the shoes, which may do some actual physical harm, and the girdles, which have a lot to do with varicose veins in some women. Some of the others turn me on. The absence of some of them turns me off. That isn't true of others. Call it taste or conditioning or both, but it's true.

If a woman could do one or another of them because she *chose* to —individually, and not as a result of the fact that everybody else does it, not because it's necessary to meet a definition—then I would say more power to her. She can shave her head, paint herself purple and wear a suit of armor for all I care—if she does it because she wants to, and if she does it as we do, to be attractive to a man (or just to men) along the way to whatever she's doing with her life.

But it is terrible to watch a young girl become an object, and if

214

you have a daughter who has passed through her teens you have probably experienced the sight of it happening to her face, as de Beauvoir describes it:

The eyes no longer penetrate, they reflect; the body is no longer alive, it waits; every gesture and smile becomes an appeal. Disarmed, disposable, the young girl is now only an offered flower, a fruit to be picked.

Possibly the reason so many men are so quickly disillusioned after marriage is that until then they see only the object—they don't meet the subject until afterward. Our most common error is to assume that *they* do it to *us,* as individuals—that they "trap" us—when in fact it is we, collectively, who leave them no option.

As women realize this, as they recognize the cultural demand that they objectify themselves, many do go to what we might call, for shorthand purposes, an opposite extreme. If we meet *them,* we stereotype women's liberation in their mold. Don't do that; it's a stage, though perhaps a necessary one. Women do come back part way to doing the same things they did before—but they do them with an entirely different attitude from that of the women who are still primarily objects.

You will recognize, as you dwell on this, that a woman who is in a sense "too much" an object—a woman who goes well out of her way to advertise her objectness—is usually regarded as "in bad taste" (in my old neighborhood the word was "cheap"). But de Beauvoir also points out that the woman who refuses to be an object is also considered to be in bad taste.

Most women's liberationists can confirm this observation from personal experience. They will be called all the things that we have discussed feminists' being called—and this phenomenon explains, in part, why some successful women, at least, express worry about the feminists' "femininity." "If she simply wants to be inconspicuous," de Beauvoir reminds us, "she must remain feminine."

I don't think there can really be any dispute about this, as much as many of us want to protest in our defense that we don't think of women as "sex objects." Of course we do. We can't help it. All that we can do is to try to break the habit, and then enjoy whatever practices a free woman chooses to engage in for her and our mutual pleasure.

A lot of men seem to believe that the definition has to do with targets: that a "sex object" is a woman we see somewhere whom we would like to *and intend to try* to fuck. Not "make love to"; fuck. A lot of other men think that it means a woman whom we fantasize fucking. But it doesn't—it means females who are regarded as objects, in the grammatical sense of which we spoke earlier, rather than as people. They are the focus for the actions of others, not people who themselves act. Kearon and Mehrhof give a sharp example:

> The "object" part of the sex object function can be seen more clearly in the street scenes between men and women: the cat-calls, obscenities, molesting, and worst of all, the conversations they start up with us on the assumption that we are their collective and always available confidantes. Here there is no question of sexual gratification. It is purely the expression of woman's "object-ness" couched in the convenience of sexual terms.

If you say that you dig blondes, you are obviously seeing women as objects. If you say that you dig Marjorie, and you love her blonde hair because it is part of Marjorie, then perhaps you are talking about a person. Simple as that.[8] If you still wonder whether you see women as objects all that often, close your eyes and try to imagine a typical day in your life in which all the women were carrying out this vision of Shulamith Firestone:

> My "dream" action for the women's liberation movement: a *smile boycott,* at which declaration all women would instantly abandon their "pleasing" smiles, henceforth smiling only when something pleased *them* [her italics].

Possibly the most confusing single thing to men about the entire women's liberation movement—certainly it is the apparent paradox I have heard brought up most often by bemused males—is the "fact" (as filtered through the simplistic stereotyping of the press) that women in the movement object to being regarded as sex objects while at the same time objecting to wearing bras. Obviously, the males say, a woman without a bra is sexier.

Stereotype No. 1: A woman without a bra is only "obviously" sexier if you are already seeing her as a sex object, which means that she has a certain kind of figure and is of a certain age. When you say that, you aren't thinking of a woman in her late forties with some-

216

thing of an obesity problem. You are, in fact, thinking of a body that conforms to an image, which is precisely *not* to be thinking of a person.

Stereotype No. 2: A woman does not "have to" give up bras in order to "belong to" women's liberation. In fact, most Americans don't yet realize that women in women's liberation don't have to "belong to" anything. They may or may not belong to any one or more of dozens of organizations; or they may not even, at any particular moment, be in a small group.

In any case it has very little to do with bras. The facts are much more prosaic. A lot of women in the liberation movement don't wear bras. A lot of them still do. A lot of women have given up wearing bras who are not in the least interested in the liberation movement. I don't mean that there's no connection; there is. I only mean to get us past one of the sillier stereotypes.

You run into it all the time. A 1970 interview with Miss California —who like most of the rest of us understands not the first thing about women's liberation and responds only to stereotypes—brought this more or less standard paragraph to readers:

> At this point a reporter brought up Women's Liberation. . . . "Is there anything Women's Lib advocates that you firmly disagree with?" he asked the 5 foot-8 inch, 36-21-36 beauty.
> "Yes," she said. "I like to wear bras." [9]

At what is in some senses another extreme, Washington reporter Betty Beale describes a meeting of women favoring the Equal Rights Amendment, gathered at a luncheon given by the famed Perle Mesta. "None of these ladies is for Women's Lib," Beale writes. " 'I want to keep my bra,' said Perle." [10]

It is obvious enough in the first story that the reporter (clearly male) is dealing not with a person but with a sex object, and that he or the rewrite man or the editor or somebody was acting quite deliberately in juxtaposing her measurements—the only identity she is given in the story—with her silly comment about bras. You will also note the capitalized form in both stories—"Women's Lib"—which gives the reader the erroneous impression that women's liberation is an organization with a position, like the American Civil Liberties Union or the John Birch Society.

As I say, the whole thing about bras is a stereotype; but it is not

217

only a stereotype. There is an argument about bras that makes some sense, if you have followed any of what has been said about sex objects and if you try to connect it all to the need, in the women's movement, for coming to terms with one's own sexuality. The point is simply that every woman's breasts are different, while all women in bras, if they are of about the same size, look alike.

Breasts are real; they are not the fantasy objects of men. We don't have them, so we picture them; a certain kind of breast becomes our idea of a sexy breast. Our pornography, whether of the dirty-pictures variety or the slightly less hard-core *Playboy* variety, deals either in drawings of women with breasts of our fantasy-ideal type, or in photographs of women chosen for their nearness to that type. And women—the overwhelming majority of women who don't even realize yet that their chief activity in life is objectifying themselves—put on bras to bring them closer to that type, instead of allowing their individual breasts to be *theirs,* with all the variety that breasts in nature have.

Some women will tell you that bras are necessary for all sorts of physical reasons having to do with sag and droop and slump. They are wrong. After a certain number of years (and depending on other exercise), the tissues, like those in that firm stomach you used to have, start to break down—differently in different women. Some doctors are certain that *pregnant* women should wear bras when their breasts are enlarged, because the additional unaccustomed weight leads to chest pains, and the unusual gravity pull sometimes leads to secretion.[11] But otherwise, the human race has come a long way without bras, and their function truly is a purely cosmetic one, related to the role function.

Difficult as it is to believe if all you know is what you read in the papers, women in the liberation movement hardly ever talk about bras, much less take positions on the subject. The distinction between being oneself and being an artificial object makes the point obvious: Men (and other women) ought to regard each person as an individual. "Men," writes Germaine Greer, "must come to terms with the varieties of the real thing," and we can only agree that to look at what is real is saner, by definition, than insisting on conformity to a fantasy.[12] Beyond that, it is up to the individual woman.

That is really all that there is to bras. It is not the biggest deal in the women's movement, or the second biggest. It is certainly not in any way a defining characteristic of women's liberation. It is a titil-

218

lating stereotype for the press, with the unfortunate effect that it misleads many women who might otherwise be tempted to learn a little more.

Where women in the movement *have* given up bras, it is for something like the reasons given above, plus the undeniable fact that a great many more women are simply more comfortable without them. What most of us don't realize is that the damned things really are, and always have been, uncomfortable (and that's why many young women not connected with women's liberation at all, but very interested in comfort, have also given them up). If you watch the bra ads, you'll see that they're always pitched at how comfortable this particular model is—a pitch that wouldn't be made unless the discomfort of bras were of particular importance. There are women who are psychologically uncomfortable without them, but just about every one nevertheless heaves a sigh of relief when she takes hers off.

Although I have never met her, I doubt whether Flossie Cato of Morrilton, Arkansas, is a flaming feminist. Mother of six and grandmother of one, Flossie Cato was fired from the Crompton-Arkansas Mills at Morrilton because she didn't wear a bra to work. Noting that some men work at the mill without undershirts and some women work in shorts, she said, "It's purely a matter of comfort." [13]

For a movement woman, even, comfort is likely to be the main consideration, especially when combined with her newfound conviction that she need not torture herself with that discomfort simply to conform to a male fantasy. Beyond that, the sometimes painful practice of coming to terms with her own sexuality—which as we have said is a different process for every woman, and which *is* an essential part of women's liberation—includes coming to terms with the fact that breasts bounce, they have nipples on the ends, and they aren't all shaped alike. Certainly a woman who tries to pretend to herself and others that those things aren't true remains unliberated; but that doesn't mean that she has to take off the bra itself in order to be free.

Whatever you do, don't start a women's liberation conversation by asking about bras. It only demonstrates how tiresomely dependent on stereotypes you are; and as of now, you're not.

After bras, the area of the greatest misinformation probably has to do with what we somewhat loosely call lesbianism. There are stereotypes more widely held—concerning marriage, man-hating and other things—but there is no other area guaranteed to put most men

219

and women uptight. In our case, it's clear enough that our own fears about homosexuality are involved, along with a feeling that I can only describe as a sort of helplessness. We can be jealous, and angry at, another man, but we are helpless in the face of sexual rivalry over a woman when the third party is another woman. We don't really know what to react *to*.

Our reaction to lesbianism is based first of all on our conditioned and damaging ideas about male and female "roles" and second on the assumption that in a lesbian relationship nothing changes except the genital structure of the male role-player. If we get rid of our role concepts, then we get rid of, first, our own concerns about our own masculinity (and thus about homosexuality), and second, our concerns about the "unnaturalness" of lesbianism.

Feminists, however, do not make it easy for us; for there are a few women who seem to argue that liberation *means* lesbianism. Ti-Grace Atkinson has been quoted as saying, "Feminism is the theory; lesbianism is the practice." A group called Radicalesbians is prominent on the East Coast (and has contributed some serious and thoughtful discussion of the whole question). But as with other issues within the movement, no one position defines "women's liberation."

Anyone who is not frightened off by the subject and who wants seriously to pursue the possible ramifications of lesbianism within the movement can hardly do without Koedt's *Notes from the Third Year,* which includes three long pieces dealing with it in one way or another —the article, "The Woman Identified Woman" by the Radicalesbians; Koedt's own "Lesbianism and Feminism"; and Koedt's interview with a woman who loves another woman. For most of us beginners, however, it's all a little heavy. We have to start with basics, like this simple statement by Golder on homosexuals of both sexes:

Our images come from movie stereotypes or whispered gossip. Hardly anything in our culture teaches us that homosexuals have jobs, celebrate birthdays, shop in supermarkets, take their children to playgrounds, own homes, put money in parking meters, root for the Forty-Niners, watch television, and are real persons who laugh, cry, argue, hurt, relax, bleed, worry and enjoy.

The women's movement doesn't really help us all that much if we're just starting out. A great many women in the movement insist that the subject is a "lavender herring." [14] A lesbian reporter on a straight newspaper told a San Francisco columnist, "We dropped out of the women's lib movement. We were put down for being gay. And they scream about discrimination!" [15] The late 1971 convention of the National Organization of Women had (according to one news story anyway) a hell of a time with lesbianism as a subject:

Philosophically they believe the lesbian is doubly oppressed—as a woman and as a homosexual, facing "injustices and degradation common to all women, plus enduring additional social, economic, legal and psychological abuses."

So they adopted a resolution, providing that

a woman's right to her own person includes the right to define and express her own sexuality and to choose her life style . . . and NOW acknowledges the oppression of lesbians as a legitimate concern of feminism.

The female reporter, however, says that "it isn't all that easy," since there are few lesbians in NOW, and "a strong segment of the NOW matriarchy, primarily from the eastern seaboard, has been fearful that support of lesbians would somehow endanger the feminist movement as a whole"—an argument not confined, within women's liberation, to NOW.[16]

Other women in the movement feel, though, that the question has to be dealt with. Some argue that unless the basic heterosexual structures are at least questioned, women will necessarily dissipate valuable energy in "trying to straighten up each particular relationship with a man" and in arriving at compromises between their own personal commitments and their affection or desire for a particular man. Others, like Koedt's anonymous interviewee, simply think that it's silly to ignore a question that must occur to anyone with normal intelligence:

Because it is a natural question, if you want to remove sexual roles, and if you say that men and women are equal human beings, well, the next question is: Why should you only love men?

Which means to us: Why should we only love women? We don't like that—but let's just keep our hands from starting to shake for a few minutes more. What we need to do right now, in pursuing the

221

relationships between women's liberation and lesbianism, is to see what it means to those women who have themselves pursued those relationships—because they're not going to come out where we would come out anyway.

It usually comes up first, of course, as an alternative. Women see, in all the ways that we've described, how they are used by men, how they are taught to objectify themselves for men, how men set not only the social but the sexual standards of the culture. They want to rebel, and one obvious way is to turn to each other—especially since at the same time they are feeling that enormous release, that fantastic euphoria, that comes with the discovery of sisterhood. For the first time they are close to other women, they *like* other women; and this happens just when they are inclined to turn against their continuing to be sex objects for men.

Most soon realize, however, that that is not the direction to liberation; for they are still defining the whole thing in terms of their relationship to men. Other women, in that formulation, are simply a substitute for men, at best an alternative. Lesbianism is (as it is for most of us) simply the definition of a sexual act—and it is a masculinist pattern of response to define human relationships as though they were merely sexual and had no other dimensions.

It is not an unimportant pattern of response, though, when it happens—because there is more than sex involved. There is the whole mixed-up, jumbled-together pattern in which sex is joined with the need for male approval; a genuine, loving lesbian relationship provides love and overcomes aloneness while breaking the Daddy's-little-girl syndrome, or at least it can do so. "I am," says Koedt's interviewee, "like an addict who has kicked the habit," and she is talking about male approval, not sex.

Beyond that, though, the same interviewee notes that a lot of the game-playing has gone out of her relationship—not that this happens with all lesbians, or even most lesbians, but it can happen. We are men, and therefore subjects; the whole bit about will I get a date this weekend? and will he think I'm beautiful? and will he approve of me? have never meant to us what they do to women. Especially, we have not grown up in this pattern; in high school, for instance, we may have been very concerned about our relationships with girls, but that was not our whole life in the way that it was often a girl's whole life, so that it remains so for the young woman. Perhaps we would have to be women really to get the full gut reaction to what this one woman says about her present life:

> One of the biggest differences is that for the first time I haven't felt those knots-in-the-stomach undercurrents of trying to figure out what's *really* happening under what you *think* is happening.

But this is a long way from where most women in the movement are, or even from where women's liberation itself is. Lesbianism is not even a serious consideration in the heads of most feminists. On the contrary, they are often as repelled by the idea as you are by its male counterpart. Robin Morgan says, "A woman who doesn't mind any other insult—'go home and take a bath,' 'what you need is a good screw,' 'dirty, Communist pinko'—will dissolve in tears because someone calls her a dyke." [17]

I don't think we can leave the subject there, though, for at least three reasons. First, lesbianism is a stereotype about the women's movement, which we have to clear up in order to understand the whole thing. Second, we are filled with stereotypes about lesbians themselves, whether they are feminists or not, and unless we clear them up a little, we cannot understand what we must understand about gender roles. And third, while lesbianism is far from the biggest question in the women's movement, the subject does raise questions which any serious discussion of women's liberation ought to examine.

In the first place, the word itself is likely to mislead us. A lesbian to most of us is not somebody who puts money in parking meters or celebrates a birthday. To call someone a lesbian is to define her entirely in a sexual way (aside from the fact that it is in a way we don't necessarily understand). To use the word when what we are talking about is two human beings who love each other is more likely to get in the way of our understanding than to enhance it.

In the second place, if we sneer at lesbianism, or somehow devalue the kind of relationship the word can describe, we are in a sneaky way demonstrating just how masculinist our definition of "woman" really is. The Radicalesbian essay makes this point about as clear as you can make it:

> A lesbian is not considered a "real woman." And yet, in popular thinking, there is really only one essential difference between a lesbian and

other women: that of sexual orientation—which is to say, when you strip off all the packaging, you must finally realize that the essence of being a "woman" is to get fucked by men.

The first time *I* read that, I sent up about six mental flags. It is just, I thought at first, a rather nasty way of saying that after all, to be male and female means that you have genitals that are "designed" to fit together. In essence, we have evolved as (and for the evolutionary moment must continue to be) heterosexual animals.

But by then I had begun to develop enough of a feminist consciousness to catch my error. We do not say, just because our bodies are in some real way heterosexual, that the essence of being a man is to fuck women. My reaction was to confuse *capacity* with *function,* in sex as in childbirth. Because we can does not mean at all that each and every one of us must (or that we must all the time), or that there will be any tragedy if we do not. You may raise moral questions if that's your bag, but you are wrong if you raise biological ones.

For most of us, the word "lesbian" is a put-down, and its function as a put-down is to remind women that they belong in a feminine, and therefore submissive, role. We admire somewhat the tomboy, we hold the sissy in contempt—and thus we show our real attitudes toward the masculine and feminine roles. In the same way, "dyke" is an entirely different kind of insult from "faggot." [18]

None of which means that lesbianism is in fact the practice of which feminism is the theory. Lesbianism, as Koedt's interviewee points out with several examples and at some length, is a masculinist drag if it is simply an imitation of the same roles; it is not a way out of any gender-role trap at all, merely a relatively unsatisfying variation on it. If that's what two women want to do, okay, but it's *not* feminism or women's liberation or anything like them.

Women who are "into" women's liberation, who are trying to ask themselves serious questions about their own sexuality and its forms, are in some parts of the country simply regarded as prey by aggressive lesbians, just as they have always been regarded as prey by aggressive males. The woman to whom we've been referring told Koedt about

refusing to be seduced by lesbians who play the male seduction game and tell you, "you don't love women," and "you are oppressing us" if you don't jump into bed with them. It's terrible to try to seduce someone on ideological grounds.

Despite the fears of many women, both non-feminist lesbians and non-lesbian feminists, there is some contact now between the two groups; and where there is such contact, often on a basis of inter-organizational cooperation, there appears to develop a genuine feeling of common sisterhood once the first hangups are past. Nor are the effects all one way; the president of one organized lesbian group told a reporter that while she used to hate straight women, she has now learned truly to like them—thanks to women's liberation. "I could change a lot more," she said. "I have even experienced a relationship with a man, more profound than ever before." [19]

Which is *not* to say that women's liberation is "therapy" for lesbians. Lesbians, like the rest of us, need therapy only when they're sick. As Koedt points out in her essay, they may be sick, if they are locked into role-playing imitations of heterosexual relationships; but that is because all role-playing is sick. Or, as de Beauvoir suggests, a lesbian may be sick if lesbianism is a place to hide rather than a place for facing reality:

Homosexuality can be for woman a mode of flight from her situation or a way of accepting it. The great mistake of the psychoanalysts is, through moralistic conformity, to regard it as never other than an inauthentic attitude.

And not just the psychoanalysts; you and me. We have to fight our way through that last triple negative and recognize that (in men as in women) homosexuality is sometimes a perfectly authentic attitude. Koedt's interviewee says that when she first thought about lesbianism in terms of herself, she was sure that very little about it would be physical, that it would be mostly "warm and affectionate." This, she said, was because her relationships with men had led her to think of the really physical as somehow related to conquest.

But one of the things I discovered was that when you really like somebody, there's a perfectly natural connection between affection and love and sensuality and sexuality. That sexuality is a natural part of sensuality.

We men are learning that a little, I think. We are not as afraid to touch each other as we used to be. Most of us aren't up to it ourselves, but it is possible to see two otherwise ordinary-looking men embrace each other in public with affection without feeling those old rumbles of suspicious revulsion. The biggest hurdle we have yet to overcome is the simple admission that expressing our affection in that way is sensual—and that there is nothing whatever wrong with that.

There is the biggest reason for devoting so much space to the word "lesbianism" (for we have really talked more about the word and the idea than the practice). It is to bring it through the stereotypes and the hangups to the recognition of that "perfectly natural connection between affection and love and sensuality and sexuality."

Among women in the movement who have never attempted a physical sexual act with another woman—among women in the movement who are not more than abstractly interested in ever doing so—that connection *is* recognized, and it is an important part of the movement. What is important is that the women's own fear of lesbianism is being overcome, so that even though they may do nothing overtly sexual, they are increasingly less afraid openly to display their affection for one another and their new understanding of each other's sensuality.

To some extent, women even use the word "lesbianism" to refer to this feeling, this willingness. It confuses the rest of us (and other women, sometimes), but if we are to try to understand women's liberation we must understand that when an adherent refers to lesbianism she may not be talking about mutual sex at all. She may be talking about the willingness to walk in the park with another woman, holding hands because they are no longer afraid of the fact that they like the touch and the affection it conveys.

An interview with a Gestalt psychologist quotes her as saying that many women, who for any of a number of reasons are not having good experiences with men, thereby cut themselves off from having any good experiences *at all*—when they could quite easily have them with women by overcoming their fears. "They are afraid," says Dr. Stella Resnick, "that if they really get close and let themselves love another woman, they will have to have sex with her." [20]

The women's liberation movement is breaking down this fear, the fear of love, and a lot of the time, when the word "lesbianism" is kicked around, it is this breakdown, not mutual masturbation or tribadism, that is being talked about. It is sensuality, and as Negrin says, "Sensuality is whole-oriented—total rather than local, human rather than genital, expansive rather than merely repetitive." [21]

It is a hell of a note that our cultural conditioning leaves us all, female and male, with a fear of loving each other unless it happens in certain, narrow, dominance-submission ways. I was well past the age at which one ought to be an adult before I could say outright—without allowing myself any soothing qualifying phrases—that there are a couple of men whom I love. I was rather older than that before, in a burst of affection, I was able to embrace one of them in public and thereby to discover that the world didn't end. I still regret the necessity—and it *is* a necessity—to refrain from physically expressing the love I feel in some cases because the other man in question is—well, he's not ready for it.

And I can even ask, now: If there were not this cultural role hangup, might it not seem as natural to go on to a complete and fulfilling sexual expression of that love with another man as it now does with a woman? Could it just barely possibly be that no label would suddenly appear printed on my forehead, that I would not then become *an* anything, that I would simply be the same guy, but with one more gratifying experience of physically expressing the love I feel? After all, I'm just as old, if not quite as wise, as the woman Koedt interviewed:

Both of us are equally strong persons. I mean, you can ask yourself the question, if there were going to be roles, who'd play what? Well, I certainly won't play "the female," and I won't play "the male," and it's just as absurd to imagine her in either of them. So in fact what we have is much more like what one gets in a friendship, which is more equalized.

Unless you're an unusual male, you can't *imagine* a sexual relationship (much less a homosexual relationship) that fits that description. If somebody doesn't play "the male" and somebody "the female," then what do you *do*? The only possible answer I can give you is that you have to overcome the meaning of the roles to find out. Since I am by no means sure that I have done that myself yet, I can't advise you. I can only say that I'm convinced that it's both possible and desirable.

The Radicalesbians say that "in a society in which men do not op-

227

press women, and sexual expression is allowed to follow feelings, the categories of homosexuality and heterosexuality would disappear." In her related essay, Koedt says that even the term "bisexuality" might disappear, since it perpetuates a psychological (not the biological) division, and we might "finally return to a simpler word like 'sexuality,' where the relevant information is simply 'sex among persons.' "

Person. Engrave that word somewhere in your mind, for it is the key word in all of this talk of women's liberation, and indeed in all talk of liberation of any kind. It is not the best word we could have etymologically—it comes from a Latin word for an actor's mask, which is just contrary to what we want to mean—but it is the word we have, used in its simple normal English-language sense.

To be a *person* is ultimately the goal of every woman in every branch of the women's liberation movement—a goal not only for herself but for each of her sisters. More than that: It is their goal for us as well, for unless we become persons they cannot.

18

THE trouble with marriage, as we know it, is that it depersonalizes women.

We talk a lot about 50-50 relationships in marriage, and about mutual respect, and about a lot of other things that camouflage the effects of the institution, but no matter how much we believe them, they are camouflage. The individual marriages that are exceptions are so rare that it is pointless even to try to consider them.

The fact is that married women are not defined in our culture as persons, but as adjuncts, satellites, to men. Their names are taken away. A surprising number of legal rights suddenly disappear. Their social and economic status comes from their husbands. In most cases the wife's friends are the husband's friends (or their wives), or the neighbors who are neighbors because of where he lives.

Two books in the Bibliography—one by Gallen, one by Pilpel and Zavin—delineate a startling change in the new wife's legal status. She can have no independent credit rating. She can be separately wealthy and own stock, but in most cases she can't sell it without her husband's permission. In ways that few husbands or wives find it comfortable to contemplate, you *own* your wife.

You don't think so. She certainly doesn't think so. The idea makes you both bristle. But it's instructive to read over Kenneth Stampp's *The Peculiar Institution,* a standard academic work on slavery in America. This is from his description of two clauses, which were juxtaposed, in the Alabama legal code of 1852:

> The first clause confirmed his [the slave's] status as property—the right of the owner to his "time, labor and services" and to his obedient compliance with all lawful commands. . . .
> The second clause acknowledged the slave's status as a person. The law required that masters be humane to their slaves, furnish them adequate food and clothing, and provide care for them during sickness and old age. In short, the state endowed masters with obligations as well as rights and assumed some responsibility for the welfare of the bondsmen.

You don't have to rely, in reading that, on some metaphorical parallel. It is a literal description of the husband-wife relationship in America, whether we like it or not. Here is Gallen in 1967 on the legal position of a wife:

> The legal responsibilities of a wife are to live in the home established by her husband; to perform the domestic chores (cleaning, cooking, washing, etc.) necessary to help maintain that home; to care for her husband and children.
> The legal responsibilities of a husband are to provide a home for his wife and children; to support, protect and maintain his wife and children.

It repels us to say it, we resist as doggedly as we can saying it, but it is true: Wives (and incidentally children) *are* property. If you still doubt it, consider this single fact: You cannot be convicted in any court in the United States of raping your wife. We all say that we detest rape and the rapist; but in fact, in America, rape is the forcible sexual assault, against her will, of anybody but your wife. She is, legally, yours to do with as you will.

The major oppressions, however, are not legal but conventional.[1] The all-pervasive effect of the marital "role," the stifling, foot-binding result of the ways in which we define wives—we have already discussed how these affect female children and developing young women. Girls want to become, not biologists or carpenters or artists or in any way *people,* but wives—assistants to, supporters of, sexual objects for, ego-boosters on behalf of, men. The few women who to some extent escape the foot-binding are plagued, because of the cultural insistence on this submissive role, with anxieties and with outside social tribulations that they can never entirely avoid.

The single (or divorced) woman will find, for example, that unless she is wealthy enough not really to need one, she will have trouble obtaining a mortgage; she will have credit difficulties; landlords will often regard her as an undesirable tenant; prospective employers worry about her for fear she will leave to marry (although in fact turnover is much higher among male employees); she will tend to think of herself at times as a burden on her married friends; and virtually every male she meets will regard her as prey in one sense or another. She does not "fit" where she is "supposed" to be—attached to a man.

Meanwhile, the wife herself, like Mother in the children's books, is isolated from the real world if she does not work, lives her whole life in a context of husband and family with little understanding of, or interest in, the outside world. Any creative spark goes into the kind of pathetic "innovation" one finds described in *Hints from Heloise*. She becomes a caricature of a human—that sad creature of the television commercial who knows two dozen ways to fix hamburger, or whose outstanding characteristic as a human being is that she is one of a group of "sniffers."

If she works, she works for less money (less than black men, as we have seen) and at lesser jobs, because the cultural role says— regardless of the facts of her individual life—that she has somewhere else to go, a "natural" place to fall back into. Only the very wealthy woman or the rare woman professional escapes these depersonalizations to some degree, and then only partly. Caroline Bird calls them "loophole women."

There is no simpler and more obvious symbol of the subjection of female to male than the evident surrender of identity symbolized in the surrender of a name. Betty Smith does not even, in conventional usage, become Betty Jones. She becomes Mrs. John Jones—in effect, a woman named John. When you register at a hotel, she becomes a couple of tossed-off conventional symbols in front of *your* name,

We have all heard of "primitive" cultures (Jews especially will recognize remnants of the pattern in their religious practices) in which the real name is kept a secret, so important is its personal symbolic importance. There is something almost magical about our names which is deeper than our own culture. Yet we insist that women surrender them, showing the extent to which they surrender themselves.

It is virtually impossible in this culture, even in this relatively enlightened age, for a woman to retain her own name completely in marriage. Judith uses her own name both professionally and personally, to the extent that people are often surprised to discover that she is married (the fact that we aren't in the same profession helps). But if you have ever traveled you will understand why we glumly surrender the principle whenever we have to stay at a hotel.

Legal complications and documents aside, there are other problems. When we go to another city on *my* business—when for example I have a speaking engagement—you can imagine the problem of introductions when the only name anyone knows is mine. Possibly you can imagine (though not so easily) the problem when the situation is reversed. The more conventional among the people we meet (who might include prospective employers of hers) are likely to wonder whether we really are married, and to apply conventional— and inapplicable—ideas of what they call "morality" to our behavior.

And this is the case of a woman who does have some separate identity, who does have a circle of her own in which she moves. The wife who is only an adjunct to her husband would meet even greater difficulties if she insisted on her own name.

But what would we feel if we had to give up our identities on marriage? Suppose that you, John Jones, suddenly had to be known for the rest of your life as Mr. Betty Smith? Really: Use your real names and try to imagine it. You would almost never be introduced to anyone as John Jones, the stockbroker; or John Jones, the reporter; or John Jones, the man next door; or even John Jones, an interesting person. You would almost always be introduced as, "And this is Betty's husband, John"—and that's *all*. No matter what you do, no matter what you are.

Don't tell me about how you would be proud to be known as Betty's husband. You are proud to be known as Betty's husband only if you are also known as yourself. It is easy enough for a few successful and well-known women to say that they're "proud" to use their husband's names—especially if their husbands are not nearly so well-known. But I wonder how that guy in Chicago likes being introduced all the time as Abigail Van Buren's husband, even if in that case it *is* his name. Yet that's what happens routinely to women.

Men want to insist that this question is trivial. It is not. "Trivia" is who played the British officer in the Randolph Scott version of *The Last of the Mohicans*.[2] "Trivia" is not a word you can apply to a cultural construct which not only symbolizes the subjection of women, but helps to perpetuate it.

It is itself a part of the conditioning of every new individual who grows up into it. You break down conditioning by breaking down the processes by which it happens; and to do that you have to pursue those processes into every detail that shows how deeply the conditioning is imbedded in our culture.

That is the importance of the prefix "Ms.," about which it is currently so fashionable to make jokes, or to point out that few women on a percentage basis are really concerned about it. Of course few women care—they are as conditioned as we are. But we would not be so determined to shrug it off, to ridicule it instead of thinking about it, except for the fact that it *does* matter to *us,* we really do believe, on some level, that a woman ought to be defined socially by whether she is married. When we meet a woman for the first time, a lot of us are actually a little uncomfortable until we know her marital status—even though we may have no plans toward more than a casual relationship.

There is a direct connection between the use of "Ms." and the sorry business of asking kids what they want to be when they grow up. Both are directly connected to the cultural idea that a man may be a businessman or a professional or a worker or an artist, but a woman's principal purpose in life is marriage—and the self-objectification and submission that go with preparing for it and "succeeding" at it.

If you don't really think that the "Ms." prefix and the issue it symbolizes touch something of deep psychological importance to women in this culture—even women who shrug off the prefix itself —try a little experiment with me. You must know a woman somewhere who has nothing to do with women's liberation, who has been married for, say, eight or ten years or more, who is not a relative of yours, and whose "maiden name" (itself rather obviously a masculinist term) you happen to know.

Think up some kind of excuse, and write her a note or send her a message, using *her* name, and not her husband's. When you hear from her, should she ask why you did that, ask her innocently, "It's *your* name, isn't it?" She may think you're a kook, but you can bet your last Christmas necktie that a part of her response will be pleasure; I'll almost guarantee that she'll be pleased that you know it and remember it. And if you're watching closely, you'll see that a part of that pleasure comes, whether she knows it or not, from your recognition of her *as a separate person,* apart from her husband.

But be careful. I can also almost guarantee that her husband won't like it at all. Aside from any idea he may have that you are somehow flirting, you have poached on the fact that he owns his wife. You have seen her as something other than *his* possession—and if you ask him innocently, "It's her name, isn't it?" you are as likely as not to get a punch in the mouth. A couple of these experiments, and you will quickly change your mind about the idea that a woman's use of her own name, or her insistence on "Ms.," is "trivial." It hits very deep.[3]

This possessiveness, this ownership, aside from its sexual connotations, shows itself in so many ways in our culture that for our own comfort we don't even notice them. One of the simplest is physical location. Another personal example may make it clearer.

As I've said, I am married to a professional woman. We live in Berkeley as I write this, but it is entirely possible that tomorrow morning she will get a job offer from Pittsburgh or Missoula or Jacksonville—a job offer representing a genuine advance, in terms of money or status or both, in her work. Aside from the desirability of living in any particular place (I have a special prejudice against Chicago, for instance), what do we do?

Now, as it happens, I am a writer, and self-employed. I could presumably live and write anywhere. Ours may be the easiest situation of this kind that any feminist could imagine. But I don't want to leave the San Francisco Bay Area, where I was born and where I have done most of my best work, where my family lives, where I have more friends than anywhere else, where there are several other people (female and male) whom I love. I probably would go, but I would decidedly not like it.

I would go (I think), because I would rather live with my wife in a place I like less than live without her in a place I like more. But

234

even so, I have a choice. Given the usual situation—in which it is the husband who gets the job offer in another location—a woman usually has none.

My situation is seen by everyone (including you) as unusual. A few years ago, when I was employed locally as a magazine editor in a job I liked and one which was genuinely helpful to *my* career, the conflict would have been much greater, the required sacrifice on my part much larger. One of us would have had to yield a step (perhaps a crucial step) in her or his professional career, or we would have had to live apart, at least for a time.

But no matter what choice we had made, I would not have been criticized by anyone except perhaps a feminist or two. Had I stayed, most people would have said, "Well, of course he had to." Had I gone, most people would have said, "How noble!" Had she turned down the job and stayed, most people would have said that she was doing the proper thing. And in fact, not only prospective employers but colleagues are surprised to learn, once they know that she is married, that she is willing to consider employment in another area at all. The first question is always a startled, "But what about your husband?"

Most wives are not professionals with their own careers. But when the husband decides to move—and make no mistake, he decides— the wife may still have to leave the place where her family lives, where there are people she loves, where she has familiar associations. She may still have to go to a place not only where she is a stranger but where she may have no desire to live. And if she does not go, if she insists on her right to live where *she* wants to live, society will almost unanimously say that she is wrong.

The law, of course, agrees. The husband cannot "desert" his wife by taking a job somewhere else. But a wife "deserts" her husband if she does so against his will, *or* if she refuses to move with him to a new location. He owns her, as clearly as he owns his razor or his golf clubs.

There is even more to it than that—for so strongly do our cultural roles dominate our thinking that even in a marriage which is not going too well, she does not have the choices for quitting that are available to him. If the couple has been together for any time at all, our definitions of the masculine and feminine roles put her at such a disadvantage that his side of the disagreement can only continue to gain ascendancy. Inge Bell, for instance, reminds us of a simple cultural fact:

> Let us take . . . a couple who divorce when both are in their thirties. . . . The man can choose among all women his own age or younger. . . . The woman, by contrast, is limited by custom to men her own age or older . . . the awareness of this difference makes divorce a much more painful option for women than for men and thus puts many women at a continuous disadvantage within a strained marriage.

The result being, of course, that in such a strained marriage she is likely in fear or despair to become *more* submissive, and the roles get sicker.

Some of us, female and male, do the best we can within these roles. Most of us Americans are not intellectuals who go around analyzing our cultural roles anyway; we are much more likely not even to see them, but to work out the conflicts of our lives within their limits without even thinking about the fact that that's what we're doing. And we have all seen happy marriages—marriages of which we might even say offhand that the partners seem to have achieved some sort of mutual respect, as well as a continuing love.

But maybe, while we're trying to struggle and to break sets, we ought to take a closer look at "love" and "respect." It does seem, doesn't it, that genuine love and genuine respect ought not to require a dominance-submission pattern—ought in fact to break it? How many marriages do? Don't most of the marriages we know about that have "lasted" depend less on love and respect than on a kind of mutually tolerant affection? Consider this charmingly stilted description written in 1907 by W. I. Thomas:

> An examination . . . of so-called happy marriages shows very generally that they do not, except for the common interest of children, rest on the true comradeship of like minds, but represent an equilibrium reached through an extension of the maternal interest of the woman to the man, whereby she looks after his personal needs as she does after those of the children—cherishing him, in fact, as a child—or in the extension to woman on the part of the man of that nurture and affection which is in his nature to give to pets and all helpless (and preferably dumb) creatures.

He regards her affectionately as dependent and not really all that bright (and "explains" her in conversations), and she regards him

236

affectionately as just a little boy under all that bluster. It may be better, for a lot of people, than being alone; but it's a poor definition of "love."

As a matter of fact, there is another description of married life, by Brenton, that fits most present-day middle-class marriages a lot better than the child-and-pet affection that Thomas wrote about—a description of the ongoing mutual misunderstanding to which couples may adjust, but within which neither partner can ever feel complete, much less fulfilled:

> The husband expects his wife to bring him pipe and slippers and make him a cooling drink while he eases off the day's tensions. The wife expects him to listen to her troubles, to fix the things that need fixing. He can't understand what kind of tensions *she* could have gone through in the cozy nest that for him represents—or, he feels, ought to represent—a retreat from the day's cares and worries. She can't understand how he could have had it so tough because at least he got to meet new people, talk about interesting things, and face the kinds of challenges she feels such a dearth of in her own intellectually barren life. He insists that she doesn't appreciate how hard he works, how much he's knocking himself out for her and the kids. She insists that he doesn't appreciate how hard *she* works, how much she's knocking herself out for him and the kids.

Obviously, much of this pattern is a description of what our particular society does to both of them, locking them as it does into this sterile choreography, a weird caricature of life, so that they can meet what are actually the goals of other people—his boss, the people who sell her appliances, and so on. But it is their own masculinist conditioning that makes that locking-in possible; Brenton goes on to note that "they have a whole series of the old sex-role stereotypes so firmly fixed in their minds that they can't see each other as flesh-and-blood human beings."

So of course, as I keep trying to say, it happens to both of us. But it is harder on a woman. We men do in fact have lives outside the house and the family and the housework, challenges at least more interesting than sorting the dirty clothes into three piles, some opportunity for continuing to *become* instead of merely continuing to *exist*.

It is not boredom—it is not a matter of filling time. And it is not a matter of the usefulness of what she does, either (she can become a community volunteer for the finest cause in the world, and she will

237

still find herself doing somebody else's shit work). It is a matter of not being anyone real, of not having any individual, separate importance.

As people grow older, these marital roles have deep psychological effects. Take a few people, female and male, whom you know and who are in their fifties; the chances are that they are willing to think of themselves as "middle-aged." Ask them how they first perceived that they were becoming "middle-aged." If some of them are people whose chief identity is "wife," and some are not, you will learn what Bernice Neugarten learned:

> Women, but not men, tend to define their age status in terms of timing of events within the family world, and even unmarried career women often discuss middle age in terms of the family they might have had. . . .
>
> Men, on the other hand, perceive the onset of middle age by cues presented outside the family context, often from the deferential behavior accorded them in the work setting. One man described the first time a younger associate helped open a door for him; another, being called by his official title by a newcomer in the company; another, the first time he was ceremoniously asked for advice by a younger man.[4]

If you're old enough (and you don't have to have reached your fifties), you will recognize the male pattern for yourselves—and your own gut response. But you will see, too, I'm sure, that it is not that way for women—one more example of how a wife is cut off from being a whole person.

What is perhaps a little more difficult for men to recognize is that there are actual *physical* effects of this role-playing on women. As long ago as 1957, Doris Menzer-Benaron and her colleagues found that the deleterious effects of the "woman's role" aren't just confined to those that are socially desirable or undesirable. Friedan, who found this study and others, generalized about some of them (the internal quotation is from Menzer-Benaron):

> Studies have been made of women recovering from hysterectomy, women with menstrual complaints, and women with difficult pregnancies. The ones who suffered the most pain, nausea, vomiting, physical and emotional distress, depression, apathy, anxiety, were women "whose lives revolved almost exclusively around the reproductive function and its gratification in motherhood."

Pauline Bart has spent several years studying the menopausal period in women in America and elsewhere, and has come to a similar conclusion. In the first place, she found that women in other cultures (she studied the literature on about thirty-five other cultures) don't seem to have the menopausal troubles that women in our culture have. A closer study of women in our culture showed that roles do, indeed, have a lot to do with physical problems.

Women in our culture who have a lot of trouble, physically and/or psychologically, during menopause are women whose only identities as persons, in their own minds, are as wives and mothers. Their physical troubles (which are quite real) appear to be a result of role loss—they had no identities left, no concept of themselves as human beings, once they could no longer be mothers.[5] It is not just a far-out idea that we must learn to regard childbearing as a capacity rather than a function.

But for us, that means that we have to overcome the dominance-submission bag, which means in turn that we have to realize how deeply we are caught in it. We have to overcome the idea that the only way we can quit being dominant is to submit. And if you don't think that we do in fact believe that, somewhere not very far beneath our consciousnesses, you have only to think about doing the dishes.

"I was constantly astounded," Brenton wrote, "by the number of men who, when the topic of equality in marriage was introduced into our discussion, spontaneously—and bitterly—responded, 'I don't see why a man has to wash the dishes at night after working hard all day.'" What is it about the idea of *doing the dishes* that bothers us? Has it become, in our minds, some sort of unconscious symbol of submission, or degradation? Does doing the dishes mean to us, in some weird way, being *dominated?*

Maybe. Men wash dishes in restaurants, but there is something about the public image of even that dishwasher that involves such a low status that the rest of us almost automatically characterize the dishwasher as a loser. It is tempting to go spinning off into high-level abstractions about the dishwasher-as-failure, and to connect that with our masculine (and absurd) equation of material success and potency. There is also a possible train of thought having to do with children's books, aprons, and transvestism. It's hard to say what weird things may go on in our heads.

In any case, we seem to have the idea that women's liberation means that we have to do the dishes. Possibly the best way to begin to tackle *that* misconception is to say that that is exactly what it is: a misconception. Who does the dishes, or any other piece of "housework," is something that two people, if they decide that they want to live together, work out according to the particular patterns of their lives.

In our house, for example, Judith does the dishes and the vacuuming and the rest of that boring but, I suppose, necessary work when I am trying to meet a usually overdue deadline. I do them when she is under a similar pressure. The rest of the time, we both avoid them until we can't avoid them any longer, but we acknowledge simply that somebody has to take a little time off from *living* and do the chores. And, of course, that they are no more her responsibility than mine.

That is the point. They are not "woman's work." They are dull jobs that have to be done so that both of you can live your lives in whatever comfort and sense of accomplishment that you can achieve. It is the idea that a woman is somehow a different species, who can achieve fulfillment and completeness and some meaning in her life by running a vacuum cleaner or setting the table, that we have to overcome.

About our male resistances to this idea, Pat Mainardi has said all that there is to say, and I urge you to hunt up her essay and to read it *with your wife*, if you are married. Assuming that there has ever been a time when she asked for some help around the house, you will recognize yourself; and if you are not afraid of the recognition, you may even come up with a rueful laugh. But it is an essay to be learned from; it's cheating to let the laugh substitute for the learning.

It *is* the woman's *role,* in our culture, to do this dirty work. If you are old enough, there is at least some chance that Sunday dinner was once a big deal in your house; it was in mine. It was when the "extended family" got together. I don't know when that practice started to die out among the middle class or people more fortunate, but it was extremely common throughout American society in the early years of the century; and shortly before I was born, Inez Haynes Irwin described graphically the effect of all those Sunday dinners on her:

The midday Sunday dinner seemed in some curious way to symbolize everything that I hated and dreaded about the life of the middle-class woman. That plethoric meal—the huge roast, the blood pouring out of it as the man of the house carved; the many vegetables, all steaming; the

240

heavy pudding. And when the meal was finished—the table a shambles that positively made one shudder—the smooth replete retreat of the men to their cushioned chairs, their Sunday papers, their vacuous nap, while the women removed all vestiges of the horror.

We all gathered once—my extended family—for a meal like that, shortly after one of my nephews got married. For some time afterward, to my puzzlement, I became increasingly aware that the women in my family did not like my nephew's new wife. Finally, one day, I discovered that her sin had been committed that day. After the "plethoric meal" had been reduced to a "shambles," she had failed to break off an interested conversation with one of the men in the family in order to rush and help the women to "remove all vestiges of the horror." Her peculiar idea that the conversation might be as important as the dishwashing had put her, temporarily at least, outside the circle of approval.

Women who have better things to do, in fact, are more likely to meet censure from role-trained other women than they are from men. Edith Clark, a writer who lived in a small town (because her husband got a job there) and who tried to combine her career with marriage and motherhood, had a housekeeper; but, she wrote, "I am the only woman in the knowledge of most of our neighbors who attempts to 'hire her work done and to write instead,' as one of them neatly phrased it." That is how most of us look at any attempt by a married women to be a *person,* and that is what most of us who are husbands must overcome in order to accept, without feeling threats to our masculinity, the idea that there are a certain number of dirty jobs that have to be done, and that they have nothing to do with gender.

We of course condition our children to this role-based idea of who does the dirty work; they "share the chores," but *she* helps with the dishes, and *he* takes out the garbage, because we're so trapped in our roles that we can't even keep ourselves from making masculine-feminine divisions in even that sharing. And in addition, of course, we are their models.

But, you will say, what of the usual pattern, in which the man works and the woman does not? If he must do eight (or more) hours of outside work, when she does not, must he do half the housework as well?

Well, first of all, that isn't the "usual" pattern—it's the stereotyped pattern, which is not the same thing. Forty per cent of American adult women have jobs. Most of those who are married come home and do the housework *too*. Remember those schoolgirls who wanted to be teachers so that they would be home in time to cook dinner and do the chores?

Second, the pattern is not what it ought to be. It is when that pattern *does* exist that the woman is most isolated from real life, most forced into turning her consciousness inward, most blocked from her development as a real person. Your problem is not to worry about who does the dishes but to worry about getting out of the way of your wife's freedom, and even helping her toward it where you can.

Third, one of Friedan's most perceptive observations was that housewifery expands to fill the time available. If you both have something else to do with your lives, and if you don't regard housework as woman's work, you will be amazed to discover in how little time it all gets done. If each of you has a genuine life *as a person,* your standard-housewife neighbor will be astonished to discover that you can keep your house quite clean and neat with an expenditure of about ten per cent of the time she spends on hers. When some men say that some women exaggerate the difficulties of housewifery, they are exactly right. Beyond that, the woman who has nothing else to do is likely to feel, after a time, that a house ought to be six times as clean as there is any real reason for it to be.

You cannot, of course, regard yourself (nor can she regard you) as "helping." You are not helping. You are doing your part of the work. Not long ago I was talking on the phone with a woman who is a former colleague, and who has been struggling, along with her husband, for a better definition of their relationship. "The other night after dinner," she said, "my husband said, 'I'll help you with the dishes.' I suddenly realized that with the best intentions in the world, he's said that every night for three years—and he always does part of the dishes. And all of a sudden I blew up and started to yell at him. Poor guy—he couldn't figure out what was wrong."

Apparently he *did* figure it out, though, and so must you. It *isn't* the dishes. It's the definition.

The one thing that remains to overcome is the conditioning of the woman herself. Regardless of what she may have become, her girlhood conditioning has been toward housewifery, and yours has not.

242

She will see things in the house that you will not see, and if she points them out you'll get impatient.

"I'm getting tired," a movement woman told Anita Micossi, "of having to point out to him something that's so obvious to me, like what around the house needs attention." But she does have to point it out; it is her area of expertise, in many cases the only one for which she is trained, and you have to learn from her just as she, or any other apprentice, would have to learn from you the details of whatever you have been trained for.

Beyond that, things will bother her that simply will not bother you. Despite herself, she may get bugged by the presence of one meal's dirty dishes, where you would be willing to let them stand for a day or two; her tolerance of the dust level on a windowsill is likely to be lower than yours. These are problems of personal adjustment like any others, and they can be worked out like any others—but only if you have *both* broken the idea that underneath there somewhere, they are *her* responsibility.

And remember always: Doing the dishes, dividing the housework, breaking that concept of what is "woman's work," is *not* women's liberation. "Having their husbands share the housework," Friedan wrote, "didn't really compensate women for being shut out of the larger world." And Dana Densmore is more explicit; shifting the housework burdens around, she points out, doesn't change the political fact of masculine power:

As long as men are the superior caste and hold the political power in the class relationship between men and women, it *will* be a favor your lover is doing you, however imperiously you demand it. And beyond that one thing, nothing else need have changed.

So by all means, do the dishes some of the time without worrying about your masculinity. But don't think that that makes you a feminist hero. If your feminist consciousness is working, the housework thing will fall into place where it belongs—as part of a larger cultural pattern, as much symbolic as real. If it isn't, doing the dishes won't help much.

You can see, I'm sure, that the whole housework-is-woman's-work bit goes back to the wife as property, to the similarity we noted earlier between the rights and responsibilities of a husband and those of a slave-owner. It is her job, her role, her function, to take care of *his* needs and wants, which includes cleaning up whatever mess results from those needs and wants. It's reflected in our everyday language (and it's a good idea to remember that the usages of our everyday language are rarely accidental): We speak of her as taking care of *his* house, being *his* "helpmate," even being the mother of *his* children. Earlier we found that "happy" marriages are found to depend on her meeting *his* expectations, but not the opposite.

A little more difficult for us to see, perhaps, is the fact that so long as your wife, and the woman next door, accept this definition, another woman who does not accept it cannot be free to break the pattern. So long as that vision of the cultural role remains dominant, the woman who wants to be free will encounter the potential employer who is convinced that she has marriage to "fall back on," that her dedication to her own life must be different from that of a man, that somehow her "real" role will sooner or later claim her. The arrangement that you and your wife make together for your private life is your own business; but neither of you can escape responsibility for its effect on the lives of other women in your culture.

Sometimes, indeed, we men wish, too, that this housewife-and-mother role were not so rigid. The women's magazines are full of advice to women, telling them that to "save their marriages," they must remember to go on being sex objects as well as housewives; and even if we have no more feminist consciousness than is implied in that advice, we at the very least do deplore, at times, the loss of the *woman* and her replacement by the *wife*. "Two years after he marries a lovely sexy girl," says Ellen Peck, "she turns into somebody's mother. 'My God,' he thinks, 'I'm married to Betty Crocker.' " [6]

Ah, but the society allows for that—not officially (the result is deplored officially), but *really*. That's where we get the old sexual double standard.

Whether you ever do it or not—whether you would even consider doing it or not—it's true that the culture (including the women in it) takes one view toward a man who does a little sexual dabbling on the side, and quite another view toward the woman who does the same thing. It tolerates to a greater degree what we call "infidelity" if a man does it; and it isn't all that hard to figure out that this tolerance is related to the cultural conviction that the woman is in fact the possession of the man.

Most writers on the subject seem to be convinced that there is a valid societal reason for this. The idea is that in a society in which inheritance is through the male line, men have to be sure that the children to whom their possessions will pass are in fact *their* children.

This seems to me to be rather silly. One might want to leave one's possessions to the children one loves, but you can love an adopted child, and many people do. And anyway, what difference does it make—you're going to be dead anyway, aren't you? But whatever I think, it does make a difference to a lot of people; enough so that at various times in history, men have gone to such elaborate lengths as the invention of chastity belts to be sure that their children were *their* children.

This is not to say that that is what we think about, consciously, when we think about the possibility of our wives' making it with other men. We think, almost literally, about somebody invading our territory, about somebody taking something that belongs to us. And a lot of us, in addition, leap immediately to the idea of comparison. Is there something wrong with *me*? Don't *I* satisfy you? The fragility of our confidence in our own masculinity is sometimes downright pitiable.

Of course the whole thing about paternity, whatever its historical meaning, is academic now. No woman needs to have a baby she doesn't want, except as we may force her into that position by permitting her to live in poverty or in ignorance or both. No man needs to worry about his wife's having another man's baby unless he thinks that she will do so deliberately—which in fact most of us do *not* think. If "fidelity" ever had that kind of function in society, it has it no longer.[7]

I am not saying that free women always and inevitably means free love. It *does* mean freedom *to* love, which is something else.

I am not saying that women's liberation insists on your wife's having a merry sequence of affairs with the neighbors. The movement *does* insist on her right to do as she chooses with her body, just as we now have that right "unofficially" while we solemnly frown at it conventionally. The movement would also like to take some of the hypocrisy out of the whole thing. And incidentally, the right to do as she chooses with her body includes the right to do nothing with it—at home as well as elsewhere.

I am not saying either that you ought to walk out to the kitchen and say, "Hey, honey, why don't you go over and make it with old Sam?" I am saying that if she *does* go over and make it with old Sam, it is as much her choice to make as if you go over and make it with old Henrietta.

I am not saying that you must now rush out and join the nearest wife-swapping club (but if men don't own women, why don't we call it "husband-swapping"?). I am not saying anything about your private life, and your private arrangements with your wife, at all—except that she is entitled to whatever you are entitled to.

There are people with religious and moral and ethical convictions about sex and marriage, and I respect them—if they're real. But there are far more people to whom religious and moral and ethical "convictions" are really an unconscious cover-up for possessiveness, ownership, fear and jealousy; and if you are one of them, women's liberation demands of you that you face and deal with that fact—whatever sexual adventures you and your wife may or may not engage in.

For if there is no dominance and no submission, no role-playing, no conscious or unconscious concept of ownership—if, in other words, both parties to a sexual relationship (semi-permanent or otherwise) are *free*—then the whole idea of "adultery" is meaningless. The free person gives only what she or he wants to give, and gives it only when she or he wants to give it, and for only that long. If *you* are free, then you don't need her "fidelity" to prove your masculinity. If *she* is free, she doesn't need your "fidelity" to prove her "success" as a wife.

You will even be able to recognize the rather simple and not too important fact that another sexual partner can be fun once in a while, not because he or she is "better" but just because he or she is different—and you will not be threatened, on all sorts of other personality levels, by what may be nothing but a taste for occasional variety. Whatever other aspects there are to your relationship will remain just as strong—and if there aren't enough other strong aspects, then maybe you're both in the wrong relationship in the first place.

We think of adultery as dirty. It is sordid and troublesome and usually in some way unsatisfying. The third party—the "other man" or the "other woman"—moves in an aura of fear or dissatisfaction or second-bestness or all of them. The married partner "cheats"—lies and subterfuge become part of her or his life, and more often than not bring a sort of self-disgust with them.

And yet, though we feel this, it happens all the time. It happens often, I think, not because the husband or the wife is unsatisfying, or repellent, or even boring, but simply because the husband or the wife, perfectly pleasant most of the time, is not always *enough*. I don't mean "enough" in quantity, as in "often enough." I mean "enough" in the sense of meeting every need, physical and psychological, all the time.

Love and marriage do not, alas, go together like a horse and carriage, and often do not go together at all, at least not after a time.[8] Affection, as we have noted, is not the same thing; and there is nothing but a cultural frown to keep a woman or a man, otherwise contentedly married, from loving someone else, even if only for a while. Why not, then, refuse to frown?

We know, we men, that we can have a sexual relationship with another woman, even a relationship that lasts for a time, and still be a good husband and father. Why not sit down with a woman (preferably *before* we marry her, but not necessarily) and talk about it—and talk, at the same time, about the fact that *she* can have a sexual relationship with another *man* and still be, if she so chooses, a good wife and mother? Only fear and guilt, only those omnipresent oppressive roles we insist on playing, keep us both from this recognition—and from richer, fuller and freer lives. De Beauvoir, one woman who does recognize that "a man can make an excellent husband and yet be inconstant," argues that "we could concede the same for the wife," and adds:

What makes adultery degrading is the compromise of character made necessary by hypocrisy and caution; an agreement based on liberty and sincerity would do away with one of the defects of marriage.

That defect, she says elsewhere, is that marriage as we know it "transforms into rights and duties those mutual relations which should be founded on a spontaneous urge." And of course it does. The idea that a human being should be thought to have a *duty* to go to bed with another human being degrades not only the idea of sex but the idea of love—and incidentally makes as clear as does any other concept the relationship between being a wife and being a slave.

If we can sincerely and deeply question our imposed gender roles, we will not have to play the possessive and jealous husband; we can instead rejoice in the knowledge that whatever we have from a woman (sexual or otherwise) is freely given—presumably because she likes us the way we are. And she will not have to play the pitiably desperate game of "working at her marriage," lest she lose it: for it will be for her as it is for us a part of her life, not her life's meaning.

Women do not, in general, like this sort of talk about marriage any more than, in general, men do. They are afraid of it, just as we are, since they are conditioned into their roles just as we are (and they know, too, that in most cases we have more opportunities for meeting interesting other women than they have for meeting interesting other men). They, like us, are even threatened if they find that *someone else* has broken the roles—which is why so many women who are quite willing to recognize some discriminatory patterns are so quick to pull back from any identification with "women's lib."

Judith and I once had a brief discussion of the women's movement with a young woman who had already achieved some success as a professional in public relations. "I like some of their ideas," she finally admitted, "but I could no more go out without shaving my legs than I could go out naked."

I cannot say too often that virtually no one in women's liberation says that she has to stop shaving her legs; virtually no one in women's liberation says that any woman has to quit wearing a bra; and virtually no one in women's liberation says that anyone, female or male, has to go to bed with anyone else for any reason whatever. No one has to leave her husband (or his wife), or even widen her (or his) sexual experience, unless she or he wants to. The only thing that we have to do is to break enough of our conditioning to develop at least the beginnings of a feminist consciousness. The only thing that women have to do is to break through their own *false* consciousness.

"False consciousness" is a Marxist phrase, which you ought to know because movement women, Marxist or not, use it a lot. There are treatises about its subtleties, but its meaning is fairly simple all the same. False consciousness is the state of mind of someone who, because his picture of the world is faulty, believes that he is well off when in fact he is getting the short end of the stick.

A typical Marxist example of false consciousness is the American worker who, because his union has gotten him good wages and his life is better than it was in the 1930s, has forgotten that his interests are in fact opposed to the interests of capitalists; hence he doesn't realize that while they are paying him pretty well, they are exploiting him in a dozen other ways and keeping him from seeing that he'd be better off if they were overthrown.

You may disagree with that, of course; you may believe that the example is *not* an example of false consciousness. But the concept remains, and the fact that the phrase is Marxist doesn't make the concept untenable (de Beauvoir uses the phrase "bad faith" to mean about the same thing, but it's confusing in English). Whether it works in that example or not, false consciousness clearly exists in other areas.

It is the state in which most women in America now live. Nearly three years ago, polls like those mentioned near the beginning of the book showed about a third of American women struggling to some extent out of that false consciousness. More recently, the figure has been nearer half. But polls ask only specific questions; certainly a majority of American women still suffer from false consciousness on many issues.

They believe things that are not true—that, for example, a woman's capacity for childbearing means that childbearing is her function or that women are "made" to serve men—and believing those things, they say that they are not "for" women's liberation. On another level of false consciousness, they believe things about women's liberation itself that are not true, and therefore disagree with nonexistent positions, or with positions held by only a very few.

A doctrinaire Marxist might say that the American worker is maintained in a condition of false consciousness by capitalist control of the communication media. As a communicator, it seems a little simplistic to me. Be that as it may, however, it is certainly true that women are maintained in a position of false consciousness by masculinist control of the communication media (I said "masculinist," not "male"). They can respond only to the images and to the information that they get.

The press' practice of picking up one or another isolated quotation, or focusing on one or another particular woman in the movement, doesn't help, either; non-movement women are turned off by what appears to them to be overstatement, or extremism, or even a seeming exclusiveness. "I think 'apolitical' women," says Carol Hanisch, "are not in the movement for very good reasons, and as long as we say 'you have to think like us and live like us to join the charmed circle,' we will fail." [9]

There is something of a problem for married women, too, in the fact that the women's liberation movement grew up, for the most part, among women who are young and single. Unless she is careful, even a woman who gets as far as joining a small group may find that her life as a *wife* is foreign to her new sisters; some may go so far as to criticize her for being married in the first place.[10] The Radical Feminists, one of the most flexible of women's liberation organizations in their theoretical approaches to women's problems, limit their membership so that only one-third of the members can be married or otherwise "attached" to particular men.

False consciousness, however, keeps most women from getting that far, and there is little communication in the culture to give them any help. That will not make complete sense, of course, unless you think of the educational system (for instance) as one of the communication media, unless you think of children's books as a communication medium, unless you think of the whole process of conditioning as a result of sometimes blatant but often subtle communication from adult to child, and then among adults to reinforce the comfortably conditioned.

There is, as we found earlier, so much to overcome. This example from Komisar falls to hand:

In New York . . . a sixteen-year-old girl can be put in a reform school for up to four years for having sexual experiences with a number of boys (as many as the court decides is "promiscuous"). Such girls are considered "ungovernable and unmanageable"; there is no such penalty for boys.

It is a very long way from there to the abolition of gender roles. But we are not going to reach sanity—never mind justice—any other way. Veteran reporter Robert de Roos wrote of a woman he met, and said after describing what we would call her oppression, "My

lady is not for Women's Liberation. She just wants a fair shake." [11]
There is, however, no "fair shake" without the recognition that every
human being is a person; and there is no such recognition possible
while we refuse to face and to challenge the deep-rooted meanings,
and oppressions, of the roles we are taught to play.

Arlie Hochschild, embracing what she calls "a perspective that
might be called radical feminist," writes of that perspective:

> It assumes that, unless proven otherwise, differences in temperament,
> interest, aptitude and roles are due to nurture rather than nature, and
> that how girls are brought up has a lot to do with how women are
> brought down.

We cannot change that for them. But they cannot change it alone.

19

▼

So where does that leave *you?*

Unconvinced, reluctant, resistant, and not a little frightened. Better informed, I hope—both about your culture and about the women's liberation movement. But frightened anyway. You are being asked to be something which in your inner feelings you *are not.* You fear the change. You fear the change in yourself, because you don't know what it will feel like not to be yourself any more; and you fear the women.

To be asked to break your role is to be asked to change your entire pattern of behavior, your whole way of looking at the world—even the models you admire. It is all very well for Burris to ask impatiently, "Why are so many blind to the grotesqueness of the tough, hard, super-balls, insensitive, unemotional male image in John Wayne, James Bond, the Marines, etc.?" But John Wayne, as Dr. Charles W. Peek said, *cannot* express his feelings toward women, and James Bond doesn't have any—and those are the people we men are taught in this culture to be.[1] Peek continues:

What parents are really telling their son is that a real man doesn't show his emotions and if he is a real man he won't allow his emotions to be expressed. These outward expressions of emotion are viewed as a sign of femininity and undesirable for a male.

It is a long way to the point where we can see the John Wayne image as one of tragic repression, but that's what it is. We are not grown men when we are playing Glenn Ford playing Sam Cade. To be unable to cry is a sign of immaturity, not maturity. It is literally unsane not to acknowledge that we are dependent on women— easily as dependent as they are on us.

Many of the authorities interviewed by Brenton stress this point. When a woman steps even a little way out of the passive-submissive role, when she demonstrates independence, we are forced to admit to ourselves how much *we* are dependent on *her*. We don't like that— some of us literally can't stand it. For if we are dependent on her, then she is not completely dependent on us; and as soon as we see that she is not completely dependent on us, we start to worry about our masculinity.

We get resentful or hostile or both. Maybe it takes the form of ridicule (which in our superiority we may inaccurately label "satire") or lofty disdain, but it is resentment and hostility all the same. Then, as Brenton notes, "hostile and resentful men create women similarly disposed toward them. The result is increased competition —not cooperation—between the sexes."

We have to learn not to want what we want, a staggering idea. We can no longer justify the picture in our heads, so perceptively described by de Beauvoir all those years ago:

> The ideal of the average Western man is a woman who freely accepts his domination, who does not accept his ideas without discussion, but who yields to his arguments, who resists him intelligently and ends by being convinced.

That is a sick desire; and we have to look squarely at it and admit to ourselves that it is a sick desire. We have to look squarely at ourselves and see how sick our culture has made us—so sick, indeed, that a surprising number of us cannot deal with an adult and independent woman. "The more passive male," says Dr. B. Lyman Stewart, "eventually becomes impotent because of unconscious fear or hostility toward women." [2]

253

Okay, you don't become impotent (maybe). But let's not kid ourselves that it isn't a pattern. A sociologist, Arlene Daniels, set out to
interview military psychiatrists, and ran straight into the usual masculinist hiya-babe syndrome—whereupon, as reported by Ruthe Stein,
she counter-attacked:

> "I lost 40 pounds and began wearing make-up and tight-fitting clothes.
> I dripped with allure," she said, modestly . . . when they were con-
> fronted by an aggressive and sexually provocative woman, they backed
> off.[3]

You are, in fact, a frightened little boy under there (you and me,
friend). And just as some women have to learn not to be Daddy's
little girl all their lives, so we have to learn to quit trying to cover
up our hidden whimpers with a Superman suit. It won't fool an intelligent adult woman anyway, and even if it did, Superman bores
her almost more than he oppresses her. An intelligent woman, to borrow again from de Beauvoir, "would fain have to do with an adult
who is living out a real moment of his life, not with a little boy
telling himself stories." But *we* are able to deal with *her* only by con-
vincing ourselves that she has a knife in her hand and castration on
her mind.

To be frightened by a grown woman, to withdraw in alarm, is not
of course impotence—an extreme reaction, as Brenton found.

> More likely, he severely curtails his sexual activity, explaining he has
> simply lost interest in sex, a curtailment which may not, however, prevent
> him from resuming masturbatory practices. Then again, he may turn to
> brief homosexual encounters, affairs with other women, or visits to call
> girls.

It is easy to deal with it all in words. We get rid of the *role,*
and the fear goes with it; or we get rid of the fear, and it becomes
much easier to shuck off the role. It doesn't matter how you think of
it so long as you start working at it. It's going to take a while,
so start now. Give up the idea of "conquering" women, and they
won't frighten you if they seem too bold. You have been dominating
all this time, and it's almost impossible for you to think of any other
pattern except one in which you are dominat*ed*—but it is possible,
it has been done, it is being done.

254

And it's worth it. Adult women, independent women, women in the process of breaking *their* roles, are there to be met, to make friends with, perchance to love. If it should come to sex, you will be dealing with a woman who has struggled, is probably still struggling, to be her own sexual self instead of a picture in somebody's head— a woman who recognizes and is learning to enjoy her own carnality. But you will no longer be thinking of her solely in terms of the question whether it will come to sex; she will be a whole person, whom you can meet and enjoy and like (or perhaps, sometimes, dislike) as a person. Taken overall, you soon find passive women, vapid and submissive women, childish.

Break the role—and accept love, and even sensuality, wherever it comes. You can find not only the gruff pattern of John Wayne friendship, or the semi-frightened confidentiality of drunken confession, in the company of other men—a few other men, anyway. You can love one. You can touch him. It is a liberation, an opening, a reward. To see women as persons will almost certainly bring with it the ability to see men as persons.

Watch forever the simple things of the culture, and let the feminist consciousness grow. Remember that *male* is not *normal*, remember that the roles are not fixed—and feel your perception change as you watch television commercials (or television dramas). You'll find yourself watching *All in the Family* and asking how come, if the young couple are such left-liberals, the female continues to play the semi-dumb, passive, dependent, submissive little girl, while the male comes on with the whole *machismo* thing. Is it because not the character, but the viewers, couldn't take it? [4]

Watch, too, the reading you do, and you'll see the strangest things that you never noticed before. I found this not long ago in a famous essay by a well-known scholar:

Individuals communicate with one another by "giving." The "gifts" may be words or things, services or women, but in every case . . .[5]

You will find yourself saying, Hold on there. Aren't women "individuals"?

And watch especially how your children talk—particularly your daughters. Listen not only to what they say, but to what they don't say; a silent girl may be a bad sign. Watch them for the signs of being molded into the pattern you, as an adult, are having so tough a time trying to break.

One of the nice things about a feminist consciousness is that it gives us an immediate handle on a problem. It's different from worrying about, say, the war in Vietnam. This is something you can handle right now, on your own. In fact, you have to; you have to break your own conditioning before you can even understand the problem, before you can meaningfully listen to the rest of it—and believe me, I've given you only the most superficial of views. It touches everything you see and hear and do.

"The first significant discovery we shall make as we racket along our female road to freedom," writes Germaine Greer, "is that men are not free, and they will seek to make this an argument why nobody should be free." But we don't have to. It sounds crazy, but we *are* victimized into being oppressors. We have to understand what is done to us in order to understand what we do to them. Then we can fight back—together. Not in an old-fashioned, husband-and-wife, side-by-side, 50-50 helpmates kind of togetherness—for that is the same game in a new disguise—but together as an alliance of equals.

Like the women I have tried to describe, we can find a surprising, a startling, joy in release. But also like the women I have tried to describe, we too must first overcome our fear: our fear of each other, our fear of the society, the culture, and most of all our fear of the women themselves. If the idea of free women makes us feel "unmanned," it is the fear, not the women, that unmans us. Or, as Myron Brenton put it,

As long as men feel that the equality of women will emasculate them, it is exactly what will happen.

256

NOTES
▼

CHAPTER 1

1. I'm compelled to add that whatever one's opinion of the rest of the book, everybody should read the chapter on children.
2. *The San Francisco Chronicle*, September 28, 1971.
3. *The San Francisco Chronicle*, August 24, 1970.
4. Some feminists might argue that we make and understand jokes that are based on false views of the world—stereotypes, in many cases—and that what women are responding to is the unfamiliar perception of truth.

CHAPTER 2

1. When you hit the word "psychologist," did you picture a man or a woman? Remember your answer; it becomes important later.
2. The sneaky series here, which I borrowed before in my article "New Look at the Oldest Difference," is from Maccoby, "Woman's Intellect."
3. No citation because this comes from something I covered many years ago; but I think the psychologist in question was D. O. Hebb.
4. Many years ago I heard the philosopher, Charles Frankel, say on television that a person's sanity can be defined as the degree to

which the structure in his head matches the structure of the reality outside. Although by this definition a lot of people are functionally insane in certain areas—politically, for instance—I've never heard a better definition. It also makes sense out of the otherwise murky word "sane."

5. A lot was made of bra-burning that never took place at the Miss America protest in 1970, but nobody paid much attention to Susan Adelman's superb and definitive poem:

> Atlantic City is a town with class;
> They raise your morals while they judge your ass.

CHAPTER 3

1. When you go deeper into the intellectual analyses that are taking place within the movement, you run into the distinction between "male supremacy," a *condition,* and "male chauvinism" or "sexism" as an *ideology.* See the various writings of Koedt. For a slightly different use of the argument about ideology, see Amundsen.
2. It happens that I grew up in San Francisco before World War II, where there were very few blacks. But roughly 8% of the population was Chinese and the conditions were similar, ghetto and all.
3. What is "Spanish," what is "Mexican" and what is "Californian" in my home state's history is a special example of the same phenomenon.
4. See Knowles and Prewitt. Amundsen applies the concept to women elegantly.
5. Firestone, Atkinson and a few others do argue that much of what we regard as fundamental biology is not necessarily that at all. They discuss at some length such very real possibilities as parthenogenesis and extrauterine pregnancy. Most of the women's movement, however, is not concerned with such esoterica. From our point of view they are interesting only because you might run into the arguments and conclude, in profound error, that they are representative of all, or even most, of women's liberation.
6. Chesler's article is partly a report on the details of this "therapy" as actually practiced.
7. The San Francisco Symphony auditions applicants behind a screen, so that neither their sex nor their race is known to the conductor or the judges. Blume describes the hiring of women to play trumpet and bassoon, and the surprise of the former conductor.
8. Miriam Allen de Ford.
9. Jo Freeman, "Growing Up Girlish."
10. Quoted in Anonymous, *How Harvard Rules Women.*

258

CHAPTER 4

1. See Rubin and Hacker for a start.
2. Viola Liuzzo was of course, in a sense, "lynched" in 1965, but for her work in civil rights, not for her gender.
3. Quoted by Amundsen.
4. In Jo Freeman, "Growing Up Girlish."
5. The sentence is from William J. Goode, quoted by Jo Freeman, *ibid.*
6. It is also why, at about that time, "We Shall Overcome" gave way to "black power," but that's another subject.
7. The preference until recently (and still in many cases) of black men for lighter skin in women was so prevalent that even most whites knew about it.
8. The "Afro" hairstyle is also called "natural." Some urbane whites have been known to point out that the hairstyle is neither African nor natural. They miss the point completely. The hairstyle is a positive affirmation that the qualities of black people's hair that used to be hidden (including its *natural* "nappiness") should instead be proudly displayed. "Our standards are as good as theirs; black is beautiful."
9. Amundsen.

CHAPTER 5

1. Those who like and use statistics may be interested to know that even statistics can have a built-in masculinism if you're not careful. Theodore R. Anderson and Morris Zelditch, Jr., wrote *A Basic Course in Statistics* (Holt, Rinehart & Winston, 2d ed., 1968; 1st ed., 1958), which they describe as "probably among the most elementary of all elementary texts on statistics." A very early section contains information which they say is "easily lost or overlooked by the beginner." It concerns, in part, the definition of statistical attributes, including all-or-none attributes, regarding which it says this:

"An interesting problem occurs in the case of an attribute such as sex, with its categories 'male' and 'female.' Clearly, a female is something other than just a 'not-male,' although it turns out that practically all people who are not males are, in fact, females. Sex is ordinarily treated as a dichotomy because only two categories or classes are normal. . . . Furthermore, sex is clearly an attribute since there is no question about the quantity of any one thing that is possessed. Technically, however, if this characteristic is treated as a true all-or-none attribute, its classes should be either 'male' and 'not-

259

male' or 'female' and 'not-female,' whichever the individual prefers [or depending, a feminist might add, on what you're trying to measure]. When the categories 'male' and 'female' are both used each category possesses something not possessed by the other. In this case the attribute is a compound one, which just happens to possess only two classes in most relevant populations."

It would be nice if the sociologists who use the statistical methods taught in this book would remember in their work, and in their daily lives as well, that "a female is something other than just a 'not-male.' " Psychiatrists, too.

2. Ann Arbor, Michigan, and several other cities have female patrol-women on general duty.

3. There is a feminist argument—usually a wry joke, though again the humorless are always with us and will take anything seriously—that because the female X chromosome is full-sized and the male Y chromosome appears stunted, it must be (in contradiction to the Freudian view that women are "incomplete men") that men are somehow incomplete or distorted women.

4. *The San Francisco Examiner,* July 25, 1971.

5. Funny thing: A lot of men don't know that their breasts, like a woman's, are erogenous zones.

6. Weisstein, " 'Woman as Nigger.' "

7. I didn't invent the Indo-European language structure, and I do get tired of trying to write *around* the language I'm writing *in.* To say that "we are designed" does not imply a designer, except in a formal logical structure that turns out to be based on the language itself. It just means that however it comes about, that's how it is.

8. Columnist Herb Caen says that he wants to see their scenic checks.

9. The Koedt essay in question is "Lesbianism," the title of which is misleading. It is about a lot more than lesbianism.

10. I have been trying for months to find a source for that superbly masculinist sentence, "Anatomy is destiny." Several writers credit it to Freud—he is said to have meant it only about women, of course —but I can't pin it down. It would of course be true if it meant only that no one can do anything that is physically impossible, but that's an obvious tautology.

11. New guidelines from the Equal Employment Opportunity Commission say that it's illegal to refuse a woman a job because she's pregnant, and provide several other protections for working women who get pregnant. *The New York Times* Service story in *The San Francisco Chronicle,* March 31, 1972.

12. In rural Japan immediately after World War II, a common joke

260

held that farmers prayed for their children to be born during the
night—so that their wives wouldn't lose a day's work in the field.
Pearl Buck's *The Good Earth* describes a similar pattern in China
not too long ago. There is some disagreement about the effects of so
extreme a pattern on the woman's health; but the families rarely
limited the number of children as we do, either, or ate so well as
do most of us.
13. And one third of the males, too, of course. That will come up in a
later chapter.

CHAPTER 6

1. Those for whom Note 1 for the previous chapter was relevant
might note that where "male" and "female" are *attributes* to the
statistician, "masculinism" and "feminism" can be seen as ordinal
characteristics. That is, an individual might be some of each, to
various degrees, at least as the terms are now used in this culture.
2. I also become more concerned about my sons and other males
their age.
3. This bias in our education is sometimes startling. Every California
pupil learns about Sir Francis Drake—whose landing in California
was of minor historical importance—but they hear little of the trips
of the Manila Galleon, and of such much more important (to California history) sailors as Cermeño.
4. See Edward Hall.
5. See Komisar.
6. Mead, *Sex and Temperament in Three Primitive Societies.*
7. A plethora of television series about widows or widowers with
kids sometimes leads me to wonder—television being the profound
influence that it is—whether the "broken home" may become the
desirable middle-class norm of a later generation.
8. I didn't say she was the *best.* I'm a Pauline Frederick fan. But
then I'm old enough to remember Dorothy Thompson.
9. Quotations from a United Press International story in *The San
Francisco Examiner,* March 5, 1972. The masculinist congressman
was Lionel Van Deerlin (D.-Calif.).
10. There are some exceptions to the talk-show syndrome on local
television. Surprisingly often, these women are black; the local
station gets two tokens for the price of one.

CHAPTER 7

1. See Brenton, and his sources.
2. And one female friend has pointed out, with some practicality,

that if a tiny baby isn't wearing a diaper, you might very well *want* to hold male and female babies differently.

3. On the other hand, men who were themselves excellent athletes often want, and enjoy, the same abilities in their sons, and sons are not always better than their fathers were. Obviously it's not all that clear.

4. See Brenton, Chesler, Weisstein, Friedan, Figes and Millett, for a start, on penis envy. A more formal study is Clara Thompson's; other specific studies are cited by the authors listed.

5. The black subculture, again, shows somewhat different patterns. I'm not going into it because, regardless of what *ought to be*, the black pattern does not, at this point anyway, determine the overall cultural pattern. I do refer you, however, to the Bibliography.

6. Wilson and Banfield. There is a perfectly valid methodological reason for preferring to interview only men in this study; the slip comes when the results are taken to apply to "voters" in general. It's a common enough academic practice, particularly notable in this case because the study has to do with the respondents' attitudes —so that the results seem to incorporate either the idea that women's attitudes are indistinguishable from men's, or the idea that the "normal" voter is male.

CHAPTER 8

1. Most of the examples are from Daniel G. Brown. Of course, one of my sons had a toy which is a miniature human being, whose clothes and accessories he could change. It was called G. I. Joe, and no one ever, ever said that he was playing with a doll.

2. United Press International story in *The San Francisco Chronicle,* December 14, 1971.

3. *The Berkeley Gazette,* August 4, 1971. There is a fuller treatment of this study in Chapter 11.

4. Some doctors have already recognized a particular pattern of arm and shoulder deformity in young American males, traceable to kids' being taught to throw curves before their muscular development is ready for an act that is physiologically unnatural anyway. They call it "Little League elbow."

5. Not, of course, that grown men shouldn't cry. No adult should cry for such a stupid reason.

6. All couples living together, with or without children, should read Mainardi—together.

7. And you bloody well know I broke the habit, too.

8. Possibly a bad choice of examples. It seems fairly clear to me that

as of 1972, everybody should take typing, and very possibly everybody should take auto shop. Unless you think the auto will disappear. While we're at it, maybe everybody should take computer programming in high school too, or at least learn how to foul up computers.

9. It might take some intelligence to run a household truly well and efficiently, but it's too boring to be worth the effort—and it doesn't earn a third of the appreciation that a competent secretary gets.

10. To be rigorous, it is not certain whether a recently born baby grasps by instinct. Even if this is true, it's obviously a different kind of thing from a "maternal instinct" in other animals. There is also a difference between an instinct and a conditioned reflex—like pulling your hand off a hot stove—which some people sometimes confuse.

11. It is *possible* for a woman to regard her father as a rival to be overcome; it has happened. But it's extremely unusual.

12. Distributed by *The New York Times* Service; *The San Francisco Chronicle,* July 7, 1971.

13. The story calls the speaker "Kathleen Grady Reber, who is married but used the name Mrs. Kathleen Grady." The next paragraph begins, "Mrs. Reber, acting president of . . ." Now, really—why can't she use any name she wants to without *The New York Times* loftily deciding that the masculinist rules are "right"? Even the *Times* gave in on Muhammad Ali.

14. Hartley, "Sex-Role Pressures, etc."

15. I wouldn't have found this essay if Jo Freeman hadn't found it first.
   "Socialization" is the "correct" term in the social sciences. I've chosen to use "conditioning" partly because it dramatizes the fact that children themselves have no more choice in what happens to them than does a rat being trained to run a maze—or than does a miniature Schnauzer.

16. Hartley, "Children's Concepts, etc."

17. I first learned about this when Maccoby read the paper now collected in Farber and Wilson. I attempted to "translate" it a little more fully in my article "New Look at the Oldest Difference." Since then Maccoby has collected a mountain of evidence in her book. See also Maccoby and Rau. The studies involved include those of D. M. Levy, H. A. Witkin and others. Jo Freeman's "Growing Up Girlish" condenses much of it neatly and understandably. The Maccoby quotation that follows is from "Woman's Intellect."

18. That is not *all* that it means, but set-breaking is an excellent indicator. Maccoby in "Woman's Intellect" gives a number of other measures, each with a slightly different meaning.

19. Jo Freeman, "Growing Up Girlish."

263

20. I know of at least two strong feminists, both "intellectually active," who insist that this was not true of *them*. They *were* active and independent, though, and encouraged to be; it's the word "tomboy" that they don't think applies. Come to think of it, Jane Addams was never a "tomboy" either.

21. This required a long, protected passage for play; hence our word "mall," much used in urban planning. The game was originally called pall-mall; hence all sorts of things.

22. No great trick. I learned to read and write at three, largely due to the presence of an interested and unemployed father.

23. Also no great trick. A fellow writer, Rick Beban, now twenty-five, beat me at chess, quite legitimately, when he was six and I was twenty years older. I haven't played him since he was seven.

CHAPTER 9

1. Assuming that you can gain access to them, the best short overall reviews of gender-role treatment in children's books are in Key, Kidd and the study by the Feminists on Children's Literature. They provide other sources, besides those listed in my Bibliography. A story by Marjorie Stern in *The American Teacher,* March, 1972, mentions two new studies I have not seen: a Canadian study by a group called Women in Teaching, and a 78-page report on children's readers available for $1.50 from Women on Words and Images, Box 2163, Princeton, N.J. Stern says that the latter study found men in 147 different occupations, women in 25, which is close to the results of the Frisof study.

2. Sir Walter Scott wrote of *Ivanhoe* that clearly a man of his hero's intelligence would, in real life, have chosen the dark and intelligent Rebecca instead of the blonde and insipid Rowena—but that he, Scott, had to follow the conventions. Besides, Rebecca was Jewish (sexy-exotic-"mysterious"), and unacceptable on that ground as well. But Scott did regret it (his own words on the subject are quoted in the Heritage edition of *Ivanhoe*).

Eliot uses the convention for her own purposes: blonde Lucy, not dark Maggie, winds up with Stephen in *The Mill on the Floss.*

3. Quoted by Beard, who spends some space on Wonder Woman.

4. *The San Francisco Chronicle,* September 7, 1970.

5. Interview by Caroline Drewes, *The San Francisco Examiner,* January 25, 1970.

6. See Note 1 for this chapter.

7. See also Suelzle.

8. There are not a lot of inhabited places in California where kids

will identify much with riding sleds, either, but that's a different problem.

9. As you can go mad trying to find a copy of Merriam's *After Nora Slammed the Door,* one of the first and still one of the best of the American postwar feminist books. It's out of print. Why, in this day of fascination with women's liberation, some enterprising paperback publisher hasn't grabbed this and rushed it out, I cannot understand. It would be especially suited for the growing number of women's studies programs at the college level.

10. I am talking about running characters. Once in a great while a female doctor turns up in a particular episode; if her part is important, it usually involves some conflict having to do with her feminine role. I have never seen a female surgeon.

11. Fisher cites at this point a book called *One Fish, Two Fish, Red Fish, Blue Fish,* by Dr. Seuss. Kids, I am told, love Dr. Seuss. I don't agree with them.

12. Quoted by Feminists on Children's Literature.

13. Quoted by Key.

14. Quoted in the FCL report.

CHAPTER 10

1. Quoted by Persis Hunt.

2. Boys who are terrible at mathematics in school often have little trouble calculating earned-run averages in their heads. I've known some who keep tables of batting averages in their heads, adjusting them after each time at bat while listening to a broadcast game.

3. This is not a quotation from Figes, but it is awfully close.

4. A very bright girl who is not lazy may meet serious and prodding encouragement from an individual teacher or two, but that doesn't change the cultural pattern within the schools generally.

5. It would be considerably more difficult, however, to design the experiment. "Brilliant black pupils" is a concept almost any teacher can understand; the sets we are trying to break are much more deeply rooted. What would you tell the teacher that the pupils *are*?

6. Hariette Surovell's testimony before the National Commission on Population Growth and the American Future was excerpted in *The San Francisco Chronicle,* November 12, 1971.

7. United Press International story in *The San Francisco Chronicle,* September 25, 1970.

8. *The San Francisco Chronicle,* November 21, 1970. The photo is credited, the story isn't, but presumably both are Associated Press.

9. Jim Wood in *The San Francisco Examiner,* September 17, 1970.

10. Associated Press story in *The San Francisco Chronicle,* December 10, 1971.
11. The quotation is from the January, 1972, issue of *The Bulletin of the San Francisco Medical Society,* but I got it, and the rest of the quotations, from a story by Elizabeth Mehren in *The San Francisco Chronicle,* January 19, 1972.
12. I am all for the idea of comprehensive nutritional education. I just want to get the gender roles out of it. If a boy becomes a man who knows how to cook and does his share of it, he is not, I hope, going to do it in an all-male kitchen.
13. Both items from Friedan. A more recent report: "Although at the high school level more girls than boys receive grades of 'A,' roughly 50% more boys than girls go to college." *The Princeton Report to the Alumni on Co-Education* (Princeton, N.J., 1968).
14. I know that a lot of high school coaches also teach other courses. Insofar as they also teach English or mathematics or auto shop, they're teachers, without quotation marks. Insofar as they coach football, or stand in front of a gym class yelling "hup-two-three-four," they're jocks, pure and simple, and nothing more.

CHAPTER 11

1. Menstrual blood is no different from any other blood, and when we cut our finger we often stick it into our mouth and suck the blood. Noting this, Greer says that a woman can measure her own liberation by her willingness to taste her menstrual blood. I admit to feeling that there must be a better yardstick, but she is obviously right in her perception that most women will, indeed, regard it as "unclean."
2. People who derive right from fact, somebody said, make ideal subjects for tyrannies. Probably Rousseau.
3. Jo Freeman, "The Bitch Manifesto."
4. I think the term was invented by anthropologist Gregory Bateson, but the psychologists have made it their own now.
5. Wells goes on to say that "the Little Girl will remain caught in this circle of anger and compliancy until she learns to stop loving and nurturing the Little Girl in herself." Which is easier said than done.
6. Quoted by columnist Phyllis Battelle, *The San Francisco Examiner,* June 27, 1971.
7. *A Tan and Sandy Silence.* I won't say that MacDonald is the best novelist in America; but he is the best novelist *about* America, or

266

at least about most of it. For a portrait of a guy who is really trapped in a stock masculine role, see the first part of *Death Trap.*

8. Syndicated story in *The San Francisco Chronicle,* August 18, 1970.
9. *The Berkeley Gazette,* August 4, 1971.
10. The same survey shows this explicitly with regard to boys. Only 20% wanted to be an "average family man," and 26% wanted to be single; but asked what they *expected,* only 9% thought they *would* be single after a few years.
11. Jo Freeman's Rule again.
12. Millett has a fuller description of this "channeling" process early in her book, complete with political analysis. It seems to me that the analysis demands some knowledge of the vocabulary and techniques of political theory; it may sound like mere rhetoric to a lay reader.
13. De Beauvoir also treats this whole subject in the much deeper philosophical terminology of existentialism. It's brilliant thinking if you happen to know what she's talking about, but it demands some prior knowledge.

CHAPTER 12

1. The point is from Friedan. A very few institutions have made a very few changes to make it just a little bit easier for women in medicine, science, law, etc. But the institutional situation remains.
2. Jo Freeman, "Growing Up Girlish."
3. From a depressingly insulting Associated Press story, *The San Francisco Examiner,* March 1, 1970.
4. *The New York Daily News,* January 29, 1970; quoted by Ware.
5. *The San Francisco Chronicle,* August 26, 1970.
6. Interview by Kandy [!] Stroud, reprinted in *The San Francisco Chronicle,* July 29, 1971.
7. Quoted in *Newsweek,* March 23, 1970.
8. Hanisch, "Hard Knocks, etc."
9. Anonymous, "Questions I Should Have Answered Better."
10. Reprinted in *The San Francisco Chronicle,* March 23, 1970.
11. Kardiner quoted in *Newsweek,* March 23, 1970; Randolph from a Reuters story in *The San Francisco Chronicle,* August 27, 1970; *Chronicle* editorial, August 26, 1970.
12. Van Horne, columns in *The San Francisco Examiner,* September 22, 1968; August 24, 1969; July 26, 1970; August 23, 1970.
13. *Ibid.,* August 23, 1970.
14. *Ibid.,* July 26, 1970. This quotation is immediately followed by a

paragraph of strong praise for Millett and four more paragraphs that are straight women's liberation rhetoric.

15. *Ibid.,* August 24, 1969.
16. *Ibid.,* September 22, 1968.
17. I am tempted to go back to the original *Frankenstein* and say, "Boris Karloff is tender." But I guess that's not what she meant.
18. Willis, "Women and the Left."
19. *California Living,* January 18, 1970.
20. *The San Francisco Chronicle,* letter published on August 31, 1970. Among the signers was the *Chronicle* redwoods expert, Scott Thurber, from whom I gained much of my understanding of masculinism.
21. Quoted in *Newsweek,* May 18, 1970.
22. For more of Hunt's "expertise"—now that you have begun to have a feminist consciousness and can judge it—see Farber and Wilson.

A couple of years later, *Playboy*—increasingly uptight about its indefensible role as a purveyor of naked masculinism—gave $2500 to the Council of Economic Priorities for a study of discrimination against women by banks (*The San Francisco Chronicle,* August 1, 1971). Hefner is big on equal pay and equal opportunity. You can tell by looking at the *Playboy* masthead.

CHAPTER 13

1. The Hinckles. WSP was a fine group, but it had nothing to do with women's liberation.
2. In 1950, when Pete Seeger and Lee Hays wrote the now-familiar song "If I Had a Hammer," one line in the chorus was "love for all of my brothers." Pressure from some of the more solemn and doctrinaire among the leftists who at that time were about the only folk music fans, and who charged "male chauvinism," forced the change to "love for all my brothers and my sisters"—which is how it is universally sung now, but which still doesn't fit the meter.
3. Jordan, *The Place of American Women.*
4. Hanisch, "Hard Knocks, etc."
5. Koedt, "Politics of the Ego, etc."
6. Willis, "Women and the Left."
7. Not all movement women agree that it *should* be so, of course. "Without a programmatic analysis, the 'women's movement' has been as if running blindly in the general direction of where they *guess* the last missile that just hit them was based." Atkinson, "Radical Feminism."
8. See for example *trans/action,* November–December, 1970.

Van Allen's paper is an attempt to do the same thing in the

hazy area where anthropology touches political theory. See also Note 5 for chapter 7, and the article cited therein, as an example of what the women are trying to combat.

9. In 1966, when Stokely Carmichael took over James Meredith's march through Mississippi and thus came to national prominence, he was greeted in one Mississippi town by derisive black children chanting, "Stokely *Car*michael, the TV *star*michael!"
    On this subject, see also Mehrhof.
10. This is not an absolute technical necessity, of course, but it's hard to imagine, say, a news program handled any other way.

CHAPTER 14

1. See Densmore.
2. Sarachild's outlines read in conjunction with some of the other essays in the same publication strike me as something that might be of real interest to women who are so far unfamiliar with women's liberation.
3. And if there were a man present, he would "explain" why they "shouldn't" feel that way.
4. I have, however, seen the entire female half of a night club audience, representing a spread of age groups, break into delighted applause on hearing Carmen McRae sing "Woman Talk," which is a different song altogether.
5. Hanisch, "The Personal Is Political."
6. Quoted by Micossi.
7. Steinem, "Sisterhood."
8. Joyce Haber's column, *The San Francisco Chronicle,* March 24, 1972.
9. Hanisch says something like this of herself in "Hard Knocks."
10. Described by Schlesinger.
11. Quoted by Tax. There are other fifty-cent stamps.

CHAPTER 15

1. At the 1969 contest (for Miss America 1970) one contestant played "Bumble Boogie" on the piano. See Judith Martin's *Times-Post* Service story, *The San Francisco Chronicle,* September 9, 1969.
2. Re Miss America 1970 (Pamela Anne Eldred): "Topics on which she smiled and said 'I really couldn't voice an opinion—I don't know enough about that' included drugs, nudity in the theater, unisex fashions, student unrest, what the priorities of America should be, and whether . . . 18-year-olds should have the vote." She also

said, "I feel that the people who were voted into office must have the intelligence to know what to do and that everybody should have faith in them"—a perfectly suitable statement for a good German in the 1930s. From Martin's story cited in Note 1.

3. Quoted by de Beauvoir.
4. See for instance Jelinck, in Jelinck and Hanchett.
5. *Washington Post* Service story in *The San Francisco Chronicle,* December 14, 1971.
6. The direct complaint program is mentioned in an editorial preface to Jelinck and Hanchett. The cold speculum comes up every time the subject of medical treatment comes up.
7. Anonymous, "Are Our Doctors Pigs?"
8. The Macmillan Company, 1971.
9. *The San Francisco Examiner,* November 21, 1971.
10. "Women M.D.'s Join the Fight," *Medical World News,* October 23, 1970.
11. "Prostitutes on the street often put males in the position usually reserved for us. We are told to take uninvited touching, comments, and soliciting as 'flattery.' When it happens to men it is called 'harassment' and the wheels of justice turn." Kearon and Mehrhof.
12. I do not mean to characterize the sex lives, or attitudes toward them, of any individuals mentioned or quoted. There is no one mentioned whom I have ever met or about whom I know anything outside what they have written.
13. Within a sizable portion of the women's movement, it is an important part of women's attitude toward abortion that they are simultaneously opposed to forced, or involuntary, sterilization. This may seem startling, but many poor black women, particularly, fear to seek abortions through legal channels because they believe that in the process they will be sterilized. This is not a completely unfounded fear—some cases have been uncovered—and it is heightened by the contention of some black liberation groups that white America has an interest in keeping down the black population.

Chapter 16

1. Space forbids the extensive discussion of rape that really ought to be part of this book. We all say that we dislike rapists—but few of us bother to notice than when a woman reports a rape and a man is accused, it is the *victim* who goes on trial. Her private life, her "morals," her whole existence is dragged through the mud—to such an extent that a great many rapes are not reported because the woman regards the subsequent humiliation as intolerable. Even her

270

treatment by the police is apt to be insultingly skeptical at best. It is one of the most open and vicious manifestations of the masculinism of our society.

There is surprisingly little discussion of rape in feminist books. Millett touches on it briefly, de Beauvoir rather mystically. The Mehrhof-Kearon essay is "political" to the point of incomprehensibility. Gail Sullivan's article is good if you can get to a library big enough to have it.

2. I was tempted to intersperse, "Mrs. Peel, you're needed!" But that gets us mixed up with sex objects.

3. "An advertisement for a child's dress, sizes 3–6x, in *The New York Times* in the fall of 1960, said: 'She Too Can Join the Man-Trap Set.' " Friedan, *The Feminine Mystique*.

4. *Motivation and Personality* (1954); quoted by Greer and lifted therefrom by me.

5. Atkinson, "Radical Feminism."

6. Brenton describes a number of studies.

7. Interview by Ruthe Stein in *The San Francisco Chronicle,* November 22, 1971.

8. Figes' reference is to Maccoby, *Development.*

9. "Loving Another Woman." Koedt was reported as of early 1972 to be working on a book on female sexuality. If it's out, buy it. I recommend it sight unseen on the basis of the intelligence, clarity and restrained wisdom of her other writing.

CHAPTER 17

1. This note is by way of being a public apology. As an editor of *Ramparts* I opposed publication of Lydon's article on the ground that it took far too much space to discuss an interesting but essentially trivial subject. Since I was overruled, I don't have to apologize to the readers; but it is high time I apologized to Susan Lydon, I was very wrong.

2. Edmond Bergler, quoted by Lydon.

3. Not all straight women, or even all columnists, use this definition. Asked how she managed not to lose her femininity in view of her success, Sylvia Porter replied to a male reporter, "Did you lose your masculinity because you work?" Quoted by Millie Robbins, *The San Francisco Chronicle,* November 12, 1970.

4. In a sense it may be. The boss wants *everybody* in the office to "look nice." It is just that his concept about when a woman "looks nice" is masculinist.

5. This has nothing to do with homosexuality. To judge from his

271

television appearances, for instance, Merle Miller is gentle but in no way effeminate.

6. That was on January 23, 1970. The story, and the quotation, are from "Julia."

7. A sex symbol can be a sex object, of course.

8. This is a paraphrase of Firestone.

9. *The San Francisco Chronicle,* June 24, 1970. Apparently nobody was willing to sign the story.

10. Betty Beale in *The San Francisco Examiner,* September 13, 1971. The story doesn't say so, but the Beale column originates in *The Washington Star.*

11. Unusually heavy women can also suffer from chest pains because of breast weight. But if it doesn't actually hurt, it's probably okay. It's curious that the same people who insist on what they think is women's "natural" role also tend to insist on bras.

    We should also note that some doctors will tell you *anything*; but they are often speaking not as doctors but as males, whether they know it or not.

12. Greer also welcomes attention to the nipple, which she says is "absent from the breast of popular pornography." Possibly they had different pornography in Greer's Australia than they had where I grew up.

13. Associated Press story in *The San Francisco Chronicle,* January 23, 1970.

14. I first encountered the phrase in the Radicalesbian essay, but I've since found that it has been in actual use for some time.

15. Merla Zellerbach's column in *The San Francisco Chronicle,* September 29, 1971.

16. Carolyn Anspacher's direct report from Los Angeles to *The San Francisco Chronicle,* September 7, 1971. Anspacher provided thorough, excellent coverage of the convention to the usually hopelessly masculinist *Chronicle.*

17. Quoted by Dudar.

18. The paragraph is paraphrased from the Radicalesbians.

19. Story by Norda Strout and William J. Drummond in *The Los Angeles Times,* reprinted in *The San Francisco Chronicle,* August 2, 1971.

20. Story by Ruthe Stein in *The San Francisco Chronicle,* July 20, 1971.

21. "A Weekend in Lesbian Nation." Negrin describes herself as "heterosexually oriented."

CHAPTER 18

1. Except for obvious legal differences, most of what is said here about "wives" applies equally whether or not the couple in question is formally married. The role doesn't change all that much in most cases.
2. Henry Wilcoxon.
3. An example of how difficult it is to break conditioning was spotted by *The New Yorker* cartoonist who showed a harried clerk, using the strange pronounced version of "Ms.," asking, "Is that *Miss* Miz or *Mrs.* Miz?"
4. Quoted by Inge Bell.
5. Bart also found that a lot of the same symptoms hit men when they retired from work. That was *their* role. The still unpublished work by Jessie Bernard listed in the Bibliography deals in large part with the effects of the "housewife role" on the mental health of American women.
6. Interview by Caroline Drewes, *The San Francisco Examiner,* July 11, 1971.
7. It can also be argued, on similar grounds, that the taboo on incest no longer has the function it once had, but that would get us into all sorts of psychological quicksand.
8. It is well to remember that attachment to a carriage is an artificial, man-imposed position for a horse.
9. Hanisch, "Hard Knocks, etc."
10. The essay by "Dair Struggle" is devoted to this question.
11. *The San Francisco Chronicle,* October 25, 1970. The same writer has shown a little more understanding of women's liberation since then.

CHAPTER 19

1. Material about and quotation from Peek is from a *Chicago Daily News* story in *The San Francisco Examiner,* September 20, 1970.
2. Quoted by Van Horne, *The San Francisco Examiner,* November 28, 1971. She uses it to "prove" that "women's libbers" are "castrators," apparently under the impression that men who lose their potency at any sign of aggressiveness in a female are somehow healthy.
3. *The San Francisco Chronicle,* July 7, 1971.
4. Edmund Leach.
5. The original pilot film for *Star Trek* (never seen by the public) called for a woman, not a Vulcan, as the spaceship's executive

officer—a woman described in the first outline for the series as "expressionless, cool . . . probably [the captain's] superior in detailed knowledge of the equipment, departments, and personnel aboard the vessel." But producer Gene Roddenberry found that test audience reaction "ranged from resentment to disbelief." Whitfield says that the audiences "resented the idea of a tough, strong-willed woman as second-in-command," and found her "too domineering"; Roddenberry said sadly, "I decided to wait for a 23rd Century audience before I went that far again." The role was combined with that of the already existent character of "Mr. Spock" before the show went on the air. See Whitfield and Roddenberry.

BIBLIOGRAPHY
⬇

(with a few comments along the way)

Aberle, David F., and Kaspar D. Naegele, "Middle-Class Fathers' Occupational Role and Attitudes toward Children," *The American Journal of Orthopsychiatry,* April, 1952.

Abrams, Judy, "I'm Not That Kind of Girl," *Leviathan,* June, 1970. Adventures of an organist in the masculinist world of rock.

Addams, Jane, *Twenty Years at Hull House* (The Macmillan Company, 1910).

Advisory Commission on the Status of Women, Report, *California Women, Textbooks* (1971).

Allen, Pam, *Free Space* (The Times Change Press, 1970). Reprinted in Koedt, *Notes.*

American Political Science Association, *Women in Political Science: Studies and Reports of the APSA Committee on the Status of Women in the Profession, 1969–71* (APSA, 1971).

———, Committee on the Status of Women in the Profession, "Final Report and Recommendations," *PS,* Summer, 1971.

Amir, Menachim, *Patterns in Forcible Rape* (The University of Chicago Press, 1971).

Amundsen, Kristen, *The Silenced Majority* (Prentice-Hall, Inc., 1971). This is one of the books you should read. Has all the figures about working women and job discrimination, but also goes into politics and ideology.

Andreas, Carol, *Sex and Caste in America* (Prentice-Hall, Inc., 1971).

Annan, Noel, "Heroine," *The New York Review of Books,* January 2, 1969. Among other things, points up the dangers of easy assumptions about "lesbianism" in female behavior.

Anonymous, "Are Our Doctors Pigs?" *Rat,* June 5–19, 1970.

———, "Lesbians As Bogeywomen," *It Ain't Me, Babe,* June 11–July 1, 1970.

———, "Questions I Should Have Answered Better," *It Ain't Me, Babe,* March 15, 1970. Originally from *Notes from the First Year* (1968), of which you'll never find a copy if you don't already own one.

Anonymous member of Redstockings, "Them and Me," in Firestone and Koedt.

Anonymous women's collective, *How Harvard Rules Women* (New University Conference, 1970).

Arlen, M. J., "The Girl with the Harvard Degree," *The New York Times Magazine,* June 10, 1962.

Atkinson, Ti-Grace, "The Institution of Sexual Intercourse," in Firestone and Koedt.

———, "Radical Feminism," in Firestone and Koedt.

Babcox, Peter, "Meet the Women of the Revolution, 1969," *The New York Times Magazine,* February 9, 1969. *See also* responding letters in subsequent issues.

Baker, Elizabeth Faulkner, *Technology and Women's Work* (Columbia University Press, 1964).

Baker, Melba, "Women Who Work," *The International Socialist Review,* Summer, 1963.

Balswick, J., and C. Peek, "The Inexpressive Male: A Tragedy of American Society." A paper presented at the Annual Meeting, American Sociological Association, August, 1970. This is the same Dr. Peek who is quoted in the final chapter of this book.

Bambirra, Vania, "The Chilean Women," *Punto Final* (Santiago), March 22, 1971; partially reprinted in English translation in The NACLA Chile Project, *The New Chile* (The North American Congress on Latin America, 1972). Bambirra is a Brazilian social scientist in political exile.

Barbara (pseud.), "Consciousness-Raising," *It Ain't Me, Babe,* June 11–July 1, 1970. Originally distributed by Redstockings, New York City.

Barry, H., M. K. Bacon and I. L. Child, "A Cross-cultural Survey of Some Sex Differences in Socialization," *Journal of Abnormal and Social Psychology,* 1957.

Bart, Pauline, "Mother Portnoy's Complaints," *trans/action,* November–December, 1970. On what happens to women in middle age as a result of their conditioning when younger. Written for the lay reader. Women especially should read it.

Baumgold, Julie, "You've Come a Long Way, Baby," *New York,* June 9, 1969.

Baym, Nina, "Hawthorne's Women: The Tyranny of Social Myths," *The Centennial Review,* Summer, 1971.

Beard, Mary A. [Ritter], *Woman as Force in History* (The Macmillan Company, 1946).

Beasley, Edna, "What a Young Man Can Learn from an Older Woman," *Eye,* December, 1968.

Beauvoir: *see* de Beauvoir.

Bell, Inge Powell, "The Double Standard," *trans/action,* November–December, 1970.

Bem, Sandra, and Daryl Bem, "We're All Non-Conscious Sexists," *Psychology Today,* November, 1970. You may find that this one helps your feminist consciousness a bit.

Benston, Margaret, "The Political Economy of Women's Liberation," *Monthly Review,* September, 1969. A standard reference, now, on the economics of what happens to women in America. The politics are subject to argument; the figures aren't.

Bernard, Jessie, *Academic Women* (The Pennsylvania State University Press, 1964). A solid study.

———, *The Future of Marriage.* Unpublished but in galley proofs as this is written; it's probably out as you read this. An unsensational, scholarly work on the truly devastating effect of marriage and motherhood on the mental condition of American women. Includes research figures covering more than a generation.

———, *The Sex Game* (Prentice-Hall, Inc., 1968). This sociologist has been fighting discrimination for a long time.

———, *Women and the Public Interest* (Aldine-Atherton, Inc., 1971).

Bernstein, Judi, Peggy Morton, Linda Seese and Myrna Wood, *Sisters, Brothers, Lovers . . . Listen . . .* (New England Free Press, 1967). One of the first documents from the feminist movement within The Movement. Anthologized in Roszak and Roszak.

Bettelheim, Bruno, "Commitment Required of a Woman," in Mattfeld and Van Aken.

———, "Growing Up Female," *Harper's,* October, 1962. A fine example of masculinist Freudianism in more or less lay language.

Bieri, J., "Paternal Identification, Acceptance of Authority, and Within-Sex Differences in Cognitive Behavior," *Journal of Abnormal and Social Psychology,* 1960.

————, Wendy M. Bradburn and M. D. Galisky, "Sex Differences in Cognitive Behavior," *Journal of Personality,* 1958.

Binger, Carl, "The Pressures on College Girls Today," *Atlantic Monthly,* February, 1961.

Bird, Caroline, *Born Female: The High Cost of Keeping Women Down* (David McKay Company, Inc., 1968; Pocket Books, 1969). Another book it wouldn't hurt you to read. Lots of facts. You need it especially if you ever hire people.

Blom, Gaston E., Richard R. Waite and Sara Zimet, "Content of First-Grade Reading Books," *The Reading Teacher,* January, 1968. *See also* Waite *et al.*

Blood, Robert O., Jr., and Donald M. Wolfe, *Husbands and Wives: The Dynamics of Married Living* (The Free Press, 1964). Not a popular-type book, but it has a lot of good stuff in it.

Blume, Walter, "They Passed the Symphony's Screen Test," *California Living,* February 2, 1969. *California Living* is a magazine section in San Francisco's weird hybrid Sunday newspaper.

Bonaparte, Marie, *Female Sexuality* (Grove Press, 1965; orig. publ. 1953). Discussed in the text. Not recommended.

Borgese, Elisabeth Mann, *Ascent of Woman* (George Braziller, Inc., 1963). Well written, but a little strange. Save it for later.

Boston Women's Health Course Collective, *Our Bodies, Our Selves* (New England Free Press, 1971). Originally titled *Women and Their Bodies.*

Bradley, Mike, Lonnie Danchik, Marty Fager and Tom Wodetzki, *Unbecoming Men* (Times Change Press, 1971). A dialogue in which four "Movement" men try to deal with their masculinism. A noble try, but there is little to learn from reading it.

Bread and Roses Working Women's Collective, "You Can't Fire the Revolution," *Off Our Backs,* May 16, 1970. On bringing women's liberation to the office. Funny and important.

Brecher, Ruth, and Edward Brecher (eds.), *An Analysis of Human Sexual Response* (The New American Library, Inc., 1966). Masters and Johnson made relatively easy in paperback form. Good.

Brenton, Myron, *The American Male* (Coward-McCann, Inc., 1966; Fawcett Premier Books, 1970). This is an absolute must for you, and your old lady might like it too. The original dust jacket, incidentally, calls it a "penetrating" book, which is interesting.

Bronfenbrenner, Urie, "Some Familiar Antecedents of Responsibility and Leadership in Adolescents," in Luigi Petrullo and Bernard M. Bass (eds.), *Leadership and Interpersonal Behavior* (Holt, Rinehart and Winston, 1961).

Brown, Charles H., *William Cullen Bryant* (Charles Scribner's Sons, 1971).

Brown, Daniel G., "Sex Role Development in a Changing Culture," *Psychological Bulletin,* April, 1958.

Brownmiller, Susan, "Best Battles Are Fought by Men and Women Together," *The Village Voice,* May 22, 1969.

———, "Speaking Out on Prostitution," in Koedt, *Notes.*

Buck, Pearl, *Of Men and Women* (The John Day Company, Inc., 1941).

Buhler, Charlotte, "The Curve of Life as Studied in Biographies," *Journal of Applied Psychology,* August, 1935. Some earlier support for Pauline Bart's findings about menopause, and some other set-breaking on the same subject.

Bunting, Mary I., "A Huge Waste: Educated Womanpower," *The New York Times Magazine,* May 7, 1961.

Burris, Barbara, "The Fourth World Manifesto," in Koedt, *Notes.* The byline reads: "In agreement with Kathy Barry, Terry Moon, Joann DeLor, Joann Parent, Cate Stadelman."

Buytendijk, Frederik J. J., *Women: A Contemporary View* (Newman Press [Glen Rock, N.J.] and Association Press, 1968). Translated by Denis J. Barrett. Weighty continental psychology. You can skip it.

Cade, Toni (ed.), *The Black Woman* (The New American Library, 1970). Readily available paperback. Recommended.

Caldwell, Taylor, "Women Get a Dirty Deal," *The Saturday Evening Post,* May 25, 1963.

Calverton, V. F., and S. D. Schmalhausen, *Sex in Civilization* (MacCauley [New York], 1929). Teutonic-Marxist, but more or less on the right side.

Canary, Betty, *Surviving as a Woman* (Henry Regnery Company, 1970).

Carroll, Berenice, "The Professional Status of Women in History." A paper delivered at the 66th Annual Meeting, American Political Science Association, September 9, 1970.

Carson, Josephine, *Silent Voices* (Delacorte Press, 1969; Delta Books, 1971). On the contemporary Southern black woman.

Catt, Carrie Chapman, and Nettie Rogers Shuler, *Woman Suffrage and Politics* (Charles Scribner's Sons, 1926). The first feminist movement, in America anyway.

Chapman, J. Dudley, *The Feminine Mind and Body* (The Citadel Press, 1968).

Chesler, Phyllis, "Men Drive Women Crazy," *Psychology Today,* July, 1971. The title is meant to be taken literally. Look this one up.

Child, Irvin L., Elmer H. Potter and Estelle M. Levine, "Children's Textbooks and Personality Development," *Psychological Monographs,* 1946.

Clark, Edith, "Trying to Be Modern," *The Nation,* August 17, 1927. A delightful report on the tribulations of a female writer in a very small town in the Midwest.

Clark, Mae Knight, *Lands of Pleasure* (The Macmillan Company; California State Department of Education, 1969).

Coffey, Warren [untitled review], *Commentary,* November, 1965.

Coleman, Kate, "Carnal Knowledge: A Portrait of Four Hookers," *Ramparts,* December, 1971. Surely the most dedicated piece of journalism in recent years.

Converse, Philip E., and Jean M. Converse, "The Status of Women as Students and Professionals in Political Science," *PS,* Summer, 1971.

Cooke, Joanne, Charlotte Bunch-Weeks and Robin Morgan (eds.), *The New Women* (The Bobbs-Merrill Co., Inc., 1970; Fawcett World Library, 1971). One of the basic collections. Read it.

Cronan, Sheila, "Marriage," in Koedt, *Notes.*

Cussler, Margaret, *The Woman Executive* (Harcourt, Brace and World, Inc., 1958).

Daly, Mary, *The Church and the Second Sex* (Harper and Row, 1968). Masculinism among the Catholics.

Dean, Heather, "The Sexual Caste System," *Random,* October, 1966. *Random* is a publication of the University of Toronto.

De Baggio, Thomas, "Puffery or Effrontery?" *The Nation,* January 17, 1972. Partly about gender roles in advertising.

de Beauvoir, Simone, *The Second Sex* (Alfred A. Knopf, Inc., 1953; Bantam Books, Inc., 1961 and ever since; originally published in France in 1949). *The* book. You'll probably have to read it sooner or later, and if you really care, you ought to. It isn't easy, and a little of it is outdated, but it's worth it.

De Crow, Karen, *The Young Woman's Guide to Liberation* (Pegasus Books, 1971). For girls between 13 and 18, depending on how bright they are, who don't otherwise have contact with the women's movement, this is a good one. Keep it around for your daughter and take a peek at it once in a while yourself. Deals with roles; doesn't go into politics much.

Decter, Midge, "The Liberated Woman," *Commentary,* October, 1970. A woman should probably evaluate this; it sounds fatuous and condescending to me. Terrible on men.

de Ford, Miriam Allen, "Women against Themselves," *The Humanist,* January–February, 1971. Nice.

dell'Olio, Anselma, "The Founding of the New Feminist Theatre," in

Firestone and Koedt. As I said, the feminist consciousness, once it gets started, gets into everything. This is good on how it gets into art.

Densmore, Dana, "Independence from the Sexual Revolution," in Koedt, *Notes.*

de Rham, Edith, *The Love Fraud* (Clarkson N. Potter, Inc., 1965; Pegasus Books, n.d.). Pretty good. Very good for you if you think childbearing is "creative."

Deutsch, Helene, *The Psychology of Women* (Grune and Stratton; Vol. 1, 1944; Vol. 2, 1945). The basic Freudian work on the subject. Discussed in the text and by Friedan and Millett.

Devlin, Bernadette, *The Price of My Soul* (Alfred A. Knopf, Inc., 1969; Vintage Books, 1970).

Dinerman, Beatrice, "Sex Discrimination in the Legal Professions," *American Bar Association Journal,* October, 1969.

———, "Women in Architecture," *Architectural Forum,* December, 1969. As you may have guessed, Dinerman is a student of sex discrimination in the professions.

———, "Women in Engineering Firms: Their Status and Prospects," *Consulting Engineer,* February, 1969.

Dingwall, Eric, *The American Woman* (Rinehart and Company, 1956).

Dixon, Marlene, "The Rise of Women's Liberation," *Ramparts,* December, 1969. A standard of the women's movement. Included in Roszak and Roszak.

Dixon, Ruth B., "Hallelujah the Pill?" *trans/action,* November–December, 1970.

Drabble, Margaret, "Doris Lessing: Cassandra in a World under Siege," *Ramparts,* February, 1972.

Dreifus, Claudia, *Radical Lifestyles* (Lancer Books, 1971).

———, "The Selling of a Feminist," *The Nation,* June 7, 1971; reprinted in Koedt, *Notes.* If you have read Germaine Greer, you should read this.

Dresser, Mary, "Newsroom Bias: Establishment Style," *Off Our Backs,* April 25, 1970. Colleagues in journalism please copy.

Dudar, Helen, Judith Gingold and Nancy Dooley, "Women in Revolt," special section, *Newsweek,* March 23, 1970. Excellent, sensitive reporting.

Duvergé, Maurice, *The Political Role of Women* (UNESCO [Paris], 1955). "Political" in the narrower sense.

Edwards, Allen, and R. E. L. Masters, *The Cradle of Erotica* (The Julian Press, 1963). Not the Masters of Masters and Johnson. This is more about Eastern and African sex practices than about women.

Efron, Edith, "Is Television Making a Mockery of the American Woman?" *TV Guide,* August 8–14, 1970. The answer is "yes." This is Efron the good reporter, not Efron being a right-wing news "analyst," in case you've encountered her book.

Eisenberg, Ira, "The New Feminists," documentary for KPIX, San Francisco, telecast March 21, 1972. A rare serious effort, and done well. If there's a Westinghouse outlet in your town, get them to telecast it; they can get it.

Eliasberg, Ann, "Are You Hurting Your Child without Knowing it?" *Family Circle,* February, 1971.

Ellis, Havelock, *Man and Woman* (Houghton Mifflin Company, 1929).

Ellis, Julie, *Revolt of the Second Sex* (Lancer Books, 1970). Strictly a rip-off. Don't even steal it.

Ellmann, Mary, *Thinking about Women* (Harcourt, Brace and World, Inc., 1968). Not about liberation, but has some good stuff. You might read this one on the side.

Epstein, Cynthia Fuchs, *Woman's Place* (University of California Press, 1970). One of the more serious studies. Lots of data. Good.

Erikson, Erik, "Womanhood and the Inner Space," *Daedalus,* Spring, 1964. You'd have to call this psychoanalytic essay "notorious." Millett is only one of many writers who have demonstrated its absurdity, but it continues to be influential among psychiatrists. It claims to prove some things "natural," but clearly doesn't.

Esquire, "The American Woman," special issue, July, 1962.

Evertts, Eldonna L., and Byron H. Van Roekel, *Crossroads* (Harper and Row Basic Reading Program; California State Department of Education, 1969).

Fanon, Frantz, *The Wretched of the Earth* (Grove Press, 1963). If you've read it, *see* Burris.

Farber, Seymour M., and Roger H. L. Wilson (eds.), *The Potential of Woman* (McGraw-Hill Book Company, Inc., 1963). A standard, available in paperback. Worth buying for Maccoby's essay alone, but do get it and read it all. A few essays are nonsense, but you can spot them by now.

Farnham, Marynia, and Ferdinand Lundberg, *Modern Woman: The Lost Sex* (Universal Library, 1947; originally published 1942). Some more nonsense, more or less Freudian. Friedan polishes it off pretty well.

Farrell, Warren, "The Resocialization of Men towards Women's Role in Society." A paper delivered at the 66th Annual Meeting, American Political Science Association, September 9, 1970.

FCL; *see* Feminists on Children's Literature.

The Feminists, position paper on membership requirements, August 8, 1969.

Feminists on Children's Literature, "A Feminist Look at Children's Books," *School Library Journal,* January 15, 1971; reprinted in Koedt, *Notes*; originally a presentation at a symposium during the joint meeting of The Children's Book Council and The Authors Guild of America, October, 1970.

Feminists on Children's Media, "Little Miss Muffet Fights Back." This is an annotated bibliography of children's books which avoid masculinism. Copies of this pamphlet as well as reprints of "A Feminist Look at Children's Books" are available, each at 50¢ plus a stamped (16¢), self-addressed envelope (4 x 9½ or larger), from Feminists on Children's Media, P.O. Box 4315, Grand Central Station, New York, N.Y. 10017.

Ferguson, Charles, *The Male Attitude* (Little, Brown and Company, 1966). Recommended.

Ferro, Nancy, Coletta Reid Holcomb and Marilyn Salzman-Webb, "Setting It Straight," *Off Our Backs,* April 25, 1970. About the attitude of a part of the women's movement toward news media.

Figes, Eva, *Patriarchal Attitudes* (Stein and Day, 1970; Fawcett World Library, 1971). You're ready for this one right now. It's on the "must" list.

Finck, Henry T., "Are Womanly Women Doomed?" *The Independent,* January, 1901. Masculinist arguments never change.

Firestone, Shulamith, "The Bar as Microcosm," in Tanner. About drinkers, not lawyers; but she has much to learn about bars.

———, *The Dialectic of Sex* (William Morrow and Company, 1970; Bantam Books, Inc., 1971). Exciting, exasperating, brilliant, wildly opinionated, deeply probing, arrogant, challenging—a fascinating mind too strongly convinced by too few data. And she should have stayed away from ecology. The best word is "precocious." Read it with your mind wide open, but your skepticism alert. But read it.

———, and Anne Koedt (eds.), *Notes from the Second Year* (Radical Feminism, 1970). Primarily for intelligent "women not yet in the feminist movement," and nearly essential to them. Many of the contents anthologized; some listed separately herein.

Fisher, Elizabeth, "Nature and the Animal Determinists," *The Nation,* January 17, 1972. Read this if you have ever read anything by Lionel Tiger. *See also* Judith Shapiro.

———, "The Second Sex, Junior Division," *The New York Times Book Review,* May 24, 1970. On children's books.

Fisher, Karen, "Women's Magazines: Cashing In on Fear and Fantasy," *The Nation,* October 11, 1971.

Flexner, Eleanor, *Century of Struggle* (The Harvard University Press, 1959; Atheneum Publishers [paper], 1968). The best history of the earlier feminist struggle in America; you need it to counter all the nonsense you were taught.

Ford, Clellan S., and Frank A. Beach, *Patterns of Sexual Behavior* (Harper and Brothers, 1951).

Ford, Hal, "Mail and Female," *California Living,* October 31, 1971.

Foster, Anne Tolstoi, "Is That Really Me?" *TV Guide,* June 19, 1971. On the image of woman in television commercials.

Fowler, Herbert B., "Police Handling of Emotionally Disturbed People," *FBI Law Enforcement Bulletin,* January, 1971. Describes three types of emotionally disturbed people; all three sections illustrated with photos of policemen dealing with women.

Freeman, Barbara, "The Polemic of an Ex-Shit-Worker," *Velvet Glove,* December, 1971–January, 1972. She was an office worker at *Rolling Stone.*

Freeman, Jo, "The Building of the Gilded Cage," in Koedt, *Notes.*

——, "Growing Up Girlish," *trans/action,* November–December, 1970.

——, "The New Feminists," *The Nation,* February 24, 1969.

——, "The Revolution Is Happening in Our Minds," *College and University Business,* February, 1970. Discrimination in academia.

——, "Women's Liberation and Its Impact on the Campus," paper delivered at the 66th Annual Meeting, American Political Science Association, September 12, 1970.

——, [as "Joreen"], "The Bitch Manifesto," in Firestone and Koedt.

Friedan, Betty, *The Feminine Mystique* (W. W. Norton and Company, Inc., 1963; Dell Publishing Co., Inc. [paper], 1964). A lot of this is still as good as new. If you haven't read it—or read it lately—by all means do.

——, "Women Are People Too!" *Good Housekeeping,* September, 1960.

——, "Woman: The Fourth Dimension," *Ladies' Home Journal,* June, 1964.

Frisof, Jamie Kelem, "Textbooks and Channeling," *Women: A Journal of Liberation,* Fall, 1969.

Gallen, Richard T., *Wives' Legal Rights* (Dell Publishing Company, 1967).

Galligan, Edward, "Marriage on the Rocks," *Ramparts,* February, 1967. A takeoff on those "marriage manuals." Hilarious—and the book he's reviewing really exists.

Gallup, George, and Evan Hill, "The American Woman," *The Saturday Evening Post,* December 22, 1962.

Gans, Herbert J., *The Urban Villagers* (The Free Press, 1962). Includes good portrayals of gender roles, even when he's not being explicit about them.

Gardner, Jennifer, "False Consciousness," in Firestone and Koedt; originally published in *Tooth and Nail*. This is really for women, but it may help you to grasp the concept.

Gardner, Jo Ann, "Sesame Street and Sex-Role Stereotypes," *Women: A Journal of Liberation*, Spring, 1970. Just what it sounds like.

Garskof, Michele H. (ed.), *The Psychology of Women's Liberation: Readings* (Brooks, Cole Publishing Company [Belmont, Calif.], 1971).

Gasiorowska, Xenia, *Women in Soviet Fiction, 1917–1964* (University of Wisconsin Press, 1970).

Gilman, Charlotte Perkins, *Women and Economics* (Small and Maynard [Boston], 1898). An amazingly contemporary book.

Ginzberg, Eli, and Alice M. Yohadem, *Educated American Women: Self-Portraits* (Columbia University Press, 1966).

Glass, David C. (ed.), *Biology and Behavior* (The Russell Sage Foundation, 1968).

Goldberg, Philip, "Are Women Prejudiced against Women?" *trans/action*, April, 1968. A report on a fascinating experiment demonstrating the power of conditioning (and the importance of remembering Jo Freeman's Rule).

Golder, Evan, "A Glimpse of the Gay Life," *California Living*, January 2, 1972.

Goode, William J., *World Revolution and Family Patterns* (Prentice-Hall, Inc., 1964).

Gornick, Vivian, "The Next Great Moment in History Is Theirs," *The Village Voice*, November 27, 1969.

———, and Barbara K. Moran (eds.), *Woman in Sexist Society* (Basic Books, Inc., 1971).

Goulden, Joseph C., "A Peek at the Books," *The Nation*, January 10, 1972. On the government's investigation of the exploitation of women by the phone company.

Gray, Madeline, *The Normal Woman* (Charles Scribner's Sons, 1967).

Gray, Susan W., "Masculinity-Femininity in Relation to Anxiety and Social Acceptance," *Child Development*, June, 1957.

Green, Constance, *A Girl Called Al* (The Viking Press, Inc., 1969). Example of an almost-good children's book that cops out at the end.

Greer, Germaine, *The Female Eunuch* (McGraw-Hill Book Co., 1971; Bantam Books, Inc. [paper], 1972; originally published in Great Britain, 1970). *Newsweek* called it "a dazzling combination of erudition, eccentricity, and eroticism." That'll do. If you've already read it, be sure to read Dreifus' *Nation* piece. If not, by all means read both. I

285

would recommend this book much more heartily if I weren't convinced that Greer doesn't really like women.

Guetzkow, H., "An Analysis of the Operation of Set in Problem-solving Behavior," *Journal of Genetic Psychology,* 1951.

Hacker, Helen Mayer, "Why Can't a Woman . . . ?" *The Humanist,* January–February, 1971.

———, "Women as a Minority Group," *Social Forces,* October, 1951. An early, and scholarly, examination of some ways in which women are treated like blacks or other minorities.

Hall, Edward T., *The Silent Language* (Doubleday and Company, Inc., 1959).

Hall, Trish, "Pauline Bart—The Sociology of Women's Oppression," *the every other weekly,* May 12, 1970.

Hamilton, Alice, *Exploring the Dangerous Trades* (Little, Brown and Company, 1943).

Hanisch, Carol, "A Critique of the Miss America Protest," in Firestone and Koedt.

———, "Hard Knocks: Working for Women's Liberation in a Mixed (Male-Female) Movement Group," in Firestone and Koedt.

———, "The Personal Is Political," in Firestone and Koedt.

Harding, M. Esther, *The Way of All Women* (David McKay Company, Inc., 1962).

Hardwick, Elizabeth, "A Doll's House," *The New York Review of Books,* March 11, 1971.

———, "Ibsen and Women II: Hedda Gabler," *The New York Review of Books,* March 25, 1971.

———, "Ibsen and Women III: The Rosmersholm Triangle," *The New York Review of Books,* April 8, 1971.

Hare, Nathan, and Julia Hare, "Black Women 1970," *trans/action,* November–December, 1970.

Harper's special supplement on "The American Female," October, 1962.

Harris, Marvin, "Warfare Old and New," *Natural History,* March, 1972. A somewhat different approach to the idea of how masculinism "originated" in primitive cultures.

Hartley, Ruth E., "Children's Concepts of Male and Female Roles," *Merrill-Palmer Quarterly,* January, 1960.

———, "Sex-Role Pressures and the Socialization of the Male Child," *Psychological Reports,* 1959.

———, "Woman's Roles: How Girls See Them," *A.A.U.W. Journal,* May, 1962. The entire issue is on "Change and Choice for the College Woman."

Hays, H. R., *The Dangerous Sex* (G. P. Putnam's Sons, 1964).

Heer, David M., "Dominance and the Working Wife," *Social Forces,* May, 1958.

Heidensohn, Frances, "The Deviance of Women: A Critique and an Enquiry," *The British Journal of Sociology,* June, 1968. About how masculinist sociologists go about studying female "deviance."

Henry, Jules, "Education for Stupidity," *The New York Review of Books,* May 9, 1968.

Hentoff, Margot, "The Curse," *The New York Review of Books,* January 16, 1969.

————, "Even My Name Is Not My Own," *The Village Voice,* October 5, 1967.

Hernton, Calvin C., *Sex and Racism in America* (Grove Press, 1965).

Heyn, Leah, "Children's Books," *Women: A Journal of Liberation,* Fall, 1969.

Himber, Charlotte, "So He Hates Baseball," *The New York Times Magazine,* August 29, 1965.

Hinckle, Warren, III, and Marianne Hinckle, "Woman Power," *Ramparts,* February, 1968. Listed as "reporters on this project" are Peter Collier, Art Goldberg, Sandy Levinson and Marilyn [Salzman-] Webb, some of whom would certainly rather not be reminded. The article is inaccurate, condescending, masculinist and absurd; this one I *don't* apologize for having opposed.

Hobbs, Lisa, *Love and Liberation* (McGraw-Hill Book Company, 1970).

Hochschild, Arlie, "The American Woman: Another Idol of Social Science," *trans/action,* November–December, 1970.

Hole, Judith, and Ellen Levine, *The Rebirth of Feminism* (Quadrangle/ World, 1972).

Holiday, Billie (with William Dufty), *Lady Sings the Blues* (Doubleday and Company, Inc., 1956; Lancer Books, 1965).

Honigmann, John J., *Personality in Culture* (Harper and Row, 1967).

Horner, Matina S., "Fail: Bright Woman," *Psychology Today,* November, 1969. Listed in some bibliographies as "Woman's Will to Fail." A report on how young women have been trained to see themselves as non-achievers, regardless of the level of their intelligence.

Horney, Karen, *Feminine Psychology* (W. W. Norton and Company, Inc., 1967).

Houghton, Walter E., *The Victorian Frame of Mind, 1830–1870* (Wellesley College-Yale University Press, 1957).

Howe, Florence, "The Education of Women," *Liberation,* August–September, 1969.

———, "Liberated Chinese Primers (Let's Write Some Too)," *Women: A Journal of Liberation,* Fall, 1970.

———, "A Talk with Doris Lessing," *The Nation,* March 6, 1967.

Hunt, Persis, "Feminism and Anti-Clericalism under the Commune," *Massachusetts Review,* Summer, 1971.

Irwin, Inez Haynes, "These Modern Women: The Making of a Militant," *The Nation,* December 1, 1926.

Iverson, Lucille (interviewer), "A Female Junkie Speaks," in Firestone and Koedt.

Jelinek, Estelle, and Lucinda Hanchett, "Body and Soul: Two Letters to Gynecologists," *Libera,* Winter, 1972. *See* Judith Wells.

Jennings, M. Kent, and Richard G. Niemi, "The Division of Political Labor between Mothers and Fathers," *The American Political Science Review,* March, 1971.

Jones, Beverly, and Judith Benninger Brown, *Toward a Female Liberation Movement* (New England Free Press, 1968). Another early and extremely influential essay in the beginning days of the women's movement. Originally printed by the Southern Students Organizing Committee, Nashville, Tenn. Reprinted in Tanner.

Jordan, Joan, *The Place of American Women* (New England Free Press, 1969; originally published in *Revolutionary Age,* 1968). A Marxist analysis containing much hard information on working women.

———, "Working Women and the Equal Rights Amendment," *trans/action,* November–December, 1970.

Joreen: *see* Jo Freeman.

Josselyn, Irene M., "Cultural Forces, Motherliness and Fatherliness," *American Journal of Orthopsychiatry,* April, 1956.

Julia (pseud.), "The Pill . . . ?" *It Ain't Me, Babe,* January 29, 1970.

Kael, Pauline, "Winging It," *The New Yorker,* November 27, 1971.

Kagin, Jerome, "The Acquisition and Significance of Sex-Typing," in M. Hoffman (ed.), *Review of Child Development Research* (The Russell Sage Foundation, 1964).

Kanowitz, Leo, *Women and the Law: The Unfinished Revolution* (The University of New Mexico Press, 1969).

Kaplow, Susi, "Getting Angry," in Koedt, *Notes.*

Karlinsky, Simon, "Fiction and Policy: The Hard-Worked Heroines," *The Nation,* September 21, 1970.

Karp, Richard, "Newspaper Food Pages: Credibility for Sale," *Columbia Journalism Review,* November–December, 1971.

Kazin, Alfred, "Heroines," *The New York Review of Books,* February 11, 1971.

Kearns, Karen, "The Great Toy Shuck," *Liberation News* Service story in *It Ain't Me, Babe,* January 29, 1970.

Kearon, Pamela, "Man-Hating," in Firestone and Koedt.

———, and Barbara Mehrhof, "Prostitution," in Koedt, *Notes.*

Keller, Marti, "Women and Film," *the every other weekly,* November 10, 1970.

Kennedy, Florynce, "The Whorehouse Theory of Law," in Robert Lefcourt (ed.), *Law against the People* (Random House, Inc., 1971).

Key, Mary Ritchie, "Male and Female in Children's Books—Dispelling All Doubts," *The American Teacher,* February, 1972. Reprinted from *The Wilson Library Bulletin.* The article reports a study by an interdisciplinary group including Marguerite Pinson, Marguerite Sharpe, Marjorie Taylor and Laura Wright.

Kidd, Virginia, "Now You See, Said Mark," *The New York Review of Books,* September 3, 1970.

Kinsey, Alfred C., *et al., Sexual Behavior in the Human Female* (Saunders, 1953).

———, *Sexual Behavior in the Human Male* (Saunders, 1949).

Klein, Viola, *The Feminine Character* (Kegan Paul, Trench, Trubner and Company, Ltd. [London], 1946).

Knowles, Louis, and Kenneth Prewitt, *Institutional Racism in America* (Prentice-Hall, Inc., 1969; Spectrum Books [paper], 1970). Amundsen shows how these concepts apply to women.

Koch, Adrienne, "Two Cheers for Equality," in Farber and Wilson.

Koedt, Anne, "Lesbianism and Feminism," in Koedt, *Notes.*

——— (interview), "Loving Another Woman," in Koedt, *Notes.* Excerpted in *Ms.,* Spring, 1972.

———, *The Myth of the Vaginal Orgasm* (New England Free Press, 1969). Reprinted in Tanner.

——— (ed.), *Notes from the Third Year* (Notes from the Second Year, Inc., 1971). Most bookstores that carry a lot of paperbacks will have this, and so should you.

———, "Politics of the Ego: A Manifesto for New York Radical Feminists," in Firestone and Koedt.

———, "Some Male Responses," *Lilith #2,* Spring, 1969. Reprinted in Tanner.

Kollontoi, Alexandra, *The Autobiography of a Sexually Emancipated Communist Woman* (Herder and Herder, 1971).

Komarovsky, Mirra, *Blue-Collar Marriage* (Vintage Books, 1962). If you want to see gender roles at work, read this one.

———, "Cultural Contradictions and Sex Roles," *The American Journal of Sociology,* November, 1946.

———, "Functional Analysis of Sex Roles," *American Sociological Review,* August, 1950.

————, *Women in the Modern World: Their Education and Their Dilemmas* (Little, Brown and Company, 1953).

Komisar, Lucy, *The New Feminism* (Franklin Watts, Inc., 1971). Put this one on your list, too. It's a little more "liberal" than "radical," but to most of us *any* feminism is radical.

Koss, Linda, "Women's Liberation in the Media: Feminists or Female Hitlers?" *Libera,* Winter, 1972. Another one for my fellow reporters to pay attention to. *See* Judith Wells.

Kraditor, Aileen S., *Up from the Pedestal* (Quadrangle Books, 1968).

Lagemann, John Kord, "The Male Sex," *Redbook,* December, 1956.

Lang, Frances, "The Sickle Cell and the Pill," *Ramparts,* February, 1972. If you ever even think about "birth control" and "blacks" in the same instant, regardless of your color, then look this up. But see also letters in subsequent issues.

Lang, Theo, *The Difference between a Man and a Woman* (The John Day Company, 1971).

Langer, Elinor, "Inside the New York Telephone Company," *The New York Review of Books,* March 12, 1970.

————, "The Women of the Telephone Company," *The New York Review of Books,* March 26, 1970.

La Rue, Linda J. M., "Black Liberation and Women's Lib," *trans/action,* November–December, 1970. It's a little presumptuous to say so, but I know some blacks I wish would read this.

Lasch, Christopher, "Feminist Ideology," *Commentary,* April, 1966.

Lawson, John Howard, *Film in the Battle of Ideas* (Masses and Mainstream, 1953). Includes some comments on the portrayal of women.

Leach, Edmund, "Telstar and the Aborigines," in Dorothy Emmet and Alasdair MacIntyre (eds.), *Sociological Theory and Philosophical Analysis* (Macmillan and Company, Ltd. [London], 1970).

Leary, Mary Ellen, "The New State of California," *The Nation,* March 27, 1972.

Leo, André, "ADC: Marriage to the State," in Koedt, *Notes.*

Lessing, Doris, *Children of Violence.* See especially the first four novels of this five-novel series—*Martha Quest, A Proper Marriage, A Ripple from the Storm* and *Landlocked.* All were issued in paperback as Plume Books by The New American Library in 1970. The second is a particularly devastating description of the frustrations of an intelligent woman in a "respectable" marriage.

————, *The Golden Notebook* (Simon and Schuster, 1962; Ballantine Books, Inc., 1968). A novel beloved of feminists, with reason.

Levy, D. M., *Maternal Overprotection* (Columbia University Press, 1943).

Life, "The American Woman," special issue, January 7, 1957.

Lifton, Robert J. (ed.), *The Woman in America* (Houghton Mifflin Company, 1965).

Limpus, Laurel, *Liberation of Women: Sexual Repression and the Family* (New England Free Press, 1969).

Lippincott, Helene, "Male Chauvinism at Candlestick Park," *The San Francisco Bay Guardian,* December 22, 1971.

Lippmann, Walter, *Drift and Mastery* (Mitchell Kennerly, 1914).

Lopata, Helena Znaniecki, *Occupation: Housewife* (Oxford University Press, 1971).

Luce, Clare Boothe, "But Some People Simply Never Get the Message," *Life,* June 28, 1963.

Luce, Gay Gaer, *Body Time* (Pantheon Books, 1971). Men have periods too.

Lydon, Susan, "Understanding Orgasm," *Ramparts,* December, 1968. Included in Roszak and Roszak. Revised and expanded for inclusion in Morgan, *Sisterhood,* as "The Politics of Orgasm."

Maccoby, Eleanor (ed.), *The Development of Sex Differences* (Stanford University Press, 1966).

————, "Woman's Intellect," in Farber and Wilson.

————, and Lucy Rau, *Differential Cognitive Abilities* (Owen House, Stanford University, 1962).

MacDonald, John D., *Death Trap* (Fawcett Gold Medal Books, 1957).

————, *A Tan and Sandy Silence* (Fawcett Gold Medal Books, 1971).

Macfarlane, Jean, and Lester Sontag. A paper delivered to the Commission on the Education of Women, Washington, D.C., 1954.

Mailer, Norman, "The Prisoner of Sex," *Harper's,* March, 1971. How can a man who writes so beautifully be such an idiot?

Mainardi, Pat, "The Politics of Housework," in Tanner (in a revised 1970 version of the original 1968 essay) and in Morgan, *Sisterhood* (ditto). You absolutely *must* read this hilarious, but perfectly serious, essay.

Malinowski, Bronislaw, *Argonauts of the Western Pacific* (E. P. Dutton and Company, Inc., 1922).

————, *Sex, Culture and Myth* (Harcourt, Brace and Company, Inc., 1962).

Mann, Nancy, *Fucked-up in America* (New England Free Press, 1969).

Mannes, Marya, "Female Intelligence—Who Wants It?" *The New York Times Magazine,* January 3, 1970. *See also* subsequent discussion in the issue of January 17.

————, "Forgive Me, But My Mind Shows," *Vogue,* May, 1963.

————, "I, Mary, Take Thee, John, as . . . What?" *The New York Times Magazine,* November 14, 1965.

291

Marine, Gene, "New Look at the Oldest Difference," *The Nation,* March 23, 1963.

———, "Who's Afraid of Little Annie Fanny?" *Ramparts,* February, 1967.

———, with Art Goldberg, "Abortion Reform: A Big Step Forward? No," *Ramparts,* July, 1967.

Martyna, Wendy, "How to Degrade, Demean and Distort in Less than 25 Steps," *Libera,* Winter, 1972. More lessons for the press (but I wish she'd said "fewer"). *See* Judith Wells.

Maslow, A. H., "Dominance, Personality and Social Behavior in Women," *Journal of Social Psychology,* 1939.

Masters, W. H., and Virginia Johnson, *Human Sexual Response* (Little, Brown and Company, 1966).

Mattfeld, Jacquelyn A., and Carol G. Van Aken, *Women and the Scientific Professions* (MIT Press, 1965).

McAfee, Kathy, and Myrna Wood, "Bread and Roses," *Leviathan #3,* June, 1969. Reprinted in Tanner.

McCracken, Glenn, and Charles E. Walcutt, *Basic Reading* (J. D. Lippincott Company, 1963; California State Department of Education, 1969).

McKee, J. P., and A. C. Sherriff, "The Differential Evaluation of Males and Females," *Journal of Personality,* 1957.

Mead, Margaret, *Male and Female* (William Morrow and Company, 1949; Mentor Books, 1955).

———, "New Look at Early Marriages," *U. S. News and World Report,* June 6, 1960.

———, *Sex and Temperament in Three Primitive Societies* (William Morrow and Company, 1935).

———, "A Theory of Male Superiority—Turned Upside Down," *Redbook,* November, 1969. A critical review of Tiger's *Men in Groups.*

Meade, Marion, "Miss Muffet Must Go: A Mother Fights Back," *Woman's Day,* March, 1971.

Mehrhof, Barbara, "On Class Structure within the Women's Movement," in Firestone and Koedt.

———, and Pamela Kearon, "Rape: An Act of Terror," in Koedt, *Notes.*

Menzer-Benaron, Doris, *et al.,* "Patterns of Emotional Recovery from Hysterectomy," *Psychosomatic Medicine,* September, 1957.

Merriam, Eve, *After Nora Slammed the Door* (World Publishing Company, 1964).

——— (ed.), *Growing Up Female in America: Ten Lives* (Doubleday and Company, Inc., 1971).

———, *Man and Woman: The Human Condition* (The Research Center on Woman, Loretto Heights College [Denver], 1968).

——, *Mommies At Work* (Alfred A. Knopf, Inc., 1961).

Mews, Hazel, *Frail Vessels: Women's Role in Women's Novels, from Fanny Burney to George Eliot* (Athlone Publishers [London], 1969).

Micossi, Anita Lynn, "Conversion to Women's Lib," *trans/action,* November–December, 1970.

Miles, Betty, "Harmful Lessons Little Girls Learn in School," *Redbook,* March, 1971.

Mill, John Stuart, and Harriet Taylor Mill, *Essays on Sex Equality* [Alice S. Rossi, ed.] (The University of Chicago Press, 1970; originally published 1832, 1851 and 1869).

Millard, Betty, *Woman against Myth* (International Publishers, Inc., 1948).

Millett, Kate, *Sexual Politics* (Doubleday and Company, Inc., 1970). By all means read this one, though you can stop when the literary criticism starts. The first part is the good part.

Mills, C. Wright, "Plain Talk on Fancy Sex," in *Power, Politics and People* (Ballantine Books, Inc., and Oxford University Press, 1963). A wonderful and important man, Mills, but a stone masculinist.

——, "Women: The Darling Little Slaves," in *Power, Politics and People (see above)*. Masculinist review of de Beauvoir.

Milton, G. A., "The Effects of Sex-Role Identification upon Problem-Solving Skill," *Journal of Abnormal and Social Psychology,* 1957.

Mitchell, Juliet, "Mailer's Sex Ego," *Modern Occasions,* Fall, 1971.

——, *Woman's Estate* (Random House, Inc.–Pantheon Books, 1971; originally published in England, 1971). This appeared too late for me to use; Judith recommends it as an extremely important work on the theory of women's liberation.

——, *Women: The Longest Revolution* (Bay Area Radical Education Project [San Francisco], n.d.; reprinted from *New Left Review,* November–December, 1966). Reprinted in Roszak and Roszak. One of the earliest and most important documents of the women's liberation movement.

Mitford, Jessica, *Daughters and Rebels* (Houghton Mifflin Company, 1960; Avon Books, n.d.).

Money, John, *The Psychologic Study of Man* (Charles C. Thomas [Springfield, Ill.], 1957).

—— (ed.), *Sex Research, New Developments* (Holt, Rinehart and Winston, Inc., 1965).

Morgan, Robin, "Goodbye to All That," *Rat: Subterranean News,* February 6, 1970. Reprinted in Roszak and Roszak and in Tanner. Also an extremely influential and widely read essay in the women's movement.

——(ed.), *Sisterhood Is Powerful* (Vintage Books, 1970). Although no one book will do it, this anthology is in my opinion the best single

293

book in the whole women's liberation output. Do not let yourself be without it.

Mortimer, Penelope, *The Pumpkin Eater* (McGraw-Hill Book Company, 1962). For those who prefer novels, a fine portrayal of a woman to whom the childbearing capacity has become her sole function.

Murphy, John, *Homosexual Liberation: A Personal View* (Praeger Publishers, Inc., 1971).

Murray, Pauli, and Mary O. Eastwood, "Jane Crow and the Law: Sex Discrimination and Title VII," *The George Washington Law Review,* December, 1965.

Murtagh, John M., and Sara Harris, *Cast the First Stone* (McGraw-Hill Book Company, 1957).

Mussen, Paul H., and Luther Distler, "Masculinity, Identification and Father-Son Relationships," *The Journal of Abnormal and Social Psychology,* November, 1959.

Myrdal, Gunnar, *An American Dilemma* (Harper and Brothers, 1944). See especially Appendix 5, one of the first serious attempts to draw a parallel between the condition of blacks and that of women.

Nadle, Marlene, "Radical Women: We'd Rather Do It Ourselves," *The Village Voice,* May 15, 1969.

Nash, June, "Devils, Witches and Sudden Death," *Natural History,* March, 1972.

National Organization of Women, "Sex Role Stereotyping in Elementary-School Readers," in *Report on Sex Bias in the Public Schools* (New York, 1971).

Nearing, Scott, and Nellie Nearing, *Woman and Social Progress* (The Macmillan Company, 1912).

Negrin, Su, *A Graphic Notebook on Feminism* (Times Change Press, 1971).

————, "A Weekend in Lesbian Nation," *It Ain't Me, Babe,* April, 1971.

Newton, Niles, "Trebly Sensuous Women," *Psychology Today,* July, 1971.

New York Radical Feminists. A statement of organizing principles, December 5, 1969.

Niebuhr, Reinhold (interview), *McCall's,* February, 1966.

Nilsen, Aileen Pace, "Women in Children's Literature," *College English,* May, 1971.

O'Donnell, Mabel, *All through the Year* (Harper and Row, Inc., 1969).

Olah, Suzie, "The Economic Function of the Oppression of Women," in Firestone and Koedt.

The Old Mole, "No 'Chicks,' 'Broads' or 'Niggers,' " *Nickel Review* [Syracuse, N.Y.], April 13, 1970. Reprinted in Roszak and Roszak. *The Old Mole* is a Boston women's liberation publication. The essay is on masculinism in language; recommended for writers, reporters, columnists and editors.

Oppenheimer, Valerie, "The Sex Labelling of Jobs," *Industrial Relations,* May, 1968.

Orden, Susan R., and Norman M. Bradburn, "Working Wives and Marriage Happiness," *The American Journal of Sociology,* January, 1968.

Ort, Robert S., "A Study of Role Conflicts as Related to Happiness in Marriage," *Journal of Abnormal and Social Psychology.* October, 1950.

Ozick, Cynthia, "The Demise of the Dancing Dog," in Cooke *et al.*; originally published as "An Ovarian Mentality," *Mademoiselle,* March, 1968. Short and well-written, on why there aren't more female artists, scientists, etc.

Parker, Dorothy, *The Portable Dorothy Parker* (The Viking Press, Inc., 1944).

Parsons, Talcott, *Essays in Sociological Theory* (The Free Press, 1949). Masculinism in sociology; *see also* the critique in Friedan.

Patai, Raphael (ed.), *Women in the Modern World* (The Free Press, 1967).

Payne, Carol Williams, "Consciousness Raising: A Dead End?" in Koedt, *Notes.*

Peck, Ellen, "Obituary: Motherhood," *Environmental Quality,* January, 1972.

Peslikis, Irene, "Resistances to Consciousness," in Firestone and Koedt. How some women fight their own liberation.

Pierce, James V., "Sex Differences in Achievement Motivation of Able High School Students," Co-operative Research Project No. 1097, University of Chicago, December, 1961.

Piercy, Marge, "The Movement: For Men Only?" *The Guardian,* February 14, 1970; originally published in *Liberation.*

Pilpel, Harriet F., and Theodora Zavin, *Your Marriage and the Law* (Collier Books, 1964).

Pitcher, Evelyn G., "Male and Female," *Atlantic Monthly,* March, 1963.

Plath, Sylvia, *The Bell Jar* (Harper and Row, 1971; Bantam Books, 1972). A brilliant and talented young woman in the big city, driven mad by being female. A favorite novel of feminists—witty and perceptive.

Post, Suzanne, "The ACLU and Women's Rights," *Civil Liberties,* February, 1972. A good rundown on legal discrimination, including suggestions for legal attack on some problems not usually thought of as susceptible to such an approach.

Powdermaker, Hortense, *Hollywood, The Dream Factory* (Little, Brown and Company, 1950).

———, *Stranger and Friend* (W. W. Norton and Company, Inc., 1966). Another autobiographical demonstration of the importance of early life and conditioning on the development of a talented and accomplished woman.

Pringle, Murray T., "Women Are Wretched Housekeepers," *Science Digest,* June, 1960.

Pruett, Lorine, "Why Women Fail," in Schmalhausen and Calverton.

Psychology Today, "Human Sexuality," special issue, July, 1969.

Rabban, Meyer, "Sex-Role Identification in Young Children in Two Diverse Social Groups," *Genetic Psychological Monographs,* August, 1950.

Radicalesbians, "The Woman Identified Woman," in Koedt, *Notes.*

Radke, M., *The Relation of Parental Authority to Children's Behavior and Attitudes* (The University of Minnesota Press, 1946).

Rainwater, Lee, Richard P. Coleman and Gerald Handel, *Workingman's Wife* (Macfadden Books, 1962; originally published 1959).

Ramey, Estelle, "Men's Cycles (They Have Them Too, You Know)," *Ms.,* Spring, 1972. Dr. Ramey is an endocrinologist.

Redstockings Manifesto (originally mimeographed, New York, July 7, 1969). Widely read and influential. Reprinted in Morgan, *Sisterhood;* in Tanner; and in Roszak and Roszak.

Reed, Evelyn, "The Myth of Women's Inferiority," *The Fourth International,* Spring, 1954 (reprinted in pamphlet form, New England Free Press).

———, *Problems of Women's Liberation: A Marxist Approach* (Pathfinder Press, 1971).

Reeves, Nancy, *Womankind: Beyond the Stereotypes* (Aldine-Atherton, Inc., 1971).

———, "Women's Liberation," *The Nation,* June 16, 1969.

Reiche, Reimut, *Sexuality and Class Struggle* (Praeger Publishers, Inc., 1971). If it sounds like a mix of Freud and Marx, that's because it is.

Riesman, David, "Permissiveness and Sex Roles," *Marriage and Family Living,* August, 1959.

Robinson, Patricia, *Poor Black Women* (New England Free Press, 1968).

Rogers, Katharine M., *The Troublesome Helpmate* (The University of Washington Press, 1966).

Rosen, Diane, "TV and the Single Girl," *TV Guide,* November 6, 1971.

Rosen, Ruth, "The Liberation of Clio," *Libera,* Winter, 1972.

———, "Sexism," *the every other weekly,* November 10, 1970.

Rosenthal, Robert, and Lenore Jacobson, *Pygmalion in the Classroom: Teacher Expectation and Pupils' Intellectual Development* (Holt, Rinehart and Winston, Inc., 1968). Women's liberation aside, this is an extremely important book for anyone who has children in school.

Ross, Edward A., *The Social Trend* (The Century Company, 1922).

Rossi, Alice S., "Job Discrimination and What Women Can Do about It," *Atlantic Monthly,* March, 1970.

———, "Sex Equality: The Beginning of Ideology," *The Humanist,* September–October, 1969. Reprinted in Roszak and Roszak.

———, "The Status of Women in Graduate Departments of Sociology, 1968–9," *American Sociologist,* Fall, 1969.

Rostow, Edna G., "The Best of Both Worlds," *Yale Review,* March, 1962.

Roszak, Betty, and Theodore Roszak (eds.), *Masculine/Feminine* (Harper and Row, 1969). A good anthology of women's liberation writings and related material.

Rowntree, Mickey, and John Rowntree, "More on the Political Economy of Women's Liberation," *Monthly Review,* January, 1970.

Rubin, Gayle, "Woman as Nigger," *The Argus,* March 28–April 11 and April 14–28, 1969. Another of the dozen or so highly influential essays within the movement. Reprinted in Roszak and Roszak.

Rush, Florence, "Woman in the Middle," in Koedt, *Notes.* About the often overlooked problems of women in their fifties.

Ruth (pseud.), "Women and Anti-War Work: Two Perspectives," *It Ain't Me, Babe,* June 11–July 1, 1970.

Rycroft, Charles, "What's So Funny?" *The New York Review of Books,* April 10, 1969. A British analyst on whether dirty jokes express men's hostility toward women.

Sachs, Bernice C., "Woman's Destiny—Choice or Chance," *Journal of the American Medical Women's Association,* August, 1965.

Salzman-Webb, Marilyn, "America's Comic Culture," *Off Our Backs,* April 25, 1970.

———, "Seize the Press, Sisters," *Off Our Backs,* April 25, 1970. Rules for women, unfortunately not including any about writing well.

———, "We Have a Common Enemy," *New Left Notes,* June 10, 1968.

———, "Women Face Oppression as Workers," *The Guardian,* March 15, 1969.

———, and Sue Baker (interview), "Venceremos," *Off Our Backs,* March 19 and April 11, 1970.

Sampson, Ronald V., *The Psychology of Power* (Random House, Inc., 1968).

Sarachild, Kathie, "A Program for Feminist 'Consciousness Raising,' " in Firestone and Koedt. The author was once known as Kathie Amatniek. Figure it out.

Sargeant, Winthrop, "Fifty Years of American Women," *Life,* January 2, 1950.

Sayers, Dorothy L., *Unpopular Opinions* (Harcourt, Brace and Company,

1947). Included here primarily for the essay, "The Human-Not-Quite-Human," which every male member of the press should make every effort to read and which is reprinted by Roszak and Roszak. You can disagree with the religious point at the end of the essay and still benefit from the reading.

Schary, Jill, "The Ostentatious Orgasm," *Cosmopolitan,* January, 1969.

Schiller, Anita, "Women in Library Science," paper delivered at the 66th Annual Meeting, American Political Science Association, September 9, 1970.

Schlesinger, Wendy, "The Women's Defense League," *California Living,* July 18, 1971.

Schmalhausen, Samuel D., and V. F. Calverton, *Woman's Coming of Age* (Horace Liveright, 1931).

School Library Journal (editorial), "Sugar and Spice," January, 1971.

Schreiner, Olive, *The Story of an African Farm* (Fawcett Premier Books, 1968). A startlingly contemporary novel first published in 1883. Chapter 17 is a cogent argument against the restrictions of the feminine role.

Schulder, Diane, and Florynce Kennedy (eds.), *Abortion Rap* (McGraw-Hill Book Company, 1971). Testimony by a number of women in a court challenge to New York's abortion laws.

Schur, Edwin M. (ed.), *The Family and the Sexual Revolution* (The University of Indiana Press, 1964).

Scofield, Nanette E., "Some Changing Roles of Women in Suburbia: A Social Anthropological Case Study," *Transactions of the New York Academy of Sciences,* April, 1960.

Scott, Anne Firor (ed.), *The American Woman: Who Was She?* (Prentice-Hall, Inc., 1971). Fine collection for those who think history is about men.

Scott, Jack, untitled column on female athletes, *Ramparts,* February, 1972.

Sears, R. R., Eleanor Maccoby and H. Levin, *Patterns of Child Rearing* (Row, Peterson and Company, 1957).

Sexton, Patricia Cayo, "Speaking for the Working-Class Wife," *Harper's,* October, 1962.

Shapiro, Judith, "I Went to the Animal Fair . . . The Tiger and Fox Were There," *Natural History,* October, 1971. A must for anyone who has been reading those best-sellers about how we're just like the animals—Ardrey, Tiger, Fox, Morris, *et al.* This review demonstrates their irresponsibility.

Shearer, Derek, "The FBI: Of Peace and War," *Rolling Stone,* April 16, 1970. A hip reporter takes the public FBI tour and innocently asks where the female FBI agents are.

Sheldon, W. H., *The Varieties of Temperament* (Harper and Brothers,

1942). Whenever someone argues that women aren't up to some "man's job" because they're "temperamentally unsuited," either give him this book or throw it at him.

Shelley, Martha, "Subversion in the Women's Movement: What Is To Be Done?" *It Ain't Me, Babe,* October 30, 1970.

Shepard, John P., "The Treatment of Characters in Popular Children's Fiction," *Elementary English,* November, 1962.

Sherman, Julia A., "Problems of Sex Differences in Space Perception and Aspects of Intellectual Functioning," *Psychological Review,* July, 1967.

Sigal, Regina, "Women Hold Their Own," *Off Our Backs,* March 19, 1970. A good summary of the anti-Pill evidence to that point.

Sinclair, Andrew, *The Better Half: The Emancipation of the American Woman* (Harper and Row, Inc., 1965).

Singer, J., "The Use of Manipulative Strategies: Machiavellianism and Attractiveness," *Sociometry,* June, 1964. How males and females play their sex roles in trying for good grades in college.

Slater, Philip, "Parental Role Differentiation," *The American Journal of Sociology,* 1961.

Smith, Page, *Daughters of the Promised Land* (Little, Brown and Company, 1970; paperback ed., same publisher, 1971).

Snell, John E., Richard J. Rosenwald and Ames Robey, "The Wife-Beater's Wife," *Archives of General Psychiatry,* August, 1964.

Sorensen, Virginia, *Miracles on Maple Hill* (Harcourt, Brace and World, Inc., 1956).

Spencer, Anna Garlin, *Woman's Share in Social Culture* (J. B. Lippincott Company, 2d ed., 1925; originally published 1912).

Stampp, Kenneth M., *The Peculiar Institution* (Vintage Books, 1956).

Stannard, Una, "Adam's Rib, or The Woman Within," *trans/action,* November–December, 1970.

Stanton, E. C., Susan B. Anthony and M. J. Gage, *History of Woman Suffrage* (Susan B. Anthony, 1887).

Stavn, Diane Gersoni, "The Skirts in Fiction about Boys: A Maxi Mess," *School Library Journal Book Review,* January, 1971.

Steffire, Buford, "Run, Mama, Run: Women Workers in Elementary Readers," *Vocational Guidance Quarterly,* December, 1969.

Steinem, Gloria, "After Black Power, Women's Liberation," *New York,* April 7, 1969.

———, "The City Politic," *New York,* March 10, 1969.

———, "Sisterhood," *Ms.,* Spring, 1972.

Stern, Edith M., "Women Are Household Slaves," *The American Mercury,* January, 1949.

Stern, Paula, "The Womanly Image—Character Assassination through the Ages," *The Atlantic Monthly,* March, 1970.

Stimpson, Catharine, "New Wine in New Bottles," *The Nation,* January 24, 1972. On women and current fiction.

Stokes, Gail A., "Black Woman to Black Man," *Liberator,* December, 1968. But *see also* La Rue.

Stoller, Robert J., *Sex and Gender* (Science House, 1968).

Struggle, Dair, "Consciousness for What?" *It Ain't Me, Babe,* June 11–July 1, 1970.

Suelzle, Marijean, "Women in Labor," *trans/action,* November–December, 1970.

Sullivan, Gail Bernice, "Rape and Its Neglected Victims," *California Living,* April 9, 1972. This is a magazine supplement to the Sunday newspaper in San Francisco; if you have access to it, by all means read it.

Sussman, Marvin B., "The Isolated Nuclear Family: Fact or Fiction?" *Social Problems,* Spring, 1959.

Syfers, Judy, "Why I Want a Wife," in Koedt, *Notes.* Extremely funny; particularly valuable for men.

Szasz, Thomas S., *The Manufacture of Madness: A Comparative Study of the Inquisition and the Mental Health Movement* (Harper and Row, Inc., 1970).

Tanner, Leslie B. (ed.), *Voices from Women's Liberation* (The New American Library, 1970). Another important collection of important pieces. Some are directed toward women, but it's still a book you ought to have.

Tax, Meredith, "Woman and Her Mind: The Story of Everyday Life," in Firestone and Koedt. Later published as part of a pamphlet (New England Free Press, n.d.).

Terman, Lewis M., and Catherine Cox Miles, *Sex and Personality: Studies in Masculinity and Femininity* (McGraw-Hill Book Company, 1936). The authors credit assistance by Jack W. Dunlap, Harold K. Edgerton and others.

———, and Leona E. Tyler, "Psychological Sex Differences," in Leonard Carmichael (ed.), *Manual of Child Psychology* (John Wiley and Sons, 1954).

Theobald, Robert (ed.), *Dialogue on Women* (The Bobbs-Merrill Company, Inc., 1967).

Thomas, Edith, "The Women of the Commune," *Massachusetts Review,* Summer, 1971. Consists of excerpts from *The Women Incendiaries* (George Braziller, Inc., 1966). The commune is the Paris Commune of 1871.

Thomas, W. I., *Sex and Society* (The University of Chicago Press, 1907).

Thompson, Clara, "Penis Envy," *Psychology,* May, 1943. She says there's no such thing.

Thompson, Mary Lou (ed.), *Voices of the New Feminists* (Beacon Press, 1970).

Tiger, Lionel, *Men in Groups* (Random House, Inc., 1968). Best-selling pseudo-scientific prattle.

———, and Robin Fox, *The Imperial Animal* (Holt, Rinehart and Winston, Inc., 1971). More prattle; for details *see* Judith Shapiro.

Trumbo, Sherry Sonnett, "A Woman's Place Is in the Oven," in Koedt, *Notes*; originally published by *The New York Times,* 1971.

U'Ren, Marjorie, "Sexual Discrimination in the Elementary Textbooks" (unpublished). Intended for a forthcoming anthology.

U. S. News and World Report, "Rebelling Women—The Reason," April 13, 1970. They don't know the reason.

Vaertung, Mathias, and Matilde Vaertung, *The Dominant Sex* (George Allen and Unwin [London], 1932).

Valliere, Don, "Girl Jockeys—One Year Later," *Turf,* March, 1970.

Van Allen, Judith, " 'Aba Riots' or 'Women's War': British Ideology and Eastern Nigerian Women's Political Action." A paper delivered at the Annual Meeting, African Studies Association, November 5, 1971.

Vidal, Gore, "In Another Country," *The New York Review of Books,* July 22, 1971. Review of Figes; good reading for men.

Vincent, Gail Ann, "Sex Differences in Children's Textbooks: A Study in the Socialization of the Female" (so far unpublished).

Vogel, Lise, *Women Workers: Some Basic Statistics* (New England Free Press, 1971).

von Hoffman, Nicholas, "Women's Pages: An Irreverent View," *Columbia Journalism Review,* July–August, 1971.

Waite, Richard R., Gaston E. Blom, Sara F. Zimet and Stella Edge, "First-Grade Reading Textbooks," *The Elementary School Journal,* April, 1967.

Ware, Cellestine, *Woman Power: The Movement for Women's Liberation* (Tower Publications, Inc., 1970). Duplicates some of the other books recommended, but it's good.

Watson, Barbara Bellow, "The Cloak of Invisibility," *The Nation,* February 7, 1972.

WBAI Consciousness-Raising Group, "Men and Violence," in Koedt, *Notes.*

Weaver, Polly, "What's Wrong with Ambition?" *Mademoiselle,* September, 1956.

Weightman, John, "Black Chivalry," *The New York Review of Books,* August 24, 1967.

Weisstein, Naomi, "Kinder, Kuche, Kirche as Scientific Law," in Cooke *et al.* Originally a paper delivered to Davis (Calif.) chapter, American

Studies Association, October 26, 1968; later published in *Motive,* March–April, 1969; later a pamphlet (New England Free Press, n.d.). As you can see, it's pretty important and widely read.

————, " 'Woman as Nigger,' " *Psychology Today,* October, 1969. Reprinted in Tanner.

Wells, Judith, "Daddy's Girl," *Libera,* Winter, 1972. A very fine piece, as noted several times in the text. *Libera* is new as I write this; if you can't find it, send $1.25 and a little postage to them at Eshleman Hall, University of California, Berkeley 94720. This essay alone is worth it.

Wells, Lyn, *American Women: Their Use and Abuse* (New England Free Press, 1969).

Whitfield, Stephen E., and Gene Roddenberry, *The Making of Star Trek* (Ballantine Books, Inc., 1968).

Whyte, William H., Jr., "The Corporation and the Wife," *Fortune,* October, 1951.

————, "The Wives of Management," *Fortune,* November, 1951.

Wiberg, John L., and Marion Trost, "A Comparison between the Content of First-Grade Primers and the Free-Choice Library Selections Made by First-Grade Students," *Elementary English,* October, 1970.

Willis, Ellen, " 'Consumerism' and Women," in Firestone and Koedt; also in Tanner.

————, "Letter to a Critic," in Firestone and Koedt.

————, "See America First," *The New York Review of Books,* January 1, 1970. A brilliant view of *Easy Rider* and *Alice's Restaurant.*

————, "We Are Half the Human Race," *The Guardian,* February 15, 1969.

————, "Women and the Left," in Firestone and Koedt; originally published in *The Guardian.*

Wilson, James Q., and Edward C. Banfield, "Political Ethos Revisited," *The American Political Science Review,* December, 1971. Discussed in the text as an example of built-in masculinism in the social sciences.

Wilson, John D., "The Liberal Arts College for Women: An Assessment of Current Problems," *The Centennial Review,* Winter, 1970.

Windy (pseud.), "You're Only As Good As Your Feet, or: The Importance of Being Well-Shod," *It Ain't Me, Babe,* September 17–October 1, 1970. A woman's liberation depends on her choice of shoes? A funny beginning to some good advice.

Witkin, H. A., Helen B. Lewis, M. Herzman, Karen Machover, Pearl B. Meissner and S. Wapner, *Personality through Perception* (Harper and Row, Inc., 1954).

————, R. B. Dyk, H. E. Patterson, D. R. Goodenough and S. A. Karp, *Psychological Differentiation* (John Wiley and Sons, 1962).

Wolff, Charlotte, *Love between Women* (St. Martin's Press, 1971).

Wollstonecraft, Mary, *A Vindication of the Rights of Woman* (W. W. Norton and Company, Inc., 1967; originally published 1791). Believe it or not, some libraries (including the Berkeley Public) have this filed under her later *married* name. It's Godwin.

Wolson, Godwin, "Psychological Aspects of Sex Roles," in G. B. Watson (ed.), *Social Psychology, Issues and Insights* (J. B. Lippincott Company, 1966).

Woolf, Virginia, *A Room of One's Own* (Harcourt, Brace and World, Inc., paperback edition, n.d.; originally published 1929). A "must" for writers of either gender.

————, *Three Guineas* (Harcourt, Brace and Company, Inc., 1938).

Worley, Stinson E., "Development Task Situations in Stories," *The Reading Teacher,* November, 1967.

Wylie, Philip, "The Womanization of America," *Playboy,* September, 1958. Here's a guy hung up on roles.

Zelditch, Morris, "Role Differentiation in the Nuclear Family," in Talcott Parsons *et al.* (eds.), *Family, Socialization, and Interaction Process* (The Free Press, 1955).

INDEX

Bettelheim, Bruno, 20
"Big Bang theory," *see* stereotypes
biology, biological differences, 16, 37, 38–41, 44–6, 124–7, 224, 258
bisexuality, 228
"Black Analogy," Chapter 4 *passim*, 9, 12, 21, 49, 186
"block structure," *see* Conditioning
Blume, Walter, 258
Bonaparte, Marie, 20
Bond, James, 252
books, children's, Chapter 9 *passim*, 163, 239, 250, 264–5
Borgese, Elisabeth Mann, 159
Boyer, Charles, 147
bras, 6, 28, 116–7, 144, 185, 191, 214, 248; "bra-burning," 144, 161, 185, 187, 258; discussion of not wearing bras, 216–9; *see also* breasts
Bread and Roses, 163
breasts, 213, 218, 219, 260, 272; *see also* bras
Brenton, Myron, 66, 196, 206, 237, 238, 253, 254, 256, 261, 262, 271
Bronfenbrenner, Urie, 91–2
Broverman, Inge, 16–7, 18
Brown, Daniel G., 262
Brown, Helen Gurley, 175
Brownmiller, Susan, 189–90
Bruce, Lenny, 9, 90, 176
Brynner, Yul, 84
Buck, Pearl, 261
Burris, Barbara, 143, 252

Cade, Sam, 253
Caen, Herb, 260
Caldecott Award, 106
capacity, biological (*vs.* function), 38, 42–4, 46, 81, 83, 224, 249
capitalism, 143, 159–60, 161, 180, 249
Carmichael, Stokely, 269
Carmody, Deirdre, 143
Cato, Flossie, 219
Cavanna, Betty, 108
Cavett, Dick, 14, 189
Cermeño, Sebastián Rodríguez, 261
Chambers, Whittaker, 151
Chesler, Phyllis, 16, 18, 90, 258, 262
Child, Irvin, 101
Child Study Association, 110
childbearing, 38, 81–3, 142, 224, 238,

245, 249, 260–1; *see also* motherhood
Chisholm, Shirley, 24
Chou En-Lai, 60
civil rights movement, 154, 156, 157, 163, 259
Clark, Edith, 241
Clark, Mae Knight, 109
Cleaver, Eldridge, 30
Clift, Montgomery, 84
clitoral orgasms, *see* orgasms
Coleman, Kate, 189, 190
communes, 59–60
Communist Party, 159
competition, as a value, 59; among women, 129; between sexes, 32, 59
Conditioning, Part 2 *passim*, 37, 46, 167, 169, 175–6, 177, 181, 196, 197, 198, 199, 200, 208, 230–1, 237, 241, 242–3, 248, 250, 252–3, 263; "block structure," 8, 10, 12, 58, 138, 151
consciousness-raising and "small groups," Chapter 14 *passim*, 30, 165, 191, 198, 199, 203, 250; difficulties in groups, 180–1; discussion of particular men, 181–2, 199
"contextual thinking," 94–7, 112
contraception, 39, 116, 191, 211–2
conversation, social, 69–70, 100–1, 170–1, 177, 269
cooking courses, 80, 118–9
Cosmopolitan, 175
Crocker, Betty, 224
Cronkite, Walter, 60
Curie, Marie Sklodowska, 17, 103
Curtis, Tony, 84

Daniels, Arlene, 254
Davis, Angela, 60
de Beauvoir, Simone, 21, 25–6, 37, 54, 62, 68–9, 70, 71, 74, 77, 78, 86, 122, 125, 126, 133, 145, 147, 155–6, 158, 159, 191, 199, 214, 215, 225, 247, 249, 253, 254, 267, 270, 271
de Ford, Miriam Allen, 258
Densmore, Dana, 93, 243, 269
deodorants, vaginal, *see* vaginal deodorants
dependence, men's on women, *see* men,
de Roos, Robert, 250–1

desegregation of public facilities, 185–7

desertion, legal, 235

Deutsch, Helene, 20

Devlin, Bernadette, 62

di Rivera, Alice, 119

discrimination in employment, *see* work roles

dishwashing, *see* housework

Dixon, Ruth, 213

"Dr. Seuss," 265

doctors and medicine, 139–40, 188–9, 218, 262, 272; sadism among doctors, 189

doll houses, 88–9

dolls, 81, 92, 96

dominance-submission patterns, 194–200, 201, 205, 206, 209, 224, 227, 231, 233, 234, 236, 238, 246, 253, 254, 255

"double standard," sexual, in marriage, 244–8

Drewes, Caroline, 264, 273

drugs, 178–9, 269

Drummond, William J., 272

Dudar, Helen, 4, 11, 145, 150, 164, 175, 179, 192, 272

education, college and university, 76–8, 112, 120, 132, 139–40, 161, 210, 265, 267

education, primary and secondary, *see* schools

Edwards, Allen, 194–5

Eldred, Pamela Anne, 269

Eliot, George, 98, 264

elitism, 179; *see also* hierarchy

Ellis, Albert, 205

Ellis, Julie, 4

Ellmann, Mary, 20

Emch, Tom, 150

Evertts, Eldonna L., 103

F. A. O. Schwarz, 87, 88

facts, objective, 34–6

facts, statistical, 34–6, 94

"false consciousness," female resistance to women's liberation, 127, 133, 241; definition and discussion, 248–50

family, family unit, 57–60, 142; "extended family," 58–9, 240, 241;

"isolated nuclear family," 58–60, 68; *see also* marriage

Fanon, Frantz, 27

Farber, Seymour M., 156, 158, 263, 268

Fasteau, Brenda Feigen, 141, 208

fears in men, *see* men

fellatio, 199–200

"femininity," 80, 129, 133, 197, 215; three uses of word, 207–11; in men, 79–80

The Feminists, 163

Feminists on Children's Literature, 106, 107, 108, 110, 264, 265

Ferro, Nancy, 164

Figes, Eva, 4, 37, 76, 77, 114, 127–8, 137, 145, 196–7, 262, 265, 271

Firestone, Shulamith, 3, 4, 16, 41, 57, 96, 147, 155, 158, 160–1, 212, 213, 216, 258, 272

Fisher, Elizabeth, 105, 265

Fisher-Price Toys, Inc., 88–9

Fithian, Marilyn, 196

Fleming, Peggy, 60

Ford, Glenn, 253

Frankel, Charles, 257

Frederick, Pauline, 261

Free Speech Movement, 156, 157

Freeman, Jo, 18–9, 24, 30, 46–7, 94, 129, 140, 158, 166, 258, 259, 263, 266, 267; "Jo Freeman's Rule," 46–7, 70, 93, 94, 112, 267

Freud, Sigmund, 20, 21, 201–2, 260

Freudian theories, 19–21, 27, 67–8, 85, 106, 173, 202–3, 260; *see also* psychoanalysts, and adjoining entries

Fried, Edrita, 130

Friedan, Betty, 4, 23, 70, 99, 119–20, 133–4, 137, 141, 155, 156, 158, 159, 167, 168, 172, 194, 238, 242, 243, 262, 266, 267, 271

"frigidity," 68–9, 71, 196, 202–3

Frisof, Jamie, 102, 106, 264

frustration, *see* "frigidity," orgasms

"function," biological, *see* capacity

Future Homemakers of America, 131

Gallen, Richard T., 229, 230

Gallup, George (Gallup Poll), 5, 47–8

Gender, distinguished from "sex," 53, 69–70, 85

Georgia, 27, 28, 29, 31, 89

Gifford-Jones, W., 188–9
Gilbert Youth Research, 131
girdles, 28, 144, 214
"girl talk," 171
Girl Talk, 61, 171
Golder, Evan, 220
Goode, William J., 259
Goodman, Jan, 186
Goodwin, Carolyn, 118
Grady, Kathleen, 88, 263
Graham, Virginia, 61
Grant, Cary, 147
Gray, Susan, 90–1
Green, Catherine, 61
Greer, Germaine, 4, 12, 19, 21, 137, 163, 166, 218, 256, 266, 271, 272
Grieg, Michael, 101
groups, small, *see* consciousness-raising
gynecology, 188–9

Haber, Joyce, 269
Hacker, Helen, 259
Hall, Edward, 261
Hamer, Fannie Lou, 141
Hanchett, Lucinda, 270
Hanisch, Carol, 143, 160, 171–2, 182, 250, 267, 268, 269, 273
Hare, Nathan and Julia, 23
Harris, Sara, 195
Hartley, Ruth E., 91, 92–3, 263
Hartman, William, 196
Hays, Lee, 268
Hebb, D. O., 257
Hefner, Hugh, 60, 151, 175, 187, 189, 268
Heisman Trophy, 78
Henry, Jules, 99, 100
Hernandez, Aileen, 4
Heyn, Leah, 100, 104
hierarchy, rejection of by women's movement, 163–5, 211
Hinckle, Warren, III, and Marianne, 4, 268
Hints from Heloise, 231
Hochschild, Arlie, 19, 251
homosexuality, female, *see* lesbianism
homosexuality, male, 225–6, 227, 228, 254, 255, 271–2; fear of, among males, *see* men
Honigmann, John, 101, 110
hormones, 39, 127
hostility among men, *see* men

Houghton, Walter, 98
housework, 9, 23, 93, 102, 149, 237, 263; discussed as issue in women's liberation, 239–44
Hudson, Rock, 60
Hunt, Irene, 109
Hunt, Morton, 143, 151, 268
Hunt, Persis, 159, 265
hysterectomy, 238

impotence, male, 196, 253, 254, 273
incest, 273
"infidelity," *see* "adultery"
"instinct," 44–5, 81–2, 263
Institute of Life Insurance, 131
intellectuality, 129, 175, 236
Iran, 54, 56
Irving, Clifford, 60
Irwin, Inez Haynes, 240
Island of the Blue Dolphins, 105
Iverson, Lucille, 178

Jacobson, Lenore, 114
Jelinek, Estelle, 270
"Jo Freeman's Rule," *see* Freeman, Jo
Johnson, Virginia, 69, 204
Jordan, Joan, 160, 268
journalism, *see* press
"Julia," 272

Kael, Pauline, 99
Kaplow, Susi, 176–7
karate, 144–5, 193
Kardiner, Abram, 143, 267
Karloff, Boris, 268
Kearns, Karen, 87
Kearon, Pamela, 142–3, 189, 216, 270, 271
Kennedy, Florynce, 191
Key, Mary Ritchie, 100–1, 103, 106, 107, 108, 109, 110, 264, 265
Kidd, Virginia, 101, 103, 264
King, Billie Jean, 60
King, Martin Luther, Jr., 30, 163
Kinsey, Alfred C., 69
Kirchner, Clara, 108
Kleindienst, Richard, 61
Knowles, Louis, 26, 258
Koch, Adrienne, 17
Koedt, Anne, 41–2, 160, 161, 200, 201, 205, 206, 220, 221, 222, 224, 225, 227, 228, 258, 260, 268, 271
Komarovsky, Mirra, 69, 120

309

Muhammad, Elijah, 163
Murtagh, John M., 195
Myrdal, Gunnar, 22–3, 156

Nader, Ralph, 60
Naegele, Kaspar D., 66, 93
name change in marriage, 231–4
Nash, June, 104–5
The Nation, 156
National Organization of Women, 4, 87, 141, 143, 156–7, 158, 161, 162, 163, 165, 185, 221
"natural" characteristics and roles, 37–8, 58, 80, 92, 123, 129, 133, 194–5, 220, 251, 272; meaning of "natural" discussed, 42–6; *see also* capacity
Natural History, 104–5
Negrin, Su, 226–7, 272
Neugarten, Bernice, 238
The New York Review of Books, 99
Newbery Award, 106, 109
newspapers, *see* press
Newsweek, 4, 143, 151, 164, 179, 267, 268
Nilsen, Aileen, 105, 106, 108
Nixon, Patricia, 48
Nixon, Richard, 60

objectification, 6, 132–3, 137, 188, 197, 222, 233, 244; defined and discussed, 213–8
"objective facts," *see* facts
O'Donnell, Mabel, 109
oophorectomy, 189
opportunities, future, girls' *vs.* boys', 65–7, 71–2, 76–81, 83–6, 93, 95, 107, 115, 117–8, 122, 125
oppression, 23–5, 31; as concept applied to women, 26–7, 182, 192–3, 197, 221
orchiectomy, 189
orgasms, 69, 191, 196; female orgasms discussed, 201–7
ovaries, removal of, 189
Oyler, Walter, 118

parthenogenesis, 41, 258
paternity, 245
Peck, Ellen, 244
Peek, Charles W., 252–3, 273
Peel, Emma, 271
"penis envy," 67–8
pills, birth control, *see* contraception

Pilpel, Harriet F., 229
Platt, Sherry, 117
Playboy, 151, 175, 189, 214, 218, 268
poetry, children's, 103–4
political nature of sex, gender roles, 173–5, 192–4, 199, 267
Porter, Sylvia, 271
pregnancies, difficult, 238
pregnancy, extrauterine, 41, 143, 148, 258
press and other communication media, 6, 47–8, 60, 141, 143, 149–50, 160, 163, 164–5, 175, 176, 183, 185–7, 208, 210, 216, 217, 219, 249–50; *see also* stereotypes, television
Prewitt, Kenneth, 26, 258
prostitution, 195, 254, 270; discussed, 189–91
Proxmire, William, 165
psychiatrists, 129, 130, 133, 206, 260; *see also* adjoining entries
psychoanalysts, Freudian, 75, 225; *see also* adjoining entries, Freudian theories, "therapy"
psychological tests, perception differences, 16–7, 18, 66, 92–3, 112, 131–2; sex differences, 7, 18, 28, 46–7, 90–1, 94–5, 113, 119–20
psychologists, 166, 257; *see also* adjoining entries
psychotherapists, 16–7, 19, 39, 90, 173; *see also* adjoining entries, "therapy"

racism and bigotry, 12–6, 23, 34, 138, 158; institutional or structural racism, 15–6, 26, 28, 31, 158
Radical Feminists, 163, 250
Radicalesbians, 163, 220, 223–4, 227–8, 272
Rainwater, Lee, 69
Ramparts, 271
Randolph, Jennings, 144, 267
rape, 145, 192–3, 230, 270–1
Rau, Lucy, 263
Redstockings, 163
Reik, Theodore, 20
resistance by women to women's liberation, *see* "false consciousness"
Resnick, Stella, 226
"reversal" as feminist tactic, 9, 189, 190, 232
Reynolds, Burt, 175

tribadism, 226
Troup, Bobby, 171
Tyler, Leona E., 18, 24, 28

understanding, mutual, among women, Chapter 14 *passim*, 5, 222
U'Ren, Marjorie, 99, 102, 103, 106

vaginal deodorants, 28, 89–90
"vaginal orgasms," *see* orgasms
Van Allen, Judith, 140, 268–9
Van Buren, Abigail, 197, 207, 209, 233
Van Deerlin, Lionel, 261
Van Gelder, Lindsy, 179
Van Horne, Harriet, 144–5, 146, 197, 207, 267–8, 273
Van Roekel, Byron H., 103
"verbal thinking," *see* "contextual thinking"
victimization, 24, 76, 256

Walcutt, Charles E., 103
Wallace, George, 60
Walters, Barbara, 60
Ware, Cellestine, 144, 267
Watts, Alan, 94
Wayne, John, 84, 90, 147, 182, 252, 253, 255
Weisstein, Naomi, 39–40, 260, 262
Welby, Marcus, 33

Wells, Judith, 86, 129, 130, 133, 176, 197, 266
Whitfield, Stephen E., 274
Whitney, Eli, 61
Wilcoxon, Henry, 273
Willis, Ellen, 147, 161–2, 268
Wilson, James Q., 262
Wilson, Roger H. L., 156, 158, 263, 268
Witkin, H. A., 95, 263
Women in Teaching, 264
Women on Words and Images, 264
Women Strike for Peace, 155, 159, 268
women's liberation, stereotypes, *see* stereotypes
Women's Liberation Front, 158
Women's Defense League, 183
Women's Wear Daily, 141
Wonder Woman, 99, 264
Wood, Jim, 265
Woolf, Virginia, 61, 90, 98, 150
work roles, 24–5, 36–7, 44, 93, 115, 128, 137, 177, 187, 190, 208, 231, 241–2, 244, 260
Worley, Stinson, 102

Young, Robert, 60

Zavin, Theodora, 229
Zelditch, Morris, Jr., 259
Zellerbach, Merla, 272